THE

GLOBAL

FLOOD

UNLOCKING EARTH'S GEOLOGIC HISTORY

THE
GLOBAL
FLOOD

UNLOCKING EARTH'S GEOLOGIC HISTORY

JOHN D. MORRIS

INSTITUTE FOR CREATION RESEARCH

Dallas, TX
www.icr.org

THE GLOBAL FLOOD
Unlocking Earth's Geologic History
by Dr. John D. Morris

Dr. John Morris, perhaps best known for leading expeditions to Mount Ararat in search of Noah's Ark, received his Doctorate in Geological Engineering at the University of Oklahoma in 1980. He served on the University of Oklahoma faculty before joining the Institute for Creation Research in 1984. Dr. Morris held the position of Professor of Geology before being appointed President in 1996. He travels widely around the world speaking at churches, conferences, schools, and scientific meetings. Dr. Morris has written numerous books and articles on the scientific evidence that supports the Bible. Dr. Morris is the author or co-author of such books as *The Young Earth: The Real History of the Earth — Past, Present, and Future*, *The Modern Creation Trilogy*, and *The Fossil Record: Unearthing Nature's History of Life*.

First printing: October 2012
Second printing: February 2014

Cover Design: Dennis Davidson
Interior Design: Susan Windsor

All Scripture quotations are from the King James Version.

ISBN: 978-1-935587-12-5
Library of Congress Catalog Number: 2012949341

Please visit our website for other books and resources: www.icr.org.

Printed in the United States of America.

To the memory of Dr. Henry Morris,
my earthly and spiritual father,
my valued colleague in the ministry,
and in his later years, my best friend.

TABLE OF CONTENTS

FOREWORD

I count it a high honor to have been invited to write these few words. Over 50 years ago, Henry M. Morris, the father of John D. Morris, co-authored with me a volume of over 500 pages entitled *The Genesis Flood*. There are many evidences to confirm that God has used this book to be the catalyst for the worldwide creation science movement of our day. For this, we are profoundly thankful to Him.

However, since 1961, an enormous mass of geological and paleontological information has come to light which confirms the reality and magnitude of the Flood. Henry Morris, of course, knew that this would happen, and was anxious to have his son John, also a Ph.D. geologist, produce a "layman's version" of *The Genesis Flood*. Henry entered the presence of the Lord on February 25, 2006, at the age of 87. After many delays, in "the fullness of time," John's book has appeared, in the providence of God.

The Global Flood helps to meet a great need today. It is comprehensive. It is aimed at those who are not experts in earth sciences. People everywhere need to understand the true significance of the year-long, mountain-covering Deluge that buried and fossilized trillions of marine and land animals and plants only a few thousand years ago. Over 95 percent of these fossils—even within sedimentary strata seen in the highest mountains of the world—are marine creatures! We don't need to stretch the creation week of Genesis 1 to allow for this. The fossils were formed after, not before, Adam! Without the enormous hydrodynamic work of the Flood, we could not know this. Now the Christian world has no excuse—if they ever had any—for adding millions and billions of years to earth history.

May God be pleased to use *The Global Flood* to enlighten and encourage His people everywhere, in this day of confusion and compromise, to understand as never before some of the basic realities of Flood geology.

Dr. John C. Whitcomb
Founder and President
Whitcomb Ministries

Acknowledgements

The original groundbreaking book of which this is an update, *The Genesis Flood*, involved an enormous amount of work. The two authors, my father Dr. Henry Morris and Dr. John Whitcomb, successfully tackled data from many fields, compiling and integrating the work of many others into an effective presentation of a more complete worldview. My father, now with his Lord, encouraged me for years to write this update. My good friend Dr. Whitcomb recognized the need for a less technical work on the same general subject and encouraged me to continue. He reviewed the manuscript and graciously wrote the Foreword. I acknowledge him as a mentor and colleague, and thank him.

Others have contributed greatly to my understanding of these issues, including especially Dr. Steve Austin, long a friend and co-worker at the Institute for Creation Research. Similarly, my dear friend Dr. Andrew Snelling has contributed greatly to this work by reviewing the manuscript and spurring me on to completion, even though he had published his own more technical update of *The Genesis Flood* some years before. Numerous scientists read various stages of the work, giving wise counsel, including Dr. John Baumgardner, himself mentioned in these pages as a discoverer of certain concepts. Dr. Tim Cleary also critiqued the work, as did Dr. Tas Walker, Dr. Russell Humphreys, Dr. Larry Vardiman, Dr. Jim Johnson, Mike Oard, Lee Russell, Roger Sigler, David Bassett, and John Doherty. Several on the ICR staff prepared the book for publication, most especially Beth Mull and Susan Windsor. With their expert help, the book project came to fruition.

Let me also acknowledge my dear wife of 35 years, Dalta. She has put up with my long hours of study with grace and understanding. God has truly gifted me with her, my "helper fit" for me.

INTRODUCTION

The groundbreaking book *The Genesis Flood*, co-authored by theologian Dr. John Whitcomb and my father, scientist Dr. Henry Morris,[1] catalyzed the modern creation movement. Published in 1961, it paved the way for the biblical inerrancy movement and facilitated the growing Christian school and homeschool movements. Before it was published, few tried to defend Scripture in areas of science and history, for it was thought that science had disproved the Bible. This book has served as an invaluable resource, providing many with the necessary scientific arguments to uphold the critical doctrines within Genesis.

For several decades before the publication of *The Genesis Flood*, the concept of evolution had enjoyed unchallenged prominence in education, the media, politics, and the courts. Indeed, the public arena had been saturated with evolutionary teaching and application. Surveys reveal its near total dominance in university professorships, network news, and textbooks. This needed to change. And it did change under the influence of Drs. Morris and Whitcomb's seminal book. Many Christians, including those with scientific training who had accepted evolution and long geologic ages, recognized the scientific truth and apologetic value within *The Genesis Flood*.

Now, more than 50 years later, the foundational principles of creation and the Flood need restating for new generations. Science doesn't stand still, and books need revisions to stay up-to-date. Efforts over the years, including those of this author, to update such a monumental work had stalled. The project was simply too big and groundbreaking. Each paragraph required a research project.

Finally, Dr. Andrew Snelling, a leading creation geology researcher and dedicated Christian, succeeded in 2009 with the comprehensive and compelling book *Earth's Catastrophic Past*.[2] Both that publication and *The Genesis Flood* are all-inclusive and fairly technical. This present book in no way replaces either, but gleans heavily from these and other prominent works. Technical literature will be referenced as necessary, but the interested reader will also be referred to creationist sources that will provide more detail in a scriptural context than will be given here.

The following sources—some secular, but most Christian/creationist—are freely acknowledged.

Steven A. Austin, ed., 1994, *Grand Canyon: Monument to Catastrophe*, Santee, CA: Institute for Creation Research.

John Morris and Steven A. Austin, 2003, *Footprints in the Ash*, Green Forest, AR: Master Books.

Derek V. Ager, 1993, *The Nature of the Stratigraphical Record*, 3rd ed., Chichester, NY: John Wiley & Sons.

Ariel A. Roth, 1998, *Origins: Linking Science*

and Scripture, Hagerstown, MD: Review and Herald Pub.

Harold G. Coffin et al, 2005, *Origin by Design,* Hagerstown, MD: Review and Herald Pub.

Steven A. Austin, 1984, *Catastrophes in Earth History,* El Cajon, CA: Institute for Creation Research.

Michael J. Oard, 2008, *Flood by Design*, Green Forest, AR: Master Books.

Larry Vardiman, Andrew A. Snelling and Eugene F. Chaffin, eds., 2000, *Radioisotopes and the Age of the Earth: A Young-Earth Creationist Research Initiative*, El Cajon, CA: Institute for Creation Research, and St. Joseph, MO: Creation Research Society.

Larry Vardiman, Andrew A. Snelling and Eugene F. Chaffin, eds., 2005, *Radioisotopes and the Age of the Earth: Results of a Young-Earth Creationist Research Initiative,* El Cajon, CA: Institute for Creation Research, and Chino Valley, AZ: Creation Research Society.

Don DeYoung, 2005, *Thousands…Not Billions,* Green Forest, AR: Master Books.

John Morris, 2007, *The Young Earth,* rev. ed., Green Forest, AR: Master Books.

John Morris and Frank Sherwin, 2010, *The Fossil Record*, Dallas, TX: Institute for Creation Research.

John Woodmorappe, 1999, *Studies in Flood Geology*, El Cajon, CA: Institute for Creation Research.

John Woodmorappe, 1996, *Noah's Ark: A Feasibility Study*, Dallas, TX: Institute for Creation Research.

Leonard Brand, 2009, *Faith, Reason and Earth History*, Berrien Springs, MI: Andrews University Press.

Other creationist sources of importance are *Acts & Facts, Creation Research Society Quarterly* journal, *Creation* magazine, *Journal of Creation, Answers Research Journal,* and *Proceedings from the International Conferences on Creationism.*

Thankfully, things will never return completely to the way they were before *The Genesis Flood*, when evolutionists had a virtual monopoly on education and scientific investigation. By God's grace, we now have an abundance of information supporting the creation/ Flood model. The aim of this book is to equip speakers, teachers, and students with the tools to understand the information regarding the Genesis Flood and communicate it to others.

CHAPTER 1

THE SCRIPTURAL SETTING

As we begin this study of the great Flood of Noah's day, we must make sure our presuppositions are right. An effort in any discipline, including science, must start with presuppositions, proceed to the study or gathering of relevant observations, and conclude with the interpretation of those data within the worldview held at the start. The presuppositions held before the study begins are the most influential part of the interpretation and decision-making process. Individuals may be unaware of their closely held worldview, but each person has one, especially scientists. This concept applies in every endeavor, from science to economics to politics to personal morality, etc.

Studying the evidence will never "prove" or "disprove" one's perspective. But it can help us evaluate our presuppositions, especially as we compare the interpretations stemming from competing worldviews. This is particularly true as we delve into historical subjects. Forensic scientists face enormous challenges when they try to reconstruct an unwitnessed crime that took place far in the past. The same is true for the debate between creation and evolution. No witness saw either take place, and neither takes place today. We can only compare the interpretations to see which interpretation, based on the differing worldviews, best fits the evidence.

For Christians, our worldview should begin with the authoritative truth of God's Word. A governing presupposition of the creation worldview is that Scripture is historical and true. Scripture provides a credible witness of events in the long distant past. It doesn't provide

us with all the details, but it does inform our efforts to reconstruct past unseen events. Indeed, if Scripture records truth, no effort to understand the past that denies what it claims can succeed.

A proper study of earth's geological and historical records is vital when comparing the creationist and evolutionary worldviews. For Christians, this begins with Genesis 6–10, which records events that forever changed the world. Therefore, this book seeks to provide an understanding of the great Flood of Noah's day and related subjects. A flood event of this magnitude is completely outside our experience. How could we possibly know what it was like? Only as the Sender and Observer of the Flood tells us, and as our study and interpretations are done in submission to Him—then

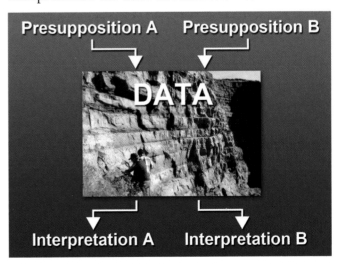

Presuppositions are the most influential part of the interpretation process.[1]

and only then do we have a chance for a correct understanding. This study will engender scientific and historical interpretations that supplement the basics we learn from God's written history.

Peter's Last-Days Warning

There is another portion of Scripture beyond Genesis that deserves our attention. It also aptly details the Flood's nature and cause, as well as the Flood's implications for today. From the pen of Peter, it is written to Christians of the latter days and merits our careful study.

The apostle Peter wrote two letters to the early Christians scattered throughout the Roman world. He wrote to encourage them in their newfound faith, to equip them for victorious Christian living, to warn them against false teachers, and to prepare them for the coming persecution. He closed his final epistle with instructions for the last days—warning believers of the type of error that would gain prevalence, training them how to recognize it, and steeling them for a victorious response.

Both Peter and his readers suspected the "last days" were upon them, but in God's sovereignty and timing the end has been delayed for these two millennia. Soon after writing this letter, Peter would lay down his pen and suffer martyrdom for his uncompromising faith and vital witness. Can his wise counsel help us as we try to discern trends in our society and in our days? Can it assist us in remaining valiant in the face of opposition?

We would particularly do well to heed his final words in 2 Peter 3. The Holy Spirit inspired his message, and the God of history has delayed its full application into our times. If Peter's "last days" instructions were important to Christians so long ago, they surely are more important to those of us who live much closer to the last days than anyone who came before us.

Peter began by calling to mind things his readers already knew (2 Peter 3:1), specifically the writings of the Old Testament prophets and the teachings of the early church leaders who themselves were personally trained by the Lord and Savior, Jesus Christ Himself (v. 2). The Old Testament Scriptures were widely available and well-studied in the Jewish culture, and early church leaders would probably have had at least partial access to them. Oral teaching by the apostles would

have been faithfully repeated, and some sections of the New Testament may have even been written, copied, and circulated by the time Peter was writing.

The Old Testament Scriptures and the apostles taught the biblical worldview—the creation of all things originally in a "very good" state (Genesis 1:31); sin and its penalty, death, as the ruination of that state (Genesis 3); the great Flood of Noah's day as God's deadly judgment of that sinful world (Genesis 6–9); the solution to the sin problem, Jesus Christ's substitutionary death that paid sin's penalty; and the future return of this same Sin-bearer to rule in righteousness. These writings and teachings were truth, and Peter thought it important that they be believed as the foundation for fruitful living and ministry.

In the seminal chapter 3 of his second epistle, Peter taught that the latter-day "scoffers, walking after their own lusts" (v. 3) had a pervasive disregard for Scripture. Today, even a meager awareness of modern society finds an attitude of "scoffing" at all things biblical. University environments breed open contempt for morality and traditional values. Professors often brag that their main job is to re-educate their students away from things previously learned at church and at home. Instead, they teach a different religion, a "naturalistic" one with no past, present, or future "supernatural" agency at work. Many are the Christian students who have abandoned their faith under the onslaught of teaching from anti-Christian zealots—self-styled "skeptics" who deny any supernatural input into the natural order. Peter says the detractors will be totally absorbed in personal interests, without regard for God's will or His Truth as revealed in Scripture.

Peter further identifies these "scoffers" by their creed that "all things continue as they were from the beginning of the creation" (v. 4), i.e., from time immemorial. They insist that the processes observed today are the only processes that have ever operated, and that they have been responsible for all that has occurred. Present processes acting at rates possible today have allegedly produced matter from non-matter, life from non-life, higher forms of life from lower forms, and man from the animals. Past process rates may have differed from today's norm at times, but only natural processes have acted in accordance with natural law as we know it. Certainly no "supernatural" processes were involved.

Uniformitarianism, "The Present Is the Key to the Past"

Students of earth history will recognize this creed as a paraphrase of the slogan of uniformitarianism, that "the present is the key to the past." The principle of uniformitarianism dominates education today, especially in those sciences that delve into the unobserved past. Applied in astronomy, uniformitarianism yields the Big Bang theory. In biology, it leads to evolution, and in geology to the concept of millions and millions of years. But by limiting possible causes to present processes, evaluating them by one's own experience, the truth may be excluded and/or missed. Naturalistic explanations are the only ones allowed in uniformitarian thinking, to the extent that science deteriorates into the "religion" of naturalism.[2]

Uniformitarianism can be considered in two veins. *Gradualism* insists that things have always proceeded just as we see today. Not much is happening. A raindrop hits the ground and leaves a little pit, rivers erode their base, freezing water opens small cracks, earthquakes occasionally occur, tornadoes sometimes drop out of the clouds, etc., but nothing out of the ordinary. Gradualist uniformitarianism averages these events to arrive at baseline process rates. Although this approach is no longer much in vogue among practicing geologists, it still dominates classroom instruction.

On the other hand, *actualism* in geology recognizes rare catastrophic events, but surrounds them with the ongoing gradual operation of processes. Indeed, geologists must acknowledge energetic events in nature, for they occasionally happen today and past evidence demands them. They hold to uniformity of process, but limited flexibility of process rate. In this way, they maintain the great ages necessary to naturalism during which natural processes reigned.

My first professional job after receiving my Ph.D. was on the geological engineering faculty of the University of Oklahoma. One of my faculty colleagues in another department (who became a good friend) was a leading evolutionary spokesman. He actually considered himself a fairly orthodox Christian, although not a practicing one. Certainly he didn't consider himself to be anti-God, but as a scientist he insisted on complete naturalism. One day in his office, as we discussed science's commitment to naturalism, he reached under his desk, removed his shoe, and began beating on his desk, exclaiming, "Science is naturalism! Even if the Bible is absolutely correct. Even if God actually created all things in six literal days. Even if the earth is really only a few thousand years old. Even if Noah's Flood actually covered the entire earth. Even if this is the way it actually happened and these things are absolutely true, the job of the scientist would be to come up with another explanation that involves no supernatural." The "religion" of naturalism and its cardinal doctrine of uniformitarianism completely dominate the academic sphere at all levels, both public and private, including many schools that call themselves Christian.

Uniformitarianism's dominance in secular thought was prophesied long ago, but it did not always dominate. Up until the mid-1800s, nearly all educated scholars recognized that non-uniform activity must have played a major role in creation and the supernatural judgment at the time of the Flood. But an anti-god philosophy began to take over, not only in science, but also in government and society. Today's ascendancy of uniformitarianism is nothing less than a fulfillment of Peter's prophecy.

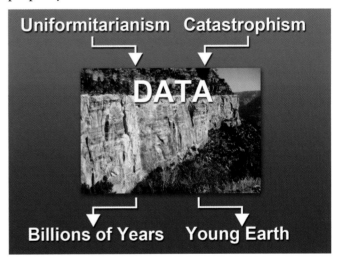

These rock units in Grand Canyon can be interpreted in more than one way, based on what presuppositions the investigator held before the interpretation began.

A uniformitarian way of thinking may be appropriate in many cases. The scientific enterprise has access today only to natural law and natural processes in the study of the way things are and how they operate. But how they originated is another matter. All science can do is study present processes and compare them to things that occurred in the past. Scientists cannot repeat the past. Are present processes capable of producing the things that were accomplished in the past?

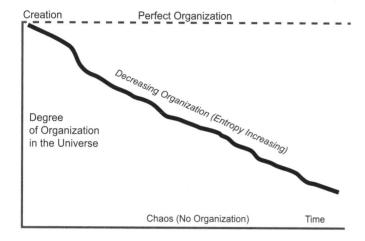

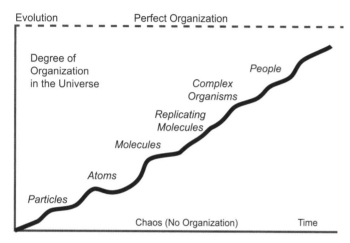

Scripture reveals that creation was "very good" when finished. It has been deteriorating since then due to the effects of the Curse. Conversely, amoeba-to-man evolution proposes a natural trend toward innovation and increased organization. Both views cannot be right.

One thing we readily observe is that present processes are totally incapable of producing life from non-life, or matter from non-matter. When nature first began to be "scientifically" studied and understood, many scientific laws were discovered—relationships that never seemed to change. In particular, two primary laws were recognized. Of course, there are many relationships now recognized as "laws," but these primary laws were discovered in the field of heat/power, or thermodynamics, and soon were seen to apply to every field and observation. Today, the two Laws of Thermodynamics are recognized as the inviolable laws of nature in general.

The First Law of Thermodynamics declares that matter/energy (everything that exists) cannot come from nothing. It cannot create itself, nor can it cease to exist. It must remain constant. The Second Law of Thermodynamics insists that the total amount of order/information in the matter/energy present cannot spontaneously increase. The entropy of a system (a measure of the disorder or randomness) will always increase, but not the order. Neither law has ever been seen to be violated. They always work.

Science must limit itself to these constraints. Scientists must not rely on miraculous events to explain observations in the present. But, as will be demonstrated throughout this book, the processes of today seem incapable of accomplishing the needed origins and developmental events of the past (and indeed, even prohibit them). Might we not be justified in assigning such events to processes not now observable? May we not acknowledge when Scripture explicitly identifies miraculous intervention into earth's normal functions, and when these instances only make sense with such a temporary overriding of natural law at specific times in the past? Natural law rigorously applies to the operation of the universe and all processes within it, but its ultimate origins must have required more.

WILLFUL IGNORANCE

A blind adherence to uniformitarianism guarantees an erroneous conclusion on at least those occasions in the unobserved past when God tells us He supernaturally intervened. Evidence would likely still be present of divine input even though the process has ended, but self-imposed blinders might keep one from acknowledging that evidence. This seems to be Peter's next point. He charges that uniformitarians "willingly are ignorant of" (2 Peter 3:5) evidence for past supernatural action. This is the cause of their inability to think

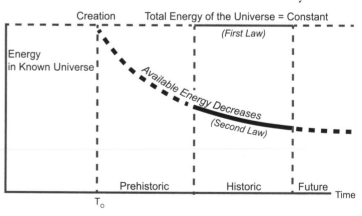

According to the first basic law of science, energy can neither be created nor destroyed. The second basic law explains that the energy's quality and usefulness constantly decrease. The universe and its components could not create or organize themselves.

| DAY 1 | DAY 2 | DAY 3 | DAY 4 | DAY 5 | DAY 6 |

The six days of creation.

correctly and of their resulting wrong conclusions. This blindness falls in two general areas, both worldwide in scope.

First, they willingly are ignorant of the fact that the original creation required supernatural input, identified here as the very "word of God" Himself. Disorder cannot, according to natural law, order itself, but by the supernatural word of God it can be done. Obviously, the First Law of Thermodynamics had not yet been enacted, for matter/energy came from God's command, and neither had the Second Law, for raw matter/energy was shaped into the exquisite order we observe, again by God's supernatural word. When earth was first called into existence, its not-yet-fully-formed matter was "standing out of the water and in the water." This is a reference to Genesis 1:2, when "the Spirit of God moved on the face of the deep" on Day One. From that point on, the Creator shaped all things into an eventual "very good" state (Genesis 1:31).

On Day Two, the oceans and the atmosphere were formed and separated, preparing the planet for life. On Day Three, the continents coalesced and/or were lifted up out of the waters, and plants began to grow. The raw matter molded by God on Days One and Two, with electrons and protons and all the other subatomic particles swirling around in order, was quite complex. But plants, which are able to receive raw energy, convert it, and utilize it, are totally unlike nonliving chemicals and required an extra-natural cause. Add to this the ability to metabolize food, photosynthesize light, and reproduce similar entities—their origin was a supernatural occurrence, quite unlike anything uniformitarian-

ism can propose. Science has conclusively proven that spontaneous generation of life is impossible, that life only comes from life. But uniformitarians insist that it actually happened—that life came from chemicals by the action of natural law alone, without any divine guidance. How unscientific.

On Day Four, the sun, moon, and stars were made, with their light and influence designed to assist man, animals, and plants in many functions, and to allow life to thrive on earth. On Day Five, animal life in the seas and sky was brought forth at God's command. If plants required the Creator's handiwork, think of the animals. Unimaginable design and variety of astonishing complexity can be seen everywhere. Land animals followed on Day Six, each one exhibiting features and functions that today's scientists can hardly understand, let alone duplicate. Obviously, natural processes alone could not have been responsible.

DESIGN
DEMANDS
A
DESIGNER

The crowning achievement of creation was "the image of God" in man, an arrangement of "chemicals" so complex and precise it defies comprehension by our finite minds, yet God's spirit infused it somehow in a way that deserved to be called "the image" of the infinite God. Only one who chooses willful ignorance could assign such magnificence to unthinking chance.

Peter's second charge of willful ignorance regards the fact that the exquisite, complex, created "world that then was, being overflowed with water, perished" (2 Peter 3:6). Sin had entered the perfect creation and had been gladly embraced by mankind. The penalty for sin (Romans 3:23) against the holy God was, even at that time, death (Genesis 2:17). Sin flourished to such an extent that the gracious Creator eventually had to act in judgment. The great Flood of Noah's day forever altered the creation.

Not only was the Flood an instrument of God's holy justice, it was a physical phenomenon as well—indeed, it was a flood similar in many ways to floods we see today. It involved rapidly moving water, and we know the power of moving water. It was also a sequence of major storms, perhaps a confluence of mega-hurricanes. Major storms plague us today, and we know something of their dynamic. Today's processes are all observations within uniformity, but the great Flood's processes were operating at rates, scales, and intensities far beyond levels we experience. Noah's Flood involved what scientists have come to call hypercanes, mega-faulting, and super-volcanoes—all similar to their counterparts of today, but multiplied by orders of magnitude. Rainfall, erosion, deposition, and other recognizable processes were all occurring, but at an off-the-scale intensity. This was no "uniform" event. Indeed, God promised there would never be a flood like this again. There have been many floods throughout history, even major or regional floods, but no year-long, mountain-covering, continent-destroying, global Flood has occurred since Noah's day.

Engineers and scientists have long appreciated the immense potential moving water possesses to do geologic work. We can observe it operate on a local scale today. Yet the past Flood, worldwide in scope, dwarfed any contemporary flood. No location on planet earth escaped its impact. Everywhere we observe the rock or fossil record, we can know that in most cases non-uniform events shaped them. The great Flood restructured the entire planet. If we attempt to interpret the geological history of any area without the great Flood in our thinking, we will arrive at error, not truth. We didn't observe the Flood itself, but we would be "willfully ignorant" to ignore the evidence it left behind.

In an important way, the doctrine of the global Flood is synonymous with the doctrine of recent creation.[3] If you were to ask an advocate of evolutionary uniformitarianism for evidence supporting evolution or the idea that the earth is old, the answer most likely would be, "It's in the rock and fossil records of earth's crust. The fossils demonstrate evolution's progress

EONOTHEM / EON	ERATHEM / ERA	SYSTEM, SUBSYSTEM / PERIOD, SUBPERIOD	SERIES / EPOCH	Age estimates of boundaries in mega-annum (Ma) unless otherwise noted
Phanerozoic	Cenozoic (Cn)	Quaternary (Q)	Holocene	11,700 ±99 yr*
			Pleistocene	2.588*
		Tertiary (T)	Neogene (N)	Pliocene	5.332 ±0.005
			Miocene	23.03 ±0.05
			Paleogene (Pg)	Oligocene	33.9 ±0.1
			Eocene	55.8 ±0.2
			Paleocene	65.5 ±0.3
	Mesozoic (Mz)	Cretaceous (K)	Upper / Late	99.6 ±0.9
			Lower / Early	145.5 ±4.0
		Jurassic (J)	Upper / Late	161.2 ±4.0
			Middle	175.6 ±2.0
			Lower / Early	199.6 ±0.6
		Triassic (Tr)	Upper / Late	228.7 ±2.0*
			Middle	245.0 ±1.5
			Lower / Early	251.0 ±0.4
	Paleozoic (Pz)	Permian (P)	Lopingian	260.4 ±0.7
			Guadalupian	270.6 ±0.7
			Cisuralian	299.0 ±0.8
		Carboniferous (C)	Pennsylvanian (P)	Upper / Late	307.2 ±1.0*
			Middle	311.7 ±1.1
			Lower / Early	318.1 ±1.3
		Mississippian (M)	Upper / Late	328.3 ±1.6*
			Middle	345.3 ±2.1
			Lower / Early	359.2 ±2.5
		Devonian (D)	Upper / Late	385.3 ±2.6
			Middle	397.5 ±2.7
			Lower / Early	416.0 ±2.8
		Silurian (S)	Pridoli	418.7 ±2.7
			Ludlow	422.9 ±2.5
			Wenlock	428.2 ±2.3
			Llandovery	443.7 ±1.5
		Ordovician (O)	Upper / Late	460.9 ±1.6
			Middle	471.8 ±1.6
			Lower / Early	488.3 ±1.7
		Cambrian (C)	Upper / Late	501.0 ±2.0
			Middle	513.0 ±2.0
			Lower / Early	542.0 ±1.0

EONOTHEM / EON	ERATHEM / ERA	SYSTEM / PERIOD **	Age estimates of boundaries in mega-annum (Ma) unless otherwise noted
Proterozoic (P)	Neoproterozoic (Z)	Ediacaran	635*
		Cryogenian	850
		Tonian	1000
	Mesoproterozoic (Y)	Stenian	1200
		Ectasian	1400
		Calymmian	1600
	Paleoproterozoic (X)	Statherian	1800
		Orosirian	2050
		Rhyacian	2300
		Siderian	2500
Archean (A)	Neoarchean		2800
	Mesoarchean		3200
	Paleoarchean		3600
	Eoarchean		4000
Hadean (pA)			4600*

The geologic column as currently understood by the U.S. Geological Survey, reflecting the uniformitarian belief in long ages of earth history

and the rocks demonstrate the earth's great age." But wait. If Noah's Flood really happened as the Bible claims, then it would at least do what large floods do today. Big floods erode and then deposit large quantities of sediments full of plant and animal remains. The great Flood would no doubt have been responsible for the majority of both rocks and fossils. And the evidence is clear—so clear that, again, only willful ignorance would conclude otherwise.

Two hundred or so years ago, advocates of uniformitarianism claimed total victory. Once the uniformitarian "doctrine" of the latter days began to gain influence, Bible-believing Christians felt a need for a response. Some stood strong, but others felt compelled to reinterpret Scripture, and downgraded the great Flood to a "local" flood that covered only the Mesopotamian River Valley, or to a nonsensical "tranquil" flood that, while global, left no discernible geological trace.

Thus, the great error of the last days hinges on misinterpretations of creation and the Flood. In both cases, uniformitarianism denies supernatural involvement and attempts to reinterpret the evidence. However, in both cases, supernatural causes are necessary to explain the data, and adequate causes are revealed in Scripture. The created "very good" world was ruined by sin, and dramatically altered by the catastrophic processes of the great Flood. Today, we study the cursed, flooded remnant of the created world, no longer "very good."

COMING JUDGMENT AND RESTORATION

Peter continues in the passage to assert that even this present world is only temporary. It currently maintains its seeming equilibrium, being "kept in store" by the "same word" of God (2 Peter 3:7), not by mere natural forces. A pseudo-uniformity reigns as sin grows once again, testing the Judge's patience. But make no mistake, He has "reserved [this world] unto fire against the day of judgment and perdition [destruction] of ungodly men." Man's sin remains, and sin requires a death penalty. The penalty will not be by water next time, but by fire. The next judgment is described as another violent violation of the uniformity we now experience.

When will this judgment come? When will His patience exhaust itself? It may come in a day, or in a thousand years (v. 8), but it will come, having been required and promised by our Just and Holy Creator/Judge/Redeemer. He stands outside of time, seeing past, present, and future unfold before Him. He can do in a day what uniform processes and rates would take a long time to accomplish.

As of yet, His patience is "longsuffering" (v. 9) toward us; especially for sinners. All deserve the just penalty for their sin, but He delays that justice so that sinners will have a little more time to respond to His gracious offer of forgiveness, based on His Son's sacrificial death on their behalf. When His purposes have been fully accomplished on earth, He will delay no longer, for He "is not slack concerning his promise" but "longsuffering to us-ward, not willing that any should perish, but that all should come to repentance." Repentance involves a changing of the mind from wrong thinking to right thinking. We must think rightly about Him, His Word, His Son's substitutionary death as payment for our sin penalty, and His supernatural plan for the creation.

His plan includes a restoration of creation to its intended "very good" state and beauty. His supernatural power will annihilate this world (v. 10) and replace it with a recreated "new heavens and a new earth" (v. 13), where righteousness can dwell once again. We can look forward to this present world passing away, as did the previous earth in the days of Noah, all by God's "non-uniform" power.

In summary, we have noticed Scripture's teaching of His past creation by supernatural processes of a perfect world that subsequently was distorted by sin, and then completely restructured by the supernaturally controlled Flood of Noah's day. This present world is upheld by supernatural power, redeemed from sin by Christ, yet dominated by anti-supernatural thinking and reserved for judgment by fire. A new and still future world will replace this one, supernaturally recreated to fulfill God's intention for creation.

Uniformitarianism, the denial of supernatural involvement in history, yields much wrong thinking. It has for too long dominated Western thought and needs to be replaced, or "repented of." We need to stand in submission to the eternal, omnipotent Creator, yielding to His authority in all areas.

CHAPTER 2

HISTORICAL DEVELOPMENT OF THE CREATION/EVOLUTION DEBATE

Throughout the centuries, nearly everyone who had access to biblical information believed in the global Flood. It wasn't questioned. To one who respects what the Bible contains, it is obvious that the Bible teaches that the Flood was global in extent. No one tried to limit the great Flood to a local region, or even a large region. Some Jewish scholars departed from a strictly literal interpretation, but they wouldn't dare take obvious historical passages and twist them into fanciful non-history. New Testament times also brought their share of controversies, but the extent of the Flood, and its companion doctrine of the young age of the earth, was not one of them.

Not only did theologians espouse the global Flood, but so did students of history, especially earth history. The rock strata were primarily understood as the work of water action, and fossils were plants and animals that perished in the Flood. In fact, the early pioneers of the fledgling field of geology were for the most part Bible-believing Christians.[1] By far, the fathers of modern science, from biology, to medicine, to physics, etc., were Christians who believed in the recent creation, the universal Curse, and the global Flood. They felt they were "thinking God's thoughts after Him" as they unraveled scientific mysteries.[2]

Throughout the "Dark Ages," God was often thought of as mysterious and capricious, but as the Reformation brought greater access to and familiarity with Scripture, many realized that God was knowable and a God of regularity and order. Scientists, in particular, attempted to know Him more fully as they better understood His grand work of creation. They recognized that as a God of order, He would have created with order, complexity, and precision, and they set about to find that order. Soon they found many laws by which nature operates, and thus was born "science" as we know it.

Moving water was found to carry enormous potential to accomplish geologic work. The great Flood of Noah's day might be beyond our experience and even our imagination, but it was understood as the cause of the area-wide layers of fossil-bearing rock.

This thinking remained until around 1800, when winds of spiritual change began blowing in England and throughout Europe. Secularists were chafing against the restraints placed upon their thoughts and actions by the teachings of Scripture. Some began promoting the radical idea that strictly natural process had formed the earth, not the hand of God. Following the lead of James Hutton (*Theory of the Earth,* published in 1795), a secular-minded lawyer by the name of Sir Charles Lyell published *Principles of Geology* in 1830. This book promoted the concept that strictly natural processes of uniform character had fashioned the earth.

Soon, the concept that supernatural input never acted on the earth captured the Western world's fancy. Lyell desired to replace belief in Scripture with his non-supernaturalism. He strategized that by exposing the Bible's supposed weak points, its grip on scholarly thought would be lessened. He felt the doctrines of the young age of the earth and the global nature of the Flood were some of the Bible's weakest points against which geological evidence could be brought. Rather than openly confronting believers, he attempted to convince minds by sowing seeds of doubt in Scripture.

Lyell bolstered his new theory by scouring the globe for evidences that could be used to support great ages. Some will be discussed in the pages to follow, but none were or are compelling, and most have been largely rejected today. However, they carried the day for those who wanted to disbelieve Scripture.

Unfortunately, Lyell's influence didn't stop there. He met and mentored a young seminary student turned amateur naturalist by the name of Charles Darwin, and helped arrange for him to join a scientific expedition around the world, where he made numerous observations of nature. Darwin carried Lyell's book with him on the *HMS Beagle*'s voyage to other lands, and acted as a geologist for the bulk of the trip, interpreting land-

forms and fossils through a uniformitarian lens.

One of Darwin's stops was in southeastern Argentina, along the shore of the Santa Cruz River. He and the other scientists present explored the broad canyon upriver, which is comparable in many ways to the more familiar Grand Canyon in America. Darwin felt the river itself was responsible for carving the wide canyon, utilizing the same processes and energy levels it now employs. He wrote in his journal:

> The river, though it has so little power in transporting even inconsiderable fragments, yet in the lapse of ages might produce by its gradual erosion an effect of which it is difficult to judge the amount.[3]

But the geological evidence of erosion along the Santa Cruz River and in its canyon was not the only important information to collect. Southern Argentina is quite far south, and glaciers cap the high mountains

in the country's interior, just upriver from where Darwin camped. We now know that the canyon was not carved by the river alone, over any length of time, but by devastatingly powerful river floods today and especially by glacial melting during and following the Ice Age, occurring just a few thousand years ago. Recent studies attribute the canyon to volcanism, glaciation, and near-instantaneous episodes of erosion, not long ages of uniform processes. In short, Darwin was wrong.

However, Darwin's erroneous thinking soon became his life message, which he greatly extended on the Galapagos Islands. This was the very next (and most famous) stop of the *Beagle's* voyage, where Darwin's pattern of wrong thinking set the stage for his claim of evolution by natural selection. There he applied his uniformitarian interpretation of the Santa Cruz River canyon to the origin of the biological diversity he observed. Neither application was warranted, however.

Upon returning to England, Darwin's ideas were not well-received by everyone. Nearly all leading scientists opposed him. Actually, his ideas were not much different from those already published by others, including his own grandfather. Knowledgeable people of the day knew them, and also knew the scriptural teachings of recent creation and the global Flood and could point to scientific support for Scripture. Unfortunately, some science professors in the universities were also Anglican clergymen who had followed Lyell's teaching and embraced millions of years. Many of them readily accepted Darwin's ideas, and jettisoned not only these doctrines, but scriptural inerrancy as well.

Scientists initially minimized the impact of Lyellian-inspired compromise in the church by bolstering support for and holding fast to creation and Flood doctrines, but the appeal of more personal and moral autonomy came to full flower when Darwin proposed his views. Disbelief reigned, and false doctrine resulted.

CHARLES DARWIN AND GALAPAGOS ANIMALS

Many people have the mistaken notion that Darwin observed evidence of animals evolving into other types when he visited the Galapagos Islands. The animals are spectacular and can be observed "up close," but evolution cannot be seen at work there. The most famous animals are the Galapagos tortoises and finches. Others include the flightless cormorants and iguanas. Instead of being a laboratory for evolution, the islands are really a shining example of God's creation truth.

The flightless cormorants are quite similar to winged birds on the mainland. These birds have adapted to life on land, but this is due to harmful mutations and adaptations that have robbed them of useful wings. Evolution should be about gaining new traits and body parts, not losing them.

Much has been made of Darwin's finches. Some count up to 17 different species living on the various islands, marked by ever-so-slight beak differences. But in times of drought or scarce food supply, the species are seen to readily crossbreed and produce fertile offspring. They are not separate species at all, merely separate communities or varieties.

Evolutionists claimed a great victory when marine iguanas were discovered, thinking that they were evolving either into or from the land iguanas. Imagine their consternation when the animals were observed to hybridize or crossbreed. They are merely varieties of the same creature, having developed different habits for the different habitats.

The giant Galapagos tortoises and turtles are divided into land and sea forms, with noticeable differences in their shells. It's interesting that they live on or visit the same isolated island group. Only minor genetic differences separate them. One wonders if even they could hybridize if given the chance.

Far from being a laboratory for evolution, the Galapagos Islands are better understood as a monument to God's creative handiwork. He created animals to fill and adapt to various environments and habitats, with no need to evolve into something new.

For further information, see the DVD *The Mysterious Islands*.

In particular, questions regarding the Flood for which science had no ready answer caused many doubts. The growing body of knowledge concerning the world's topography revealed a planet-wide pattern of high mountain chains. A lot of water must have been required to cover these mountains during the Flood. Where did it come from, and where did it go? Exotic animals were being discovered all over the globe. Weren't there far too many different animals for representatives to fit inside the Ark of Noah? Quite different people groups were being encountered in faraway places. Did all the world's ethnic groups come from Noah? These and other questions fed doubts.

There's nothing wrong with asking questions or with having doubts, for they encourage study. Finding answers may take serious study, but study can be a time of true growth. As it relates to Scripture, there will always be good answers, even if a lack of immediate answers requires that we shelve particular questions for the time being, believing that answers will someday be forthcoming. For a Christian, questions should lead to greater understanding, or a postponement of answers, not to disbelief.

Unfortunately for our theological forefathers in Europe, their doubts led to unbelief, and soon pages were being ripped from Scripture. As you'll read later in this book, there are now satisfying answers to these and other questions. We'll never have all the answers to all the questions this side of eternity, but there's no need to disbelieve. We have answers to many difficult questions now, and reason to believe we'll soon have more. Christians need no longer be intimidated by any remaining unanswered questions.

SAVING SCRIPTURE

Many people were intimidated into believing that "because science had proved it, Lyell's uniformitarian thinking must be true," even if it discredited Scripture. Striving to reach a compromise between evolution's long ages and Scripture, ardent Bible-believing Christians proposed various ways to incorporate them and thus "salvage" Scripture—concepts that still plague Christianity today. Those holding a high view of Scripture gravitated to the gap theory, which places long ages between the first two verses of Genesis 1. This theory proposes that the initial creation was followed by global destruction due to Satan's fall, and later the six days

of re-creation, and then the Flood of Noah's day. This supposedly allowed Christians to embrace both long-age geological evolution (which scientists claimed was fact) and the biological creation that the Bible clearly taught.

Other believers succumbed to theistic evolution, for the same reason. Thinking that science had proven evolution, they felt they could salvage Scripture by claiming that evolution was God's method of creation. More recently, the day-age concept has appeared, holding that the days of the creation week were equivalent to the geologic ages, during which God occasionally created some new thing. In each case, Scripture was altered. These accommodationist views compromised only Scripture. The evolution/long age/uniformitarian view was never altered at all.

All such views suffer from the same weaknesses and can be refuted at length (as they are elsewhere). First, they are bankrupt, relying on conjectures like the spontaneous generation of life from non-life. Next, all degrade Scripture by placing man's opinions above the obvious teaching of the text. None solves the Bible's imagined conflict with "scientific" pronouncements, but instead raises more serious issues. All compromising views include a downgrading of the Flood to a local or tranquil flood, one that is not responsible for the rock and fossil record. They also weaken the doctrine of God's creative majesty, substituting a trial and error approach for His sovereign, omniscient will.

A COMMON THREAD

Each view also disregards a cardinal doctrine of Christianity, that "the wages of sin is death" (Romans 6:23). Spiritual death and physical death are the consequences of man's sin, necessitating the death of Christ to pay sin's penalty, for "Christ died for our sins" (1 Corinthians 15:4). If the Curse involved only spiritual death, as these concepts' advocates claim, why did Christ need to die physically? According to all compromise views, death of conscious life predated man's appearance, and certainly was present long before man sinned, thereby incurring the Curse. But if physical death were present before sin, then it could not really be the "wages of sin," the subsequent penalty for sin. Indeed, death is thought to be the key to man's evolution, as the concluding paragraph of Charles Darwin's famous book *On the Origin of Species* directly admitted. In evolution, death produced man by causing less fit types to die and go extinct over time. Thus, death is regarded as good, and by extension Christ's death did not pay the penalty for sin.

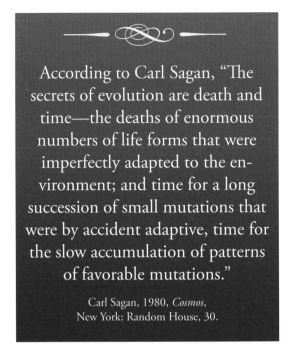

According to Carl Sagan, "The secrets of evolution are death and time—the deaths of enormous numbers of life forms that were imperfectly adapted to the environment; and time for a long succession of small mutations that were by accident adaptive, time for the slow accumulation of patterns of favorable mutations."

Carl Sagan, 1980, *Cosmos*,
New York: Random House, 30.

In this way, all compromise views negate non-negotiable Christian doctrines. While it is not impossible for someone to be a Christian and still believe in one of these compromises, it is impossible for any one of these views to be true if Christianity is true. If any are true, then Christianity's core doctrines are wrong.

Another common fallacy is the claim that Genesis was written in poetic language, and thus the account of the Flood is not to be understood literally. This concept was shown to be in error in a lengthy study that compared the verbs and verb tenses used in obvious poetic passages elsewhere in Scripture to parallel passages of obvious narrative style in Genesis.[4] Verb tenses used in narrative passages relating historical events (such as a military excursion in 1 Chronicles or a conversation with the King of Babylon in Daniel) differ from those used in poetic passages in Psalms or Isaiah.

For instance, the style used in the book of Exodus to describe the Israelites' exit from Egypt is a straightforward narrative style. The reader is expected to understand the Red Sea crossing passage in Exodus 14 as actual history. Compare it with the account in Exodus 15 in which Scripture gives a "poetic" restatement of the event—a different style of writing is employed. Colorful verbs and emotive verb tenses are used throughout,

whereas the Exodus 14 passage is written in narrative format, matter-of-factly relating a true story.

The verb study also compared the Genesis Flood account given in Genesis 6–10 to the poetic creation and Flood references in passages such as Psalm 104, and it noted differences in style and content. Similar comparisons were made throughout the Old Testament. It was discovered that the Genesis account is the *most* "narrative" and *least* poetic of all passages, and surely intended to be taken literally. This is not to imply that poetic writing is not to be understood historically, for surely God can write with flair if He chooses. But it does instruct us that God intended the Genesis accounts of creation, the Fall, and the Flood to be understood as straightforward history.

COMPROMISE TESTED

The tendency to compromise was on full display at the famous Scopes "Monkey Trial" in 1925. Anti-Christian forces gathered to strike a blow against God and the necessity of submitting to Him in life's choices. The whole affair started when the newly founded American Civil Liberties Union (ACLU) decided to use this opportunity to begin its long campaign against Christianity's influence in America. It openly advertised for any teacher who would be willing to be arrested for violating the Tennessee injunction against teaching human evolution. John Scopes was not a science teacher, but agreed to discuss evolution with one student in the back seat of a car and undergo a staged arrest. The case brought national attention. Famous lawyers lined up on both sides. The verdict actually came down in favor of the creationists, but was later nullified on a technicality.

In a bizarre and unprecedented turn of events, the lawyer defending the creation law agreed to be a witness. He was tricked by the ACLU lawyer into defending creation and the entire Bible on the witness stand. Unfortunately, he himself had already compromised with long ages and local flood concepts, and could not give a consistent defense of either creation or biblical inerrancy. Through it all, biblical doctrine and Bible believers were mercilessly ridiculed in the press, an assault that continues today. The end result? Christianity largely retreated underground and withdrew from the public arena. Today, as many believers attempt to regain an influence, they find laws blocking them and popular opinion against them, and mistakenly believe they have no right to have a say. Now education, government, the courts, the media, and many denominations and denominational schools are totally controlled by secularists.

Interestingly, all the scientific evidence supposedly supporting evolution that was scheduled for use in the trial and picked up in the surrounding media blitz has been thoroughly discredited. From Piltdown Man, to Nebraska Man, to embryonic recapitulation, to the peppered moth, to vestigial organs, etc., none are viable arguments for evolution today.[5]

The publication of *The Genesis Flood* and other creationist books countered this juggernaut, ushering in the modern creation movement. Interest in creation still flourishes today, and has spawned thousands of creation scientists, hundreds of creationist organizations, and millions of creation believers. Polls taken in America consistently show a vast majority of people, some 80 to 90 percent in most polls, hold to some form of creation, especially young earth creation.

The onslaught against the Bible continues, however. Compromise and desire of affirmation from secular peers weighs heavily. For decades, theistic evolution has been on the wane, being replaced by various forms of the day-age theory. Perhaps the most effective advocate for this today is Dr. Hugh Ross, a trained astronomer with an undue fascination with the Big Bang, which he considers God's method of creating the universe as described in Genesis 1:1. His many scientific excesses are well-documented elsewhere, but it is his grievous scriptural gymnastics that do the most harm. His view of the past is indistinguishable from that of the strictly secular view, yet he maintains that he holds to biblical

inerrancy and evangelical Christianity. But to do so, he routinely twists Scripture to make it fit secular views. Most compromise advocates merely ignore Scripture, but Ross actively teaches Christians ways to interpret the Bible to make it say things it clearly does not say. He has gained an enormous following among evangel-

The Scopes "Monkey" Trial of 1925 was purposively staged by the newly formed ACLU to challenge a Tennessee law forbidding the teaching of the evolution of man from animals. Interestingly, all the "scientific" evidences for evolution that were scheduled to be introduced are now known to be false.

ical leaders who ought to know better. No wonder the influence of the Christian church languishes so.

A NEW TACTIC

Another major movement has come to be known as the Intelligent Design Movement (ID). Arising primarily out of the insightful writings of Phillip Johnson, it sports a wide umbrella, accepting scientists from many backgrounds—including Christian, non-Christian, agnostic, cultic, evolutionist, etc. All who are involved admit the obvious need for a designer to produce life's amazing design, and decry the rather "religious" flavor of strict naturalism. Typically, they stand against evolution by natural processes only, but fully accept long ages and uniformitarianism. Some of its prominent members are Christian/creationists, but many others are quite opposed to both. The one common denominator is the tactical choice of being completely secular in their efforts and pronouncements. The identity of the designer and the method of design are left to the individual. Thus, the ID movement rigorously opposes being labeled as Christian or creationist. Indeed, it is neither.

Representatives from ID have testified at numerous court trials and school board hearings. While some success in public understanding can be cited for their efforts, several adverse and far-reaching court rulings have resulted that have done great damage. Certainly, God the Creator, officially ignored and shunned by ID, has not blessed.

Following close behind ID's minimal gains, but disavowing any ID affiliation, has come a resurgent "Christian" theistic evolution group named BioLogos. It was founded by Dr. Francis Collins, who rose to prominence as director of the Human Genome Project. Openly Christian, he has shunned any affiliation with creationists, yet banded with the many professors at Christian colleges who aggressively teach evolution and uniformitarianism. Funded by the Templeton Foundation, BioLogos has targeted Christian pastors as the way to influence Christianity and to induce church

people to accept evolution. While embracing evolution by uniformitarian processes, as well as a local flood and millions of years, they give passing lip service to God as Creator, (i.e., God the Evolver). Through teaching materials and training seminars, they desire to fully incorporate evolution into church life.

Summary

This brief review of various trends that accommodate evolution and its uniformitarian kin as they deal with earth history and the broader origins question has been noticeably incomplete, but it does point out that all such compromise efforts include uniformitarianism and local flood concepts, along with deep time. These groups and individuals raise serious issues and questions, and to these we turn our attention. Remember, the key issue in understanding earth history is the nature of the Flood. Was it regular, uniform, and local, or supernatural, catastrophic, and global in extent? Specifically, does the Bible teach that the Flood of Noah's day was global or local, and how are the scientific data best interpreted?

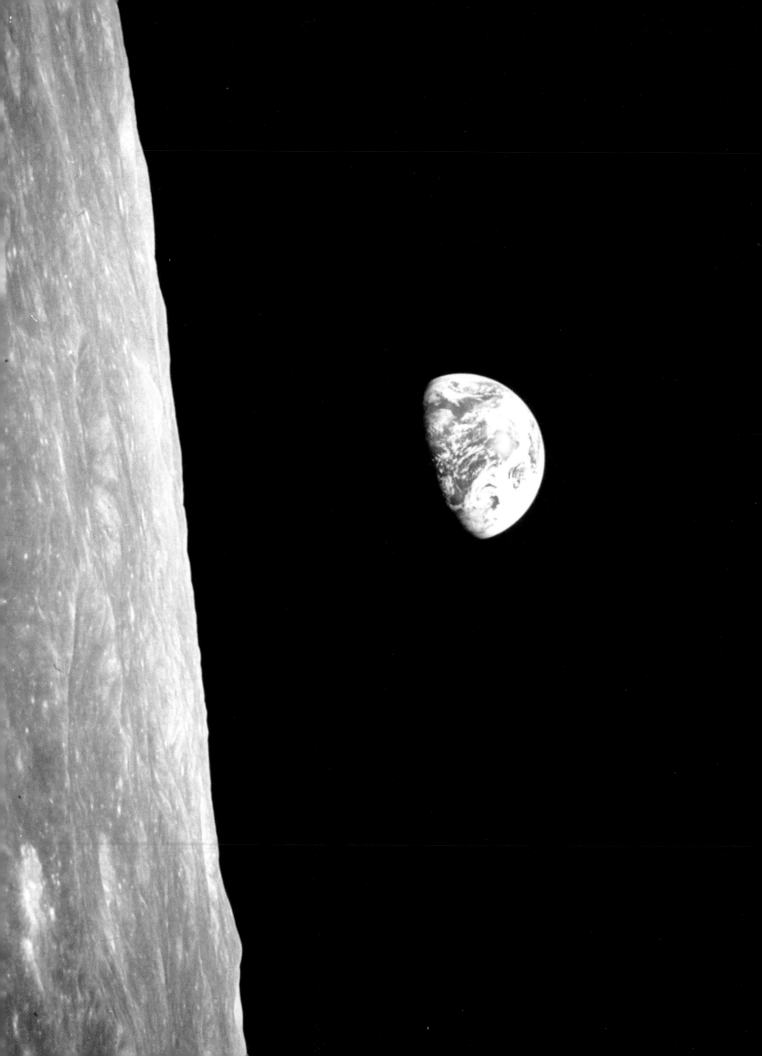

CHAPTER 3

A Scriptural Overview of Creation, the Flood, and Its Aftermath

In many different ways and in repeated fashion, the scriptural account of the Flood relates information about a worldwide flood of dynamic character. As discussed in chapter 4, this account makes little sense if it was merely a local event. It is plainly described as global and destructive, and logical inferences based on Scripture lead inexorably to the same conclusion. If the Flood of Noah's day was either local or tranquil, then God misled us, for He eloquently stated that it was global and geologically devastating.

And always remember, if the Flood really happened as stated in Scripture, then it would have been responsible for earth's present condition, including the rock and fossil records of earth's crust—evidences that have been wrongly interpreted (using uniformitarian assumptions) in support of evolution and old earth concepts. If rocks and fossils are really the result of a global flood, there is little evidence remaining in favor of evolution and long ages. Since this point is so critical, we will investigate several biblical arguments for a global flood.[1]

It will be helpful to first acquaint ourselves with the scriptural model of geology. Obviously, Genesis doesn't give all the specifics with regard to geology and earth history, but we can glean from its words much geological information, which becomes the framework on which we build our geological thinking.

The Geology of Creation

Day One

The first verse of Genesis reads, "In the beginning God created the heaven and the earth." Time was started (in the beginning) and mass/energy (the earth) was hung in three-dimensional space (the heaven). "By the word of the LORD were the heavens made; and all the host of them by the breath of his mouth....For he spake, and it was done; he commanded, and it stood fast" (Psalm 33:6, 9). An instantaneous creation event is described, with no great length of time required. All things simply sprang from the omnipotent mind of the Creator God as He spoke them into existence.

Physicists label the universe as a space-mass-time continuum, with each component necessary for the existence and realization of the others. In Romans 1:20, we are told that even the invisible nature of the Godhead is "clearly seen" in all that God has created. Might the "triune" universe be a reflection of its triune Creator God?

"God is light," Scripture tells us (1 John 1:5), so if He was all there was, we can assume that there was initially no darkness. But soon, a created darkness shrouded the primeval earth (Isaiah 45:7). "And darkness was upon the face of the deep" (Genesis 1:2), so that the Creator's next action—bathing the new earth in light from an unnamed source, under which the uninhabited orb rotated—yielded alternating periods of light and darkness. This action caused and still causes creation to give Him great glory, and illustrates His illuminating nature. The light portion of the light/dark cycle was called "Day" and the dark portion was called "Night" (Genesis 1:3-5), both necessary for earth's proper functioning.

The source of that light is enigmatic, for the sun was not made until the fourth day. There are numerous ways light can be produced, from chemical reactions to nuclear reactions to fire to friction, etc. Whatever the source, the Creator controlled and focused it. Of course, God Himself is light, so He needed no other source, but this was a newly formed source. On Day Four, a permanent light source, the sun, was made that would continually energize both organic and inorganic realms.

The Stuff of Earth

Earth materials consist of atoms, which are built from high-energy subatomic particles and held together by powerful but mysterious nuclear forces. Atoms bind together into molecules, which group together into the various minerals and compounds—solids, liquids, and gases. We know little of the shape and configuration of creation when it was first called into existence. It was called "earth," but it was yet "without form," not yet fully prepared to perform its intended function, and "void," or completely uninhabited. It could only be described as a vast unfinished "deep" (Genesis 1:2) poised for God's continuing work.

Scripture tells us that earth was completely covered by a watery layer. Remote studies of deep mantle rocks using seismic waves imply that there was a rocky earth underneath the global watery layer. The Spirit of God "moved upon the face of the waters," energizing and preparing it for the work to follow.

Day Two

On Day Two, the world's ocean separated into two zones, "the waters which were under the firmament from the waters which were above the firmament" (Genesis 1:7). Creationists debate the meaning of this zone of water above, stemming from the fact that whatever it was, it's inaccessible or gone now and can't be reconstructed. Genesis 1 refers to the firmament in more than one way—as the atmosphere in which birds fly (v. 20), and the realm of the stars (v. 14). Elsewhere, Scripture refers to a "firmament" as the faraway residence of

God (Psalm 150:1). Certainty eludes us.

The Waters Above

Many early creationists interpreted the "waters which were above the firmament" as a layer of water vapor above earth's atmosphere. Probably gaseous water, it was thoroughly transparent, neither made of liquid water (like clouds) nor of frozen water. This invisible layer of water in gaseous form would have acted as a canopy surrounding earth, producing a "greenhouse effect" on the surface below. Numerous speculative benefits to life and the environment have been ascribed to this canopy.

Just as in a greenhouse and beneath the canopies of other planets, it is postulated that the temperature within would have been evenly distributed—no polar regions, and no deserts. This would make the entire earth habitable and warm, probably similar to our modern subtropical zones. In the present world, temperature differences produce today's weather patterns, but without temperature gradients, no storms or wind would ravage the land. Without wind, there could hardly even be rainfall. Evaporation that occurred during the daytime would condense in zones directly above as nightfall cooled things off, falling back to earth as dew near where it evaporated.

Most importantly, the canopy would form a great shield surrounding earth, filtering out incoming cosmic and solar radiation. These cause mutations to living cells and to DNA. Over time, great damage builds up in cells and bodies. Damage to our organs and skin by radiation is responsible for many diseases and the aging process we all face.

Scripture doesn't give much detail for such a canopy and we can't be dogmatic, but several hints are given and cannot be ignored. Technical difficulties arise when we note that such a canopy today would likely cause global warming with such a vengeance that it would make life on earth impossible. Creationist research has tried every conceivable variable of today's conditions to make the canopy stable, with inconclusive success. Perhaps we have misinterpreted the scriptural clues, or haven't discerned the proper conditions, but most creationist scientists today hesitate to rely on canopy ideas to describe the early earth. Yet hints in Scripture remain of a radically different environment in the beginning.

In addition to the creation of "the waters above," Genesis 2:5-6 describes the environment of Eden as "the

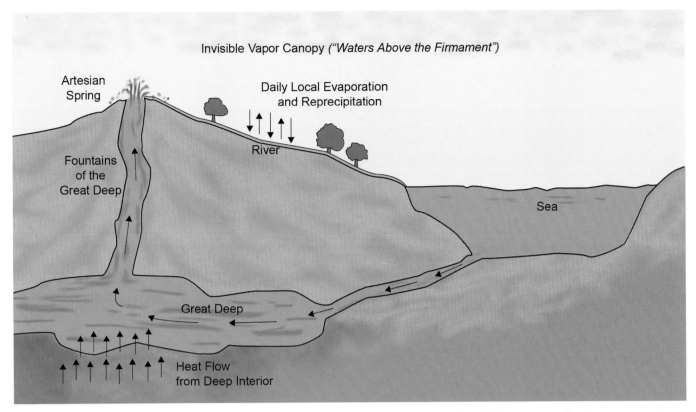

Invisible Vapor Canopy *("Waters Above the Firmament")*

Artesian Spring

Daily Local Evaporation and Reprecipitation

Fountains of the Great Deep

River

Sea

Great Deep

Heat Flow from Deep Interior

When first created, earth's hydrologic cycle must have been something like this, with fresh water flowing to the surface from below. The springs that fed the world's rivers and watered the continents evidently ruptured at the start of the Flood and no longer exist.

LORD God had not caused it to rain upon the earth.... but there went up a mist from the earth, and watered the whole face of the ground." A literal translation of the Hebrew indicates that a preferable translation would read, "God had not *yet* caused it to rain." The water cycle was radically different from today's, in which rain is collected in rivers that flow into the ocean, from which it evaporates, is transported to land, and falls again as rain. We are told that in the original creation "a river went out of Eden to water the garden; and from thence it was parted, and became into four heads" (Genesis 2:10), each river watering a different area. Dewfall could hardly have been the only source of water for large rivers. Today's rivers are fed primarily by rainfall and related groundwater, but with little rain, these early rivers would necessarily have been fed by water welling up from below and seeping from the soil. Obviously, no such system of large artesian springs remains today. Whatever they were, they were subsequently destroyed by the great Flood of Noah's day.

Such a set of rivers implies a vastly different internal "piping" system for earth. Scripture again gives only the basic facts, but it does mention underground "fountains of the great deep" (Genesis 7:11) that even-

tually broke open and contributed to the great Flood's devastation. Their eruption during the Flood not only brought hot underground water to the surface, they provided a continual source of evaporating water to the clouds that produced the intense rainfall during the Flood.

Such an environment before the Flood would likely foster abundant plant growth. Many of these plants were of great size compared to their living representatives. Before the Fall, both animals and humans were instructed to eat only plants (Genesis 1:29-30). When we study the plants from before the Flood that have been preserved as fossils, we see that they were typically those that grow in semitropical environments. From such fossils, we see the abundant nature of the biosphere and know the Creator supplied life's every need.

Benefits of Living in the Early Earth

In Genesis 5:4-32, we read that Adam and his descendants lived long lives. Those whose lifespans were recorded averaged 911 years. Obviously, things were different. We age as genetic mutations damage our cells, caused mainly by incoming radiation. With more water in the atmosphere, many such harmful particles would have been restrained from entering, resulting

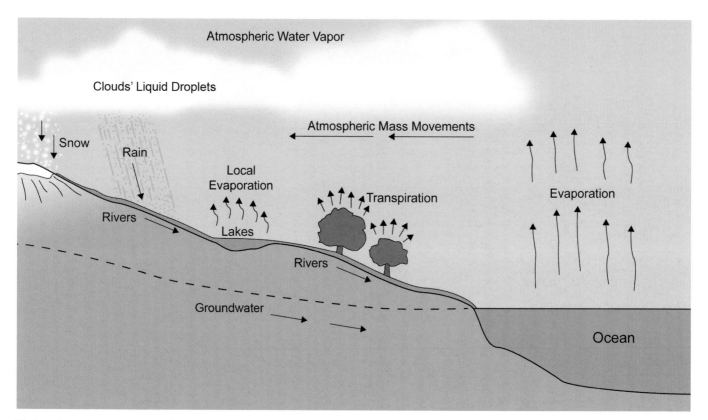

Today, the primary source of water is rainfall, fed by evaporation from the oceans.

in enhanced living conditions and a lower death rate, just as Scripture records. Perhaps there were multiple factors involved, including more complete nutrition, healthier lifestyle, increased air pressure and oxygen, etc. But those conditions are gone now, removed by the great Flood, and we can't be certain. Yet from what we can surmise, the biblical data make sense.

We might also suppose that by this time on Day Two, earth's magnetic field was also in place. The materials that make up the planet had no doubt already differentiated into zones, which we now observe as the thin surface crust, the thick mantle beneath, and the metallic core, both liquid outer core and solid inner core. Electrical currents in the core produce today's magnetic field, and with the atmosphere it provides protection for life on the surface. Without it, we would be bombarded by harmful cosmic rays. Much mystery remains about earth's interior, but at the time of its creation, all was "good."

Day Three

On Day Three, the continents were called forth from the ocean. Note that Scripture does not say God directly created the continents *ex nihilo*, but that He used a process: "Let the waters under the heaven be gathered together into one place, and let the dry land appear"

(Genesis 1:9). God the Creator used various processes to elevate some of the solid material we now call continents and relocate some of the waters into low places we now call ocean basins. He didn't simply speak continents into existence; He formed them by processes and forces, including gravity, uplift, erosion, chemical reactions, etc. In all likelihood, there was only one supercontinent, for if the waters were gathered together into one place, the land could probably be described as in one place as well.

This dynamic uplift required great power. Present evidence suggests that the pre-Flood continent (or continents) was rather similar in size (although not of similar configuration or location) to today's continents. Unless the Creator miraculously relocated the water, some period of time was necessary for it to drain off the thousands of miles of continental width. Most likely, the runoff rate was miraculously increased. If rapidly moving water had the erosive potential it does today, think of the erosion that must have resulted. This eroded material would have been deposited as sediments in low regions as the water velocity slowed. No life had yet been created, so the sediments would contain no remains of living creatures and no fossils would have resulted. This would become the necessary soil for the plants that would follow.

EARTH'S MAGNETIC FIELD

The decay of earth's magnetic field has been one of the strongest evidences for the Bible's recent creation doctrine. This concept, developed originally by Dr. Thomas Barnes in 1971, was updated and revised by Dr. Russell Humphreys over the last few decades.

Earth is surrounded by a large-scale magnetic field, generated by well-understood and well-documented electrical currents in its metallic fluid core. Uniformity considers the field to arise from postulated fluid motions in the molten outer core, but no adequate mechanism for generating such motions has been accepted. If they were ever started, internal friction would slow them down until they finally stopped, at which time they could not be restarted. Yet uniformitarians hold that a self-generating field has reversed itself many times, involving numerous "re-startings," contrary to "uniform" natural law.

Scientists have measured the magnetic field's strength on a global scale since 1835, and from 1970 onward the measurements have been accurate enough to estimate the total energy contained in the field as well. There is natural oscillation in the field's strength, but a pronounced steady overall decline, with a half-life of about 1,400 years, dominates. This means that in 1,400 years it will be one-half as strong, in 2,800 years it will be one-fourth as strong, and so on.

The earth's magnetic field protects life from incoming cosmic radiation.

Measurements of magnetized rocks and archaeological artifacts show that this decay has been going on smoothly for the past 1,000 years. Prior to that, during and after the Flood, the field at the earth's surface was more complicated. From about 2500 B.C. to 1000 A.D., the force that the field would exert on a compass needle went up and down, sometimes abruptly. During the year of the Flood, rock data show that the field actually reversed its direction, going from northward to southward and northward again within just a few days.

However, according to data and straightforward theory, the total *energy* in the field, from the core to the surface and out into space, has had a simpler history. Since creation, the energy has always decreased as least as fast as it currently does. Extrapolating into the past, 1,500 years ago the field

was at least twice as energetic. The energy would continue doubling each 1,500 years back. Based on these calculations, about 30,000 years ago the electrical heating in the core would have been more than a million times greater than it is today—enough to have destroyed the planet. The inescapable conclusion we can draw is that the earth must be less than a few dozen millennia old. If one accounts for the much greater energy loss of the magnetic direction reversals during the Genesis Flood, the field could easily be only a few thousand years old—much younger than uniformitarians insist.

Compare this "clock" with others used to estimate earth's age. This method utilizes a long period of measurement, amounting to over one-tenth of a half-life, whereas radioisotope decay has been accurately measured for only about 100 years, while its half-lives are typically measured in the billions. The short half-life should be favored by uniformitarians, for it minimizes the chances that something dramatic has happened to change things, since longer spans are more susceptible to out-of-the-ordinary events. Magnetic field decay also involves a whole earth measurement, and on this large scale it cannot be easily altered or "contaminated," as could any rock selected for radioisotope dating.

Recent creation ideas are necessarily coupled with the global Flood in the days of Noah, during which all of earth's processes and systems were severely disrupted. The rapid reversals of the global field would have recorded themselves as (the well-observed) "magnetic stripes" flanking mid-ocean spreading centers.

All things considered, the magnetic field "clock" might be the very best of geochronometers, nearly all of which indicate a maximum age for earth far too short for evolution to occur. The weight of the scientific evidence is on the side of the young earth—and of biblical doctrine.[1]

1. For more details, see John Morris, 2007, *The Young Earth*, rev. ed., Green Forest, AR: Master Books; and Andrew Snelling, 2009, *Earth's Catastrophic Past*, Dallas, TX: Institute for Creation Research, 509.

The rapid uplift would generate unimaginable heat and pressures capable of quickly hardening some of these new sediments into vast layers of fossil-free sedimentary rock of all types, and changing or melting some of these sediments into vast zones of metamorphic and igneous rocks. Under modern conditions, metamorphic processes require a lengthy time, but in the creation period, God was acting purposefully, quickly, and supernaturally to bring about His will. His miraculous processes may have been quite different from those with which we are familiar, or they may have been different only in rate, scale, and intensity from present processes. Certainly, imposing the principle of naturalistic uniformitarianism would be inappropriate during this time of miracles. We can't comprehend the processes, but He told us He did it and how long it took—part of Day Three.

The remaining part of the day, He created plants, the "grass, the herb yielding seed, and the fruit tree yielding fruit after his kind, whose seed is in itself" (Genesis 1:11). No longer were the newly formed continents barren; they flourished with plants of all kinds. These plants would provide food for the animals brought forth on Days Five and Six.

Plants were each designed with unique and intricate genetic codes, blueprints by which they would grow, function, and reproduce. This set of instructions, the seed within, would insure that the individual plants that resulted from their reproduction were substantially the same as the original ones, with differences only within the limits of variation. They were designed and equipped to survive and adapt to

Genesis tells us that God created animals and plants "according to their kinds." Much variety within each kind occurs. Limits to the created kind can be approximated by the ability to cross, or interbreed.

different conditions, able to fill the land's varied ecological niches as needed.

After Their Kind

The repeated phrase "after their kind" bears notice. Evidently, each category of plant was created as that specific category. It appeared suddenly, without having descended from another type, as evolution requires.

Note that the first type of plants mentioned was grass that, just like today, produced grass seed. The same could be said for the herbs and fruit trees created "after their kind." This information speaks to the issue of theistic evolution, which postulates that God used evolution as His "creative" method over long ages. These are seed-bearing plants, which according to evolution evolved long after terrestrial animals evolved. Thus, they would have been one of the last things to appear, but in God's account of creation they appeared first. The biblical account certainly doesn't have things created in the same order as evolution.[2]

Furthermore, in the "simple to complex" concept of evolution, early plants were "simple." However, there is nothing simple about seed-bearing plants; they are among the most complex of all plants. If evolution were true, you would think the earliest plants would have reproduced asexually and been followed by those that reproduced by various spores. But biblically, the first types of plants were complex, seed-bearing plants.

Many aspects of the creation account are incompatible with evolution and its stepchildren, progressive creation, the framework hypothesis, and the gap theory, but this is one of the most obvious. The biblical order of creation was very different from the evolutionary order of the appearance of plants and animals over long ages. No Bible-believer should

THE GLOBAL FLOOD

condone such obvious compromise and distortion of Scripture.

Presumably, Day Three is also the day when insects were created, although Scripture doesn't specifically say and Bible interpreters disagree on the subject. Insects share biological life, but not true biblical or "soulish" life, with the nonliving plants. They do not really breathe, but absorb oxygen through their thorax directly from the air. Neither do they have blood, for their body fluids are quite different. Insects are everywhere. Avoiding harming them could hardly happen without divine interference, and while this could have been the case in the pre-Curse world, it seems more likely (to this author, at least) that the death of an insect would not constitute biblical death.

From a geological perspective, plants require topsoil and a substrate for their roots. Thus, the "very good" created continents and sub-oceanic environments fulfilled these requirements. On the other hand, plants impact their environment, anchoring it and bioturbating its sediments with their various activities. This was not harmful, but constructive and supportive. Each step of creation week built on the others, preparing the planet to support animal life, and particularly the image of God created on Day Six.

Day Four

God had created "light" on Day One, but on Day Four He created "light bearers," or permanent light sources (a different Hebrew word from "light") to illuminate the earth (Genesis 1:14). Primarily, He made the sun to energize earth and the moon to reflect the sun's light. Sunlight is necessary for vital photosynthesis in plants, is the cause of the water cycle, and maintains a livable temperature, among other things. Life as we know it simply could not exist without the sun. The moon appeared also, reflecting the sun's light. In size, it is almost a companion earth, with one-quarter its diameter and a gravitational attraction large enough to produce the twice-daily tides necessary for refreshing the oceans. The stars were placed in space, too far away to affect the earth, but providing a sense of grandeur and glorifying the Creator.

A primary purpose of all heavenly bodies is timekeeping. "Let there be lights in the firmament of the heaven to divide the day from the night; and let them be for signs, and for seasons, and for days, and years" (Genesis 1:14). Even today, we measure a year as one revo-

ARE PLANTS ALIVE?

The Bible teaches that in the original "very good" creation, there was to be no death. Yet God also instructed Adam and Eve, as well as the animals, to be plant eaters (Genesis 1:29-30). Would not the eating of plants constitute death?

The answer to this seeming problem lies in a biblical understanding of "life," or "living." Note that the Bible makes a sharp distinction between plants and animals. During Day Three of creation week, God commanded the inanimate earth to *"bring forth plants"* (Genesis 1:11-12), while on Day Five He "created...every *living* creature that moveth" (v. 21). At this point, and on Day Six to follow, He instituted the concept of giving "life" (Hebrew *nephesh*) to nonliving matter—something He did not do for plants. This required supernatural *creation,* and the resultant *living* animal kingdom was something new and different from all that had gone on before.

The Bible never refers to plants as living. They may "grow" or "flourish," but they do not "live." Neither do they "die." The Bible teaches that they may "wither" or "fade" (Isaiah 40:8), but not "die," since they are not "alive." They don't have "life" *(nephesh)* or "breath of life" *(ruach)* or "blood" (i.e., "the life of the flesh is in the blood," Leviticus 17:11). This state may be analogous to lack of consciousness, so that while plants are *biologically* alive, they are not *biblically* "living." It may be that a similar argument could be made for some of the "lower" animals (such as worms, insects, sponges, etc.), and certainly for bacteria, protozoans, and viruses. Their "death" would not constitute the death of truly living organisms. This, however, is controversial among creationists.

Light from Distant Stars

Perhaps the most common argument against the recent creation of all things as revealed in Genesis involves the difficulty of light from faraway stars reaching earth within biblical time spans. How could light from stars billions of light-years away reach earth in only thousands of years? Obviously, there is much we don't understand about space, but this problem does need to be addressed.

First, we must admit that we can't directly observe how light travels through time and space. Does it take esoteric routes? Many astrophysicists think so. Has the speed of light been constant? Some point to evidence to the contrary. We cannot possibly directly measure the one-way speed, only a two-way speed as light goes out, is reflected, and then returns. Are estimates of the vast distances accurate? Multilevel assumptions are necessary to conclude so. This is not to claim that mainstream speculations are wrong, but to encourage humility on the part of those who speak with feigned certainty.

It turns out almost everything we think we know about the immense universe comes from the General Relativity equations. Relativity physics is the very best approximation of physical reality we know, but it is so counterintuitive and otherworldly that we continually look for a better system. When the equations of General Relativity are solved under the assumptions of an infinite universe without a center, the solution is compatible with an origin by a Big Bang. But if the equations are considered from the perspective of a very large but finite universe (only God is infinite, and He created all things for His glory) with earth somewhere near the center (as is now recognized by astronomy), the equations predict that light from a vast distance would arrive on earth in just two days. These more biblical assumptions predict a biblical solution to the problem. Light created anywhere in the new universe on Day Four would have arrived on earth by Day Six.

Maybe this is the solution, or maybe there's a better one yet to be conceived. But it is more biblical and uses better science than the Big Bang solution.[1]

1. Russell Humphreys, 1994, *Starlight and Time: Solving the Puzzle of Distant Starlight in a Young Universe*, Green Forest, AR: Master Books; Jason Lisle, 2006, *Taking Back Astronomy: The Heavens Declare Creation*, Green Forest, AR: Master Books.

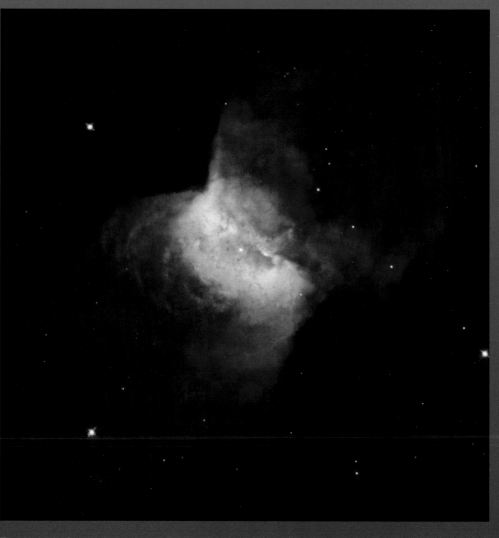

The Hubble Space Telescope's Wide Field and Planetary Camera 2 captured this image of the "butterfly wing"- shaped nebula NGC 2346, which is about 2,000 light-years away from earth in the direction of the constellation Monoceros.

lution of earth around the sun, a day as one rotation of earth under the sun, and a month closely tied to the moon's revolution around the earth. The stars' movements document even greater times, and are of use in various surveying and navigational operations. The measured pulsation of certain stars is even used for extremely small time intervals. All is "very good."

Day Five

Next, God made an abundance of life in the ocean of myriad sizes, lifestyles, and functions. Scripture says it thus: "Let the waters bring forth abundant-

ly the moving creature that hath life" (Genesis 1:20), again "after his kind" (v. 21). It could hardly have been said more accurately or succinctly, for the oceans are literally teeming with life. We may seldom interact with many of the ocean "kinds" of creatures, but all form an important link in the web of life. Most of them had never even been seen by man until recent days, yet the writers of the Bible knew.

Not only do we derive an important part of our diet from the sea, but many of our medications come directly from ocean creatures. As scientists observe certain functions in them that can be applied to us, a drug may be developed. Likewise, many modern technological discoveries are copied from behaviors and abilities of animals. Life on land could hardly continue without life in the sea.

On the same day, God created myriads of "kinds" of flying creatures to fill the skies, not only birds, but evidently flying reptiles and mammals as well. Insects fly and may be included as Day Five creations, although their lack of the "breath of life" and "blood" may better relegate them to Day Three in the thinking of some creation scientists and theologians. Each had the necessary genetic code to ensure a basic stability or "stasis" of its kind. All were uniquely designed for life in the air. Their differences speak clearly of their non-related origins. Yet their similarities with other living things form a web of symbiosis, a mutual dependency that

can best be understood as a gift from a wise Creator. Today, insects perform numerous vital ecological functions, including fertilization of plants, purging waste and carrion from the land, stabilizing habitats, etc., all the while filling the air with color and song.

Day Six

On the final day of creation, God made a dizzying array of land animals—the "beasts of the earth," "creeping things," and "cattle." He made these living creatures "after his kind" (1:24), again with the genetic specifications stipulating stasis. Each was created abruptly as that "kind," not by some process of evolution from other types.

The definition of "kind," which restricts the limits of variation within a group, is an important one for the creation/evolution controversy. Creationists believe animals (and plants) vary within their type (or "kinds"), but never evolve into other types. The Bible tells us all flesh is not the same kind of flesh (1 Corinthians 15:39), and science agrees. Often animals of similar anatomy, even though categorized as different species, can mate (hybridize) and produce fertile offspring. While limits are sometimes poorly defined, scientists—both creationists and evolutionists—generally consider the ability to hybridize proof of species relatedness.

For instance, there are many different breeds of dog, but these are known to have been developed by selective breeding among domestic dogs. Furthermore, sev-

Variety within the dog kind includes wolves, coyotes, and domestic dogs, all of which readily interbreed.

eral species of dogs can interbreed, including wolves, coyotes, foxes, dingoes, and domestic dogs, demonstrating that the dog "kind" is wide, encompassing several species. Their habits, habitats, and sizes may have diverged so far they seldom mate, but they are able to. A similar comparison could be made for most broad types, but the Flood has "reset the clock" and for many types we'll never know for sure. In general, if two species can breed either in the wild or through artificial means, they are thought to be of the same "kind."

Late on Day Six, God made man, who, in some way that is incompletely comprehended, carries the very "image of God." Within his body is a remarkable and complex genetic code, even more potent than that of the animals. Although likewise able to reproduce and adapt, mankind is quantitatively greater than the animals when his genetic abilities are considered. Other spiritual features make him qualitatively distinct from the animals. The first man and woman were given stewardship over all the earth, and mandated to care for all of creation, including the plants and animals, and to use it wisely for man's good and God's glory. God also instructed them to "be fruitful, and multiply, and replenish [literally, fill] the earth" (Genesis 1:28).

THE FINISHED CREATION

During creation week, the Creator was not playing by today's rules, but was exercising abilities from which He has rested (Genesis 2:1-3). He was using supernatural creation powers that are beyond the natural laws observed today. With the exception of the various

miracles by Christ and the prophets, physical processes abide by natural conservation laws. Creation is finished. God retains the prerogative of overriding natural law today, but seldom chooses to work in that fashion. He certainly doesn't answer to the commands of people who call for miracles, but retains sovereign control over all.

Science has discovered many basic natural laws governing the way things operate today. As introduced in chapter 1, the most basic law of all is that creation is impossible. The First Law of Thermodynamics insists that matter/energy can neither be created nor destroyed. Its form may change, but the total amount must remain the same. Obviously, the physical universe of matter/energy exists; therefore, it must have been created by processes different from those acting now. What science observes prohibits creative processes. Yet naturalistic (uniformitarian) science insists it all came together from nothing by the same processes we see. Perhaps long ago or far away, they say, laws were operating differently, contrary to observation; but all we see today confirms what the Bible has always taught.[3]

AFTER THE CREATION

We are not told how long the period of "paradise" lasted for man and his dominion, but evidently it was not long. Adam and Eve had been instructed to "be fruitful and multiply" (Genesis 1:28), but they had not yet conceived by the time they rebelled. They were completely healthy, and initially fully obedient, so the length of time was probably short.

CREATION WITH THE APPEARANCE OF AGE

Some Christian old earth advocates hold that if God created fully functioning organisms and physical systems, then He lied to us. They would have looked deceptively mature when they had, in fact, just appeared. This, they feel, is ample reason to deny six-day, recent creation and a literal interpretation of Scripture, for God cannot lie.

But how else could it be done? Would they prefer God to have created Adam as a newborn baby, or an embryo? Even an embryo would appear to have had ancestors, therefore would have an "appearance of age." Indeed, creation with no apparent history is impossible.

When Adam was created, he no doubt looked like a mature adult, fully able to walk, talk, and care for the garden. When God created fruit trees, they were already bearing fruit. In each case, what He created was functionally complete right from the start. Stars, created on Day Four, had to be seen on Day Six in order to be useful in telling time; therefore, their light had to be visible on earth. God's evaluation that the completed creation was "very good" (Genesis 1:31) necessitated that it be functionally complete and operating in harmony, with each part fulfilling the purpose for which it was created.

If a hypothetical observer from a different universe, with no knowledge of Adam's creation, traveled to earth on Day Seven and tried to determine Adam's age (or the age of a rock, or the age of a star), how could it be done? He might apply today's human growth rates (or rates of radioactive decay, or the speed of light), calculate how long it would take for this state of maturity to develop at modern rates, and come to a *wrong* conclusion.

But the world today is not as it was at creation. God's creative powers are at rest now, and He is maintaining the creation using the present laws of nature. The original created world, perfect and non-decaying at first, was subsequently cursed and made subject to decay and death (Genesis 3:17; Romans 8:20). Furthermore, even *that* world was destroyed by the Flood of Noah's day, so that the world we observe is a relic of destructive processes, not creative processes. Any effort to apply present processes and process rates to creation will not succeed.

Old-universe advocates claim that Romans 1:20 reveals that truth about creation and God's character must be "clearly seen" from the study of the creation. They say that any scientist, using valid theory and careful analysis, must be able to determine the age and origin of any object. Secular scientists have concluded the universe began with a Big Bang. Such experts insist that if that's the way it looks, then that must be the way it happened, since God could not have created with the appearance of a Big Bang if He didn't use that method.

But this position denies the clear scriptural teachings regarding creation, the Fall, and the Flood. Furthermore, it denies the very possibility of creation, for creation without the appearance of age is logically impossible.

God, in His sovereignty, knew that fallen man, living in the post-Flood world, might wrongly conclude the age and origin of things. For just that reason, He gave us a clear record of what He had done and when He did it. Furthermore, when we look at the evidence in light of what He has told us, the universe doesn't even look old, but it does look cursed and flooded. The real evidence is fully compatible with an origin only thousands of years ago.

On the other hand, if fallen scientists extrapolating present processes *are* right and the universe *is* old, then God *has* lied to us, for He clearly said He created all things in six days not too long ago.

But they chose to disobey when they first were tempted, and disobedience is sin. "The wages of sin is death" (Romans 6:23), a consequence promised when they were initially created (Genesis 2:16-17). They opted to rebel and incur God's just verdict of death (Genesis 3:14-24). All of creation, all of Adam's dominion, came under this Curse, and today all things deteriorate and die. Inanimate systems wind down, plants "wither and fade" (Isaiah 40:8), animals die, people die both physically and spiritually. Indeed, all creation "was made subject to vanity…[and] groaneth and travaileth in pain" (Romans 8:20, 22) due to the presence of sin and its penalty of death, awaiting deliverance from the "bondage of corruption" (v. 21). Science has codified this death and dying principle into the Second Law of Thermodynamics, stating that all things in nature deteriorate and die. Scientifically speaking, they increase in entropy, a measure of the disorder or randomness in a system, or the inability of its energy to be recaptured and used. Matter can be converted into energy and vice versa, but always ends up in less useful forms. The total amount remains the same, according to the First Law, but it becomes more entropic or disordered.

The Curse applied to nonliving systems as well as living. Modern processes no longer operate at 100 percent efficiency, and things run down and wear out—increasing in entropy. Evidently before the Curse, when things were still "very good," it was quite different. Today, many absolutely necessary and "good" processes and reactions are actually driven by entropy's increase, including processes like digestion and growth. Somehow God, the Creator and Lawgiver who instituted the law of entropy, ordained that while it had initially been a rule of maintenance, it became a self-consuming, in-turning construct, mandating greater entropy or randomness in every reaction. Even nonliving systems began to "die." The moon's orbit began to decay, the sun and stars began to burn out, elements began to emit radioactivity, etc. An all-pervasive "death" dominates.

We can only imagine creation before the Curse, for today entropy reigns over every process. How did animal waste and "dead" plants deteriorate? What kept the land livable? And did radioactive atoms undergo spontaneous fission, splitting and giving off high-energy particles? Locked in the present as we are, we cannot know. All we know is that in some way, things were quite different early in creation because the sin-caused death penalty had not yet been passed.

THE WORLD ALTERED BY THE CURSE

After the Curse, processes operated in ways we would recognize, and from that time until the present, uniformity of natural law has reigned. We can be certain that every time an object is dropped, gravity will pull it down. Every time wood is burned, heat is released. Every time parts move, they generate friction. In the present time, the constancy of natural law can be counted upon. However, the confidence we have in present natural law must not be over-applied to the past, before the laws of nature were fully enacted, before God's "very good" creation was altered by man's sin and the resulting penalty. It's almost like a curtain was drawn between then and now, and we can only see through it dimly.

A similar curtain was drawn at the time of the great Flood of Noah's day, an episode during which present processes were operating, but at greatly altered rates and intensities, and on wide scales. Catastrophic processes acted on regional, if not continental or global, scales, as opposed to today's uniform processes, which affect only local areas. This Flood was totally out of our experience, and we can hardly imagine it.

In total, then, three curtains have been drawn over the past. At the risk of oversimplification, the first was at the end of the six days of creation, when God "finished" His creating and making, at which time He instituted the First Law of Thermodynamics that prohibited further creation or annihilation of either matter or energy. He seldom thereafter used creative processes, and we have no access to them. The second was at the Curse, when He initiated deterioration or increasing entropy of all processes, the Second Law of Thermodynamics in its current formulation. Finally, at the great Flood, when processes used were acting at greatly accelerated rates, scales, and intensities "off the scale" of today's processes. Uniformity can address none of these three world-altering episodes, and thus cannot arrive at ultimate truth. Furthermore, if we ignore these great historical events, we cannot expect to arrive at truth regarding history.

THE PRE-FLOOD WORLD

The initially created earth was "very good," in a perpetual state of perfection. The Curse altered this, and we are told that God's judgment extended even to "the ground" (Genesis 3:17), to inanimate matter. Until the Flood, planet earth's physical systems enjoyed a period of relative equilibrium, for the biblical record contains no mention of earthquakes, volcanic eruptions, or natural disasters. However, we are told that human brutality raged during this period, and the animal kingdom was unimaginably violent. This we can see from the Flood-deposited fossil record, as well as the scriptural record. Both man and the animal kingdom participated, and together they necessitated God's intervention in the days of Noah. If things had been left to continue down this evil and violent path, there would have been little left. But God had promised to save mankind from the effects of sin through the coming seed of the woman (Genesis 3:15). In order to keep His promise, He needed to rescue godly Noah and his family, as well as representatives of the animal kinds. He sent the great Flood to judge the prevailing sin, but made provision for those He chose to save on the Ark of Noah.

GEOLOGIC CHANGES TO THE "VERY GOOD" EARTH

The Flood cataclysm morphed the early earth into the earth we know. Today, earth's surface is divided into tectonic plates that move relative to one another. The rate of movement is slow today, only discernible by sensitive, satellite-based GPS measuring equipment. The boundaries of these plates are active earthquake zones, allowing us to discern the relative direction of movement. Some plates sporadically move horizontally past the adjacent plate, such as along the famous San Andreas Fault in California. Some plates, such as those along the mid-Atlantic Ridge, are moving away from each other, leaving behind a low-lying rift valley. Others are moving toward each other, and the collisions either crumple up mountains (e.g., the Himalayas) or cause one plate to plunge beneath the other, generally resulting in volcanoes, earthquakes, and occasional tsunamis.

Catastrophists generally agree with plate tectonic theory, but propose movements much more rapid than the uniformitarians do. It may be that on the original earth, most continents were connected and there was one great stationary supercontinent, but we can't be sure. Reconstructing the former world is difficult, for the changes during the Flood destroyed much of the evidence. Whether or not they were connected at creation, it does appear that all the land masses were together sometime during the Flood. From matching rock strata traits and boundaries, creationist geophysicists consider it likely that they were indeed together at the height of the Flood, and then separated.

Rapidly raising the continents up out of the ocean on Day Three of the creation week required forces of unthinkable magnitude. But once creation was completed, forces no longer acted in a fashion and magnitude powerful enough to rend plates asunder and then move them from their original locations. Such forces were not reactivated by the Curse. Rather, the plates were set in motion by the same tectonic causes that initiated and facilitated the great Flood.

Fossils of trees living before the Flood give little evidence that they grew on high mountains. Present mountain chains were forced up by the Flood. There must have been some difference in elevation before the Flood, for rivers fed by the "fountains of the great deep" flowed by gravity to lower elevations. These rivers probably did not start on high-altitude mountain slopes, as rivers do today, fed by snow and rain. Pre-Flood rivers were supplied with water from underground sources and a nightly heavy mist.[4]

The Flood began in the oceans with the breaking open of "all the fountains of the great deep" (Genesis 7:11), causing a series of devastating reactions that forever altered the planet. Giant energy waves (tsunamis) rippled out from the quaking "fountains," forcing water inland. Earthquakes and tectonic convulsions rattled the continents. Upwelling molten magma evaporated seawater, which sprayed vapor skyward into the atmosphere. Furthermore, "the windows of heaven" were opened, inundating earth with an unparalleled downpour, with a special intensity for the first "forty days and forty nights." The extensive rainwater that fell during the Flood year needed to be constantly renewed, for the tumultuous rain didn't stop for five months. Superheated chemical brines entered the oceans, precipitating minerals and boiling seawater, replenishing the moisture in the atmosphere. Shock waves repeatedly reverberated throughout the ocean, bringing unimaginable devastation to sea life. Waves of water and loose sediments carrying sea creatures were pushed inland, over and over again.

These actions caused untold death and the eventual

fossilization of many trillions of marine organisms, as well as destroying the majority of plants and animals alive at the time. First to be affected were dwellers of the ocean depths, directly impacted as the "fountains" burst open. Then, those in the continental shelf regions were devastated, next the coastline dwellers, then those in low-lying areas, and finally the upland denizens. The waters continued rising and falling and rising again until even the pre-Flood mountains were covered. They maintained an abnormally high but fluctuating sea level throughout the Flood, as complex interaction between tectonic and hydrodynamic forces saw the water come and go in surges. Finally, the next seven months saw the waters drain off into newly deepened and widened ocean basins, exposing dry land and ending the Flood episode.

Remember that the pre-Flood world, which had been in wonderful equilibrium ever since creation, literally ruptured, fully restructuring earth's surface and even its interior. Forces were unleashed that continued for some time afterward until the relative equilibrium we now experience was reestablished. A time of post-Flood readjustment of physical systems followed, and during these few hundred years, lesser catastrophes raged. Residual catastrophism continued for centuries as human civilization reestablished itself. These residual catastrophes operated on a smaller scale than the great Flood, but were catastrophes nonetheless, devastating entire regions. In particular, the Ice Age directly followed the Flood, caused by the Flood's destabilization of climate patterns, ocean temperatures, and ocean currents. It lasted for hundreds of years, up until the approximate time of Abraham and Job, and merits several mentions in the book of Job (e.g., Job 38:29-30).

THE FLOOD'S EFFECT ON MANKIND

According to Genesis, Noah disembarked from the Ark about one year after he and his family boarded. Noah offered a sacrifice to God after he and his family left the Ark, in thankfulness for their great deliverance, and God responded by giving them the rainbow as the sign of His covenant with mankind. This was not a conditional covenant that depended on their performance, but was purely God's promise not to judge earth with a similar flood again. The promise came with the command to migrate and fill the earth.[5]

However, His hatred for man's worship of other gods and His holy nature that demands judgment for sin were not altered. It wasn't long before mankind was in full rebellion mode again. Under the leadership of wicked Nimrod, they built a tower at Babel in open disobedience to God's migration command, boldly defying Him with the assertion "lest we be scattered abroad upon the face of the whole earth" (Genesis 11:4). Most of the Noahic/Semitic clan had probably remained together while rapidly multiplying. All the rebellion-minded members spoke the same language, and working together they built the tower, likely an astrological observation station from which to worship the creation rather than the Creator. God could not leave this dual-pronged rebellion unpunished. He confused their languages, halted the cooperative rebellious building project, and enforced migration.

DISPERSAL AT BABEL

Suddenly, people found it impossible to communicate with one another, and individual language groups banded together to move elsewhere. The strongest, most prominent group probably remained where it was, forcing the others to leave. These would include the Sumerians, the Babylonians, the Akkadians, and the Assyrians. They retained the technology they had acquired and built strongholds. Other strong groups claimed fertile territory nearby with desirable natural resources, such as in the Nile River basin. The remaining clans migrated where they could, with stronger ones continually displacing the weaker ones. Some moved south to what is now the African continent, others moved east to Asia. The Ice Age was building up to the north in Europe, and some were trapped there.

Genesis 10 records these migration routes, mentioning the incipient nations and territory. In general, the Semites, the descendants of Shem, retained control of the region of Mesopotamia, while the Japhethites migrated toward the northeast and northwest in Europe and Russia, and the Hamites moved south into Africa and east into Asia. There was some mixing and extinction of family groups, but they had little choice. Language groups had to go somewhere. The Table of Nations in Genesis 10 that documents the resulting migrations is recognized as a magnificent historical document, with many of the nations recognizable throughout time up until today.

God confounded human languages at the Tower of Babel to enforce His command of worldwide migration and settlement. Today's cultures and ethnic groups are a result of this language separation.

All groups took with them the knowledge of God, the Flood, and proper worship, as well as the false worship as practiced at Babel. Many early civilizations immediately constructed similar towers or pyramids and began worshiping the stars using the same imaginary star pictures in the Zodiac. With no precursors, written scripts were suddenly developed in numerous areas, using completely different systems and symbols. All groups knew that writing was useful, and began to record information in their new language and script.

Those whose population contained individuals with special skills quickly founded technological civilizations, with construction projects, metal working, agriculture, etc., while those without such abilities fo-

cused simply on surviving. Tribes living in the harsh environment of Ice Age Europe often lived in caves for safety and warmth, all the while losing pieces of their once-common knowledge and adopting a hunter-gatherer mode of existence. In those early years, numerous budding civilizations accomplished great engineering feats that perhaps even today could hardly be duplicated. These early people were hardly ignorant sub-humans, recently evolved from the animals. Man was smart at the start.

As the Ice Age began to wane, desirable climate shifted northward into places like Europe, and once again the more dominant groups migrated into the more fertile, pleasant areas, displacing weaker, less developed tribes. The Neanderthals were such a group who had migrated north and survived in caves close to the ice sheet. They either were amalgamated into the invading peoples or were driven to extinction.

Summary

Uniformitarians mistakenly hold that the present-day pseudo-equilibrium is all that ever existed, and that it was responsible for shaping earth as we know it, as well as accounting for biological evolution. Biblical and scientific data suggest otherwise. The Creator, at His discretion, used supernatural processes and energy levels to complete His creation at least on those occasions about which He has informed us in His record. Our task is to marvel at His creative genius and try to understand Him more fully as we study His handiwork.

During the Flood year, God's objective of washing the earth clean of all the effects of man's rebellion was accomplished. He had a just purpose and redemptive goal in it all, but unlike His work of creation, He used geologic, hydraulic, and tectonic forces that we can comprehend to accomplish it. In the next chapter, we will look at Scripture's description of that global and catastrophic Flood.

CHAPTER 4

THE SCRIPTURAL NECESSITY OF THE GLOBAL EXTENT OF THE FLOOD

As Christians, we must always consider first the biblical data. And so we ask: Do the Scriptures speak of a global flood? Does its narrative make sense if the Flood was merely local? While it certainly doesn't give us all the details about the Flood, can we reasonably infer the character and extent of the Flood from what it does say? Was the great Flood of Noah's day uniform and local, or catastrophic and global? Scripture speaks to this issue in numerous ways.

THE DEPTH OF THE FLOOD

> And the waters prevailed exceedingly upon the earth; and all the high hills, that were under the whole heaven, were covered. Fifteen cubits upward did the waters prevail; and the mountains were covered. (Genesis 7:19-20)

Nearly all Bible students throughout Old Testament, New Testament, and modern times have interpreted Genesis 7–9 as describing a global flood. Not only does a plain-sense meaning imply a global flood, but details of the Hebrew grammar necessitate it, such as in the verses quoted above. The waters did not simply inundate the land, they overwhelmed it, almost as in a military conquest, and did so "exceedingly." These verses describe neither a local flood nor an insignificant flood, but a global, world-destroying event, and earth has never again been the same.

The author of Genesis used a double superlative in these verses to describe the Flood, wherein the passage literally could be rendered "all the high mountains

under all the heavens." While "all" in Scripture may sometimes be understood in a limited sense, such repeated phrasing goes out of its way to insure that a Bible-honoring reader would not mistakenly conclude that the flood being described is anything other than a global flood.

The Flood covered all the high mountains (the Hebrew word for hills and mountains used here is the same) to a depth of at least 15 cubits. God had instructed Noah to build the Ark 300 cubits long, 50 cubits wide, and 30 cubits high. Most historians consider a cubit to be the distance from a man's elbow to his fingertips, about 18 inches. Thus, the Ark was about 45 feet high. The fully loaded Ark, with the animals and foodstuffs on board, likely sank about one half its height beneath the water. Presumably, the Ark could have floated anywhere on earth at the Flood's maximum and not struck ground.

Next, consider the fact that advocates of the local flood concept consider the mountains of Noah's day, some 4,500 or so years ago, to be the same mountains we encounter today. They argue that whatever "uniformitarian" changes are currently happening to the mountains—whether rising, sinking, or eroding—would not have changed them much in "only" a few thousand years. Many mountains are quite high today, with portions of "the mountains of Ararat" (Genesis 8:4) rising some 17,000 feet above sea level, and with the world's tallest mountain, 29,000-foot-high Mount Everest, towering above the Himalayas. Nearly all of the earth's mountains and mountain ranges are composed of sedimentary rock, laid down as sediments by moving water. (Mount Ararat is a volcano, and thus is made of igneous rock.) In the uniformitarian model, these mountains could not have been covered by the Flood, but Scripture plainly informs us that all the mountains were covered. Most modern attempts to harmonize Scripture with uniformitarianism choose to ignore the problem and misinterpret the plain sense of the text.

For example, Hugh Ross, a leading local flood and old earth advocate, likes to tell of the time he biblically "confronted" the Institute for Creation Research with its "error" of teaching the young earth doctrine, and the companion doctrine of the global Flood. Accepting uniformitarianism, he knows that the mountains are too high today for a global flood, thus he concludes the Bible must be teaching otherwise. He insisted the Flood of Noah's day was quite a significant flood (he deceptively calls it "a universal flood"), but one that only covered the Mesopotamian River Valley. In his view, Noah may have thought it was global, because his vision was limited by the earth's curvature and failing eyesight. He could only see so far and mistakenly thought the Flood was global. Scripture, however, does not allow this dishonoring reinterpretation.

It should go without saying that a 29,000-foot-high flood, or a 17,000-foot-high flood, or any flood that covered the mountains for the better part of a year could not have been just a local flood, for water flows downhill. It could not pile up for months in one place without also covering everywhere else. A mountain-covering flood, deep enough to provide safe passage for the Ark, is not a local flood. The depth of the Flood argues for a global flood.

Young earth advocates interpret the 17,000-foot Mount Ararat and the 29,000-foot Mount Everest—i.e., the mountains of today—as forming toward the end of and soon after the great Flood, which occurred approximately four and a half thousand years ago. They did not exist in their present form before the Flood, and thus did not need to be covered by floodwaters. Such mountains as existed before and during the great Flood were not nearly so high, and even those were leveled by the floodwaters and crustal tectonic movements.

In short, any flood that could cover the mountains was not a local flood. If Scripture is to be taken seriously, the great Flood of Noah's day must have been global.

THE DURATION OF THE FLOOD

A similar argument could be raised concerning the year-long duration of the Flood. Some old earth advocates claim that the Genesis Flood account is not about dates and chronology, but that it's only trying to convey the fact that God hates sin and it is His nature to judge it. But the detail given in Genesis is extensive and pervasive, and Scripture specifically relates a year-long Flood, far too long to be describing a local flood. It appears that the Author of Genesis placed great store in these precise facts and intended us to know what we couldn't know otherwise. He knew the controversy that would one day arise and gave us all we needed to understand the truth and refute error.

The overall Flood episode began when Noah, his family, and the animals boarded the great ship. Seven days later (Genesis 7:10), "in the six hundredth year of Noah's life, in the second month, the seventeenth day of the month, the same day were all the fountains of the great deep broken up, and the windows of heaven were opened. And the rain was upon the earth forty days and forty nights" (vv. 11-12). It continued in its ferocity for the next five months as "the waters prevailed upon the earth an hundred and fifty days" (v. 24).

When their work was done, "the waters returned from off the earth continually: and after the end of the hundred and fifty days the waters were abated" (8:3). At this five-month juncture, the waters were "restrained" (v. 2), and the Ark "rested in the seventh month, on the seventeenth day of the month, upon the mountains of Ararat" (v. 4). Here, Noah and the Ark remained as "the waters decreased continually until…in the tenth month, on the first day of the month, were the tops of the mountains seen" (v. 5). Noah's family and the animals needed to remain on the stranded vessel until the land at the base of the mountain was dry enough to support life, and so they waited.

After 40 more days (8:6), Noah "sent forth a raven" (v. 7) and then a dove (v. 8). Seven days later, he sent out another dove (v. 10) that returned with "an olive leaf pluckt off" (v. 11). Knowing that "the waters were abated from off the earth" (v. 11), he waited another "seven days; and sent forth the dove; which returned not" (v. 12).

In Noah's "six hundredth and first year, in the first month, the first day of the month, the waters were

IN THE EARLY EARTH, WERE ALL THE MONTHS EXACTLY 30 DAYS LONG?

Thirty days hath September,
April, June and November;
February has twenty-eight alone,
All the rest have thirty-one,
'Cept in Leap Year, that's the time
When February's days are twenty-nine.

So goes the nursery rhyme that helps us remember how many days are in a particular month. Why the difference? Why aren't they all the same? Wouldn't a perfect creation as described in Genesis have a more regular pattern?

The length of the month is roughly tied to the 29½ day cycle of the moon. This has led to the lunar calendar, used by many nations throughout history. The easily recognized appearance of the "new moon" facilitates its application. The Hebrew calendar employed in the Bible is a lunar calendar. Many of the Bible's historic events and/or dates for festivals are tied to the day of the lunar month or the phase of the moon.

Our modern calendar's irregularities, with months varying from 28 to 31 days, cause some confusion. Many of the months are named after Roman gods or emperors, and some of the variety stems from less than scientific reasons. For instance, when a month was named after Caesar Augustus, he allegedly insisted it be as long as the longest month and "took" a day from February to add to August. Many have noted that a yearly cycle would be much simpler if each month were exactly 30 days, thus in 12 months there would be 360 days. Could it have been more regular in the beginning? Did it change at the Flood?

Numerous scholars have pondered this question with no agreement, but let me call your attention to perhaps the most important hint in Scripture regarding the length of pre-Flood months. The Flood started "in the six hundredth year of Noah's life, in the second month, the seventeenth day of the month" (Genesis 7:11). It "prevailed upon the earth an hundred and fifty days"

(v. 24). "And the ark rested in the seventh month, on the seventeenth day of the month, upon the mountains of Ararat" (8:4).

Between the second month's 17th day and the seventh month's 17th day were 150 days. Thus, five months averaging 30 days each were involved and a very regular order is implied in the phrase "very good" (Genesis 1:31). It seems today's 365¼-day year thereby must likely be an altered remnant of created order.

What could happen to change earth's orbit and rotation speed? Its angular momentum is vast, and just like a spinning gyroscope is hard to adjust. The earth's motion resists change. It would take a mighty force to alter it.

The Bible does speak of such an event. Without giving all the details, it indicates that the great Flood of Noah's day forever altered earth's systems. If earth's orbit has changed, this is when it happened. With the fountains of the great deep relocating a huge volume of liquid, moving continents, possible asteroid bombardment, etc., shifting the location of much mass, the length of the day, the length of the year, and the tilt of the axis could have all changed. We don't have the details as to precise amounts or forces involved, but at least we have certain knowledge of an event capable of doing the job.

dried up from off the earth: and…behold, the face of the ground was dry" (8:13). But it still needed to dry some more. It was not until "the second month, on the seven and twentieth day of the month" that the earth was dried (v. 14). Only at this time did God instruct faithful Noah, his family, and the animals to exit the Ark to begin their new lives in the new world.

Some interpretations differ slightly, but the chronology is generally understood as follows:

40 days of intense rain (Genesis 7:12)
110 additional days of "prevailing" (Genesis 8:3)
221 days of draining (Genesis 8:5-14)
Total 371 days (Genesis 7:11; cf. 8:14)

A year is a long time for a mere local flood to wax and wane, but at least a year would be needed for a global flood, and is consistent with the obvious intention of the Author to communicate its global nature and year-long timing. Several aspects of the Flood were under God's supernatural control or it would have taken longer, for it takes some time for water to ebb and flow.

Conversely, think how inconsistent the record is with a local flood. Place yourself in the Mesopotamian River Valley on the grounded Ark as the waters were abating from a local flood. The low-lying valley has two large rivers, the Tigris and Euphrates, and easy drainage to the sea. The floodwaters had filled the valley, as far as one could see. A mountain range with mountains of over 14,000-feet elevation, the Zagros Mountains, is far to the east. The Flood's maximum had passed and the Ark had landed on one of the mountains, but after 74 days of draining would the water still be covering this valley? Wouldn't it have quickly drained off? Surely the account makes little sense if describing a local flood. Logically, our only options are: Ignore the text and call the Flood local, assign it to mere allegory, or believe it as it stands.

PHYSICAL CAUSES FOR THE FLOOD

In Genesis 7:11-12, three physical causes for the Flood are given:

1) All the fountains of the great deep were broken open.

Old Faithful Geyser in Yellowstone Park. Water is heated underground by hot igneous rock. Such geysers might be reminiscent of the pre-Flood "fountains of the great deep," but were formed by the great Flood and its aftermath.

THE GLOBAL FLOOD

Before and after photos of the coast at Lampuuk devastated by the 2004 Indian Ocean tsunami, caused by underwater tectonic activity forcing water inland at great velocity. During the great Flood, tsunamis were thousands of times more energetic.

2) The windows of heaven were opened.
3) There were 40 days and nights of intense rain.

Both the "fountains" and the "windows" remained open and/or active for the Flood's first 150 days (Genesis 7:24; 8:2), all during the "prevailing" period. Interestingly, all three mechanisms for the Flood were worldwide in scope, implying a global consequence.

The fountains of the deep cannot be positively identified today. Having ruptured, they are now likely unrecognizable. Perhaps the most similar features today are the "springs of the sea" or "black smokers," underwater vents that continually belch out chemically saturated and very hot brines. Exotic communities of organisms somehow live and even thrive in this hostile environment, far below the reach of sunlight. At present, the vents are somewhat rare and localized, but are found in numerous places throughout the ocean floor. The springs possess a seemingly inexhaustible source of water, gas, and chemicals. Large ones would be comparable in size and volume to volcanoes. Could these be faded echoes of the "fountains of the great deep"?[1]

When a volcano erupts on the ocean floor or when a sub-oceanic earthquake occurs, the shaking imparts energy to the surrounding water. Since water is near-ly incompressible, it transfers that energy to the water around it and thus an energy wave, or shock wave, is transmitted through the water at an incredible speed, travelling hundreds of miles per hour. An earthquake on one side of the Pacific Ocean may generate a wave that impacts the other side in about the same time it takes a jet airplane to cross. A ship on the deep, open ocean might not even feel the wave as it passes underneath, but as the wave enters shallow water near an island or continent, it picks up the water into a huge wall that slams onto shore at great speed. This tsunami—the term "tidal wave" is incorrect, since it has nothing to do with tides—can inflict major damage for miles inland.

The Bible relates that on that one day, "all" the fountains broke open virtually simultaneously, and continued wrenching open and slamming shut and then reopening for five months. We can hardly imagine the horror of the great Flood. It included continual pulsations of tsunamis, travelling from varying directions and colliding, each one carrying various sediment types and creatures from different locations.

Perhaps the fountains are today represented by deep-seated faults, whose erupting fluids were fed by abundant sources of chemically rich brines and magmas. Often, metallic ores are associated with deep

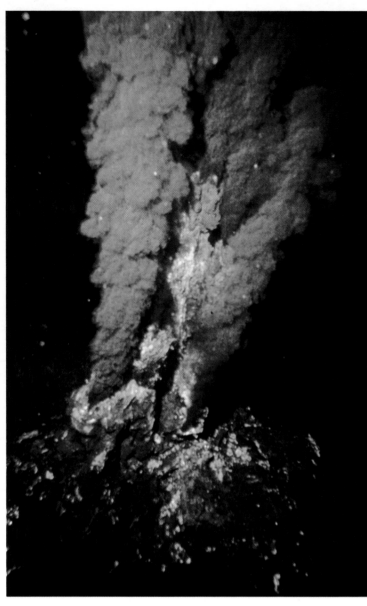
An underwater "black smoker" spewing hot water saturated with dissolved minerals and nutrients from deep inside the earth.

faults. Perhaps today we can expect remnants of fountains to be located in areas of extensive volcanism, from which underground magmas historically spewed. Some volcanic regions are covered with wide, thick layers of volcanic rock, far more extensive than modern-day lava flows.

Today, great rift zones on the ocean floor extend under the continents in some places. In total, the rift system spans an incredible 50,000 miles, not including the subcontinental portions. One can scarcely comprehend the "fountains of the great deep" spewing forth their contents for 150 days on this global scale. Each rupture would send another energy wave coursing through the water, causing unimaginable havoc on land. We must not think about the Flood as it is portrayed in pop-

ular treatments, like Noah riding in a houseboat on a Sunday afternoon. This was God's holy wrath being poured out on desperately wicked and violent sinners, with devastating walls of water, underwater mudflows, mega-earthquakes, super-volcanoes, and multiple hurricanes. The Flood waters "prevailed" on earth and did so "exceedingly" (Genesis 7:19), and the world that then was, perished (2 Peter 3:6).

The fountains that broke open at the Flood were no doubt related to the "waters which were under the firmament" (Genesis 1:7). These evidently fed the complex of artesian springs and groundwater discharges that fed the rivers flowing from Eden (2:10), supplying the needs of the pre-Flood supercontinent. Whatever they were, they are gone or different now. But the point is that the fountains causing the Flood were globally distributed. A worldwide cause argues for a worldwide effect, thus a flood global in extent.

Similarly, the "windows of heaven" opened to drop a worldwide source of water from above. Whatever these atmospheric windows were, their condensation and precipitation would have resulted in worldwide, intense rainfall.

The modern atmosphere can hardly hold enough water to cover the globe with more than just a few inches of rainfall. If it fell all at once, however, much damage would result. The present clouds certainly could not continually produce torrents of rain for 40 days and 40 nights, let alone continue for five months, but according to Scripture something of great magnitude happened. The Bible is specific that a rain of great intensity and duration inundated the earth below and contributed to the waters of the Flood. In some important way, conditions must have been different enough to allow so much water. Creation scientists have proposed that during the Flood, spreading continental plates would have caused great volumes of extremely hot rock to be emplaced along mid-ocean rifts, resulting in intense evaporation of the ocean water above. The rising vapors would have continually replenished the waters falling from the clouds.

Maybe another source of rainfall was from space. Perhaps earth encountered a vast swarm of ice meteorites. Some have speculated Saturn-like ice rings may have surrounded the "very good" earth at its creation, which melted as they fell, supplying water for the Flood. Numerous conjectures have been put forward, but such evidence no longer exists, so we cannot know.

Science knows well, however, the impact of a long torrential rainfall such as the one specifically implied in Scripture. Great volumes of water falling constantly for weeks on end would accomplish enormous geologic work and inflict a heavy toll of human casualties. Rapidly moving water has great potential for erosion of rock and transportation of sediment. Rivers would overflow and eventually merge with one another. Consider the horror inflicted on those outside the Ark.

Research has been conducted for decades by creation experts in atmospheric physics, most notably ICR's Dr. Larry Vardiman, trying to better understand pre-Flood atmospheric conditions. Gleaning from the meager hints given in Scripture, Vardiman and others have tried combinations of numerous possible conditions, all with inconclusive results. Perhaps we have incorrectly interpreted the biblical data or have not yet tested the right combinations of conditions, but problems with the proposed water vapor canopy theory have not yet been solved. The canopy theory was important at the time of the publication of *The Genesis Flood*, but is only held loosely if at all by today's creationists. Still, the biblical hints remain. Something was there, and research continues.

WHERE WAS THE GARDEN OF EDEN LOCATED?

Over the years, many have claimed the Garden of Eden has been found. The Bible describes the area around the Garden in Genesis 2, even using recognizable place names such as Ethiopia. It mentions a spring of water in the Garden that divided into four major rivers as it flowed, including the Euphrates. This has led many, including Bible scholars, to conclude that the Garden of Eden was somewhere in the Middle Eastern area known today as the Tigris-Euphrates River Valley, with its remains long ago vanishing.

It is also true that this area (the "Fertile Crescent") was the location of the ancient Tower of Babel and the patriarch Abraham's home in the city of Ur. Without a doubt, the Tigris-Euphrates River Valley plays a unique role in biblical history, but was it the location of the Garden of Eden?

First, let's examine the biblical information. While the Tigris and Euphrates both have their headwaters in the area surrounding the mountains of Ararat, they do not flow from a source like the spokes on a wheel, filling the land as mentioned. Nor are the other two rivers present. Furthermore, the mineral deposits mentioned bear no resemblance to those in this area. In short, the geography and descriptions don't match.

The key is in recognizing that through the Flood of Noah's day, "the world that then was, being overflowed with water, perished" (2 Peter 3:6). As described in Genesis 6–9, the Flood would have totally restructured the surface of the globe. No place on earth could have survived untouched.

These sediments would have been full of organic debris, which over time would either fossilize, disappear entirely, or metamorphose into oil and gas. The sediments would harden into sedimentary rock, in places bending into mountains or breaking along fault systems.

Today, the Tigris-Euphrates River Valley contains sediments over two miles thick, from which are pumped enormous quantities of oil and gas. The sediments, now rock, deeply cover and obscure any possible pre-Flood locations. No present topography or underground surface could possibly bear any resemblance to the pre-Flood world. That world is gone!

Noah and his family would have encountered the present-day Tigris and Euphrates Rivers soon after leaving the Ark. As their descendants migrated, they would probably give familiar names to the new rivers and places that reminded them of "home."

God placed an angel at the entrance to the Garden to keep pre-Flood men from returning. The Flood made even that precaution unnecessary.

Barringer Crater in Arizona, caused by a meteorite impact. Numerous craters much larger than this are seen on earth's surface, and even larger ones have been found underground by remote sensing.

Suffice it to say that whether or not the canopy conjecture has value, the biblical "windows of heaven" were real and worldwide in scope, as would have been the rainfall. As with the "fountains," a worldwide cause implies a worldwide effect. Thus, the Flood covered a worldwide area.

Another possible cause for the Flood is not mentioned in Scripture, but is implied by scientific observation. We see on earth's surface numerous "astroblemes," or meteorite craters, that impacted earth in recent post-Flood times. Others have been detected underground through seismic studies. These objects evidently hit the earth during the Flood while the strata were still being deposited and/or eroded, and thus are today partially eroded and distorted. We also notice that other bodies in the solar system (Mars, Venus, Mercury, earth's moon, and moons of other planets) were bombarded by numerous major impacts.[2] Some may date from the creation event itself, but some must have blasted earth during the Flood, perhaps having been the remnants of an exploded planet.

Lack of water erosion has preserved the craters on other

bodies. It appears at least the inner part of the solar system may have passed through a region akin to an asteroid belt or interstellar "dirty place" or something, at just the right time in God's sovereign control to trigger the Flood and add to the horror of the Flood. Think of the tsunami waves resulting from a large impact. The Flood was more devastating than we can imagine. It certainly was global in extent.

THE NEED FOR AN ARK

Genesis 6:3 tells us that God predicted one "hundred and twenty years" in advance that the Flood was coming to "destroy man whom I have created" (v. 7) because of man's sinful choices. "But Noah [already hundreds of years old by then] found grace in the eyes of the LORD" (v. 8), suggesting that God communicated the coming judgment to him at that time. Noah was instructed to "make thee an ark of gopher wood" (v. 14) for the survival of his family and the animals. A global flood of surpassing intensity was approaching, and the only way to survive was on the specially designed Ark.

But what if Noah had lived in Mesopotamia and the

How Soon after the Flood Did the Earth Return to Equilibrium?

While the Bible doesn't give us all the details, we get the impression that before the Curse there were no major storms, no earthquakes, no landslides, etc. All things were "very good." Even after the Curse, but before the Flood, these would have been minimal. However, during the Flood the earth "broke" and geological processes happened rapidly. Indeed, the entire surface of the earth was restructured by the waters of that great Flood.

Today, we live once again in a world of relative equilibrium. We experience earthquakes, hurricanes, tsunamis, and volcanoes, but, as revealed in the geologic record, to a much lesser degree than occurred during the Flood. Those early centuries after the Flood thankfully saw the devastation taper off, but it probably took several hundred years for the earth to regain the relative equilibrium that we enjoy.

Modern weather patterns are influenced by the jet streams, huge currents of air at high altitudes. These probably reestablished themselves rather quickly after the Flood. Weather patterns are likewise controlled by ocean temperatures. For example, warmer oceans result in more evaporation, and thus more precipitation. Creationists suspect that the Ice Age was a direct result of the great Flood, due primarily to the heating of the oceans by the fountains of the great deep that erupted during the Flood. Speculation since the 1970s that global warming will cause another Ice Age (although largely misguided) mirrors this creationist theory. Such dynamic weather patterns immediately after the Flood would have continued until the oceans had released their excess heat.

We also see in the centuries following the Flood that volcanism occurred on a scale dwarfing anything that we see today. Consider that during and after the Flood, the continents were rising and spreading apart as the ocean basins sank, giving rise to immense fractures in the earth's crust. Volcanic aerosols thrown into the atmosphere would have contributed to the Ice Age, shielding the earth from much of the solar radiation that we now receive, thereby cooling the continents and allowing snow to build up into great ice sheets.

As the continents rose and split late in the Flood, mountain chains buckled up, further influencing our weather patterns. Climate patterns may have been quite violent and unpredictable for several hundred years until things stabilized. Earthquakes were a common occurrence as sediments consolidated and shifted.

Creationists consider this post-Flood period one of "residual catastrophism" that would have continued through the time of the Tower of Babel and into Abraham's day. Today, we live in a world that is relatively stable but still reeling from the effects of the great Flood. Thankfully, one day there will be a new heaven and a new earth where such catastrophes will not even be remembered.

Flood was only to be a local flood covering just the region around Noah's home? Would there even have been a need for the Ark? It begs the question: "How far can you walk in 120 years?" In this length of time, one could walk around the earth several times. Certainly, even a feeble person could walk out of the Mesopotamian River Valley. Constructing the huge Ark was brutally difficult in any length of time. Why would a gracious God exercise His grace to Noah by forcing him to build an unnecessary ship? Why not tell him to migrate and return once the Flood had passed? And

why take the animals?

Local flood advocates generally think that the pre-Flood world was uniformly rather similar to today's world, with animals distributed throughout similar habitats on all continents. Most animals can migrate more easily than humans, especially the birds that were specifically mentioned as taken on the Ark. Large animals living elsewhere, like elephants in Africa and kangaroos in Australia, would hardly have been affected by a local flood in Mesopotamia. Are they not included in

Far from being merely a hydraulic episode, the great Flood of Noah's day saw atmospheric chaos and tectonic upheaval, as well. The Ark's seaworthy design allowed it to be stable among tsunamis and hypercanes.

the "every beast…and all the cattle…and every creeping thing…and every fowl after his kind" (7:14), or did they need to journey to Mesopotamia to be endangered and then saved? Some things simply don't make sense. The local flood idea is one such idea.

At 300 cubits by 50 cubits by 30 cubits (Genesis 6:15)—or approximately 450 feet by 75 feet by 45 feet—the Ark was enormous. Only in relatively modern times have ships of similar size been constructed. Why would God desire the Ark to be so big unless it was necessary to accomplish His grand purpose of saving both man and the animals? As we shall discuss more fully in the next chapter when the number of animals on board is considered, this vessel was large enough to carry "two of every sort…male and female" (6:19) of unclean animals and seven (or seven pairs) of the clean animals "to keep seed alive upon the face of all the earth" (7:2-3).

A much smaller Ark would be required if only the local animals of Mesopotamia were to be taken, or even if Noah's presumed entire flocks of animals and all his domesticated animals needed to board. But no, we are given specific details regarding size and content, and

told that outside the Ark "all flesh died that moved upon the earth" (7:21).

Furthermore, as will also be discussed later, the Ark was large enough to be stable on stormy open seas with a large cargo. A much smaller ship would be sufficient if this was only a local event. Yet God instructed His one faithful servant to build a huge vessel, which was totally unnecessary for a local flood. There is no getting around it: There was need for an Ark only if the Flood was global.

DESTRUCTION OF ALL MANKIND

Without a doubt, God's primary purpose in sending the Flood was to judge sinful mankind.

> God saw that the wickedness of man was great in the earth, and that every imagination of the thoughts of his heart was only evil continually. And it repented the LORD that he had made man on the earth, and it grieved him at his heart. And the LORD said, I will destroy man whom I have created from the face of the earth. (Genesis 6:5-7)

God's wrath was focused on rebellious mankind. As we consider the extent of the Flood, we must ask: How large was the human population at that time? How much area did the Flood need to cover in order to accomplish its primary purpose? Again, the Bible only gives glimpses into the lives and extent of pre-Flood civilization, but from these hints we can gain an estimate of the total population.

Genesis 5 lists the patriarchs in apparent father-son succession: Adam, Seth, Enos, Cainan, Mahalaleel, Jared, Enoch, Methuselah, Lamech, Noah—ten generations in all. The same list is provided in 1 Chronicles 1:1-4 and Luke 3:36-38, with no internal evidence in the list to suggest gaps in time or missing generations. The attention to detail must mean this information was important to the Author and thus to readers of future generations, including those of the modern day.

We are also given each patriarch's age at the time his primary son was born, the time span from the birth of the son to the father's death, and the father's age at death. The two numbers are added correctly so there is no confusion. In certain of the ancient texts, the numbers vary a little, but using the Masoretic Text, the one regarded as the most reliable and from which we translate our English Bibles, we can calculate times and time spans. According to Genesis, the ten pre-Flood generations encompassed precisely 1,656 years from Adam's creation to the Flood.

Many who would prefer to add time to the total insist that generations may be missing from the list. They point out that "begat" rightly means "became the ancestor of," and they are correct. Genesis speaks of "A" begetting "B," but does it necessarily mean a father/son relationship? Could it mean grandfather or distant ancestor rather than father? It is sometimes used that way, as when Christ is referred to as the son of David (e.g., Matthew 1:1). But by specifying that A begat B at a specific age, it doesn't matter whether A was the father, grandfather, or distant ancestor of B. The number of years is given, and adding a missing generation doesn't

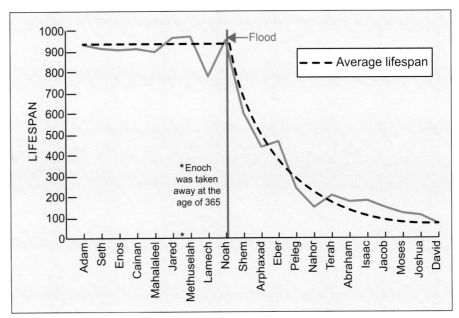

According to Genesis, lifespans before the Flood averaged over 900 years, but lifespans decreased rapidly after the Flood due to changed conditions.

add a single year to the total.[3]

Some have argued a year might be added or subtracted to the total depending on the specific month of the year a son was born. The same could be argued for the nine-month gestation period, but is this really significant? Adding a year or nine months at every possible point doesn't change the total appreciably. Hence, we can be certain that the length of time from Adam's creation to the Flood was not much different from 1,656 years.

To calculate the population at the Flood, we need to estimate the average age at death of those who died. Enoch, we are told, never died, for he "walked with God: and he was not; for God took him" directly to heaven (Genesis 5:24), "translated that he should not see death" (Hebrews 11:5). Of course, Noah didn't die until after the Flood. Of the eight who did die, the average age at death was 911.

We also know "the earth was filled with violence" (Genesis 6:11) in those days, no doubt interrupting many family lines. Thus, the conservative estimates used in the following paragraphs seem warranted.

We must also know the average family size, and we are provided that information. Of the first nine patriarchs, each is said to have sired not only the primary son, but also other "sons and daughters." Thus, each one had at least five children. There is no reason why they couldn't have had many more. In fact, Jewish legend has it that Adam and Eve had over 50 children. And why not?

Their bodies had been recently created in a "very good" state. They were commanded to "be fruitful" and fill the earth. Furthermore, they had long lifespans.

The youngest first-time father was Enoch, at 65 years old, and the oldest was Noah, who was 500 when he became a father. Thus, the potential childbearing years extended for centuries. Their bodies were strong and healthy that soon after creation, with little time to accumulate genetic damage from disease and harmful mutations. There was probably no shortage of nutritious food, and there was plenty of space for civilizations to grow. It's hard to think of any reason for them not to have had large families.

Since each family had at least five children, and probably many more, an assumption of six children is reasonable. From the data given, we could also conservatively assume that each parent was around 80 years old when the first child was born and lived, on average, 900 years.

The controlling equation is:

$$P_n = \frac{2(c^{n-x+1})(c^x - 1)}{(c-1)}$$

Where P = population
  n = generation number
  c = # of children pairs
  x = average lifespan represented as partial generations

The generation number in this case is given as ten. As Adam and Eve were one breeding pair and we have assumed six children, or three subsequent breeding pairs, this makes c = 3.

Using these reasonable assumptions, we surprisingly find that there may have been billions of people alive in the tenth generation—Noah's generation![4] So many people could not have all lived in one river valley, no matter how fertile the "crescent." They must have been distributed globally; therefore, the Flood must have been global. A local or even regional flood would not have accomplished its primary purpose.

DESTRUCTION OF EARTH AND ALL FLESH

The Flood involved more than just the judgment of man and his sin, for "the earth also was corrupt before God, and the earth was filled with violence....For all flesh had corrupted his way upon the earth. And God said...I will destroy them with the earth" (Genesis 6:11-13).

How did the entire creation that had so recently been "very good" morph into something that repulsed its Creator and merited His annihilation? We will never fully know until He informs us, but we can speculate. Perhaps Satan was so enraged at his own expulsion from God's presence and the loss of his original privileged position that he sought to destroy and twist everything God had done. He certainly spiritually attacked God's image in man by encouraging him to rebel against God, but did he also seek to foster mutations to distort that image? Satan had listened as God predicted his ultimate doom at the hand of the seed of the woman, and thus his only chance was to interrupt that lineage so that the redeemer/solution couldn't ful-

WHERE DID CAIN GET HIS WIFE?

A longstanding question many have raised is where Cain got his wife. Cain, Adam's son, was banished from the family group for murdering his brother Abel. He went to the land of Nod (Genesis 4:16), where he and his wife started their own family (v. 17). The problem is solved by simply recognizing that in addition to Cain, Abel, and Seth, Adam and Eve birthed other sons and daughters (Genesis 5:4). Cain would have safely married his sister, or maybe a niece born in a brother's line.

Actually, close intermarriage is accepted in many cultures today, as it was in Bible times, and usually results in healthy offspring. Remember, Abram married his half-sister. Isaac married his cousin with no harmful effects, and these unions fathered the chosen nation. In our day, mutations have accumulated, and close kin often carry the same inherited mutations, resulting in birth defects. In this case, so soon after creation, mutations would not have collected to a problem level, and Cain and his sister (or niece) could have married and had healthy children.

The Curse of Genesis 3 impacted plants as well as the rest of creation. From that point, the ground brought forth "thorns and thistles" (v. 18). This fossil thorn may be dated by uniformitarian thinking as millions of years old, but it surely came after the Curse just thousands of years ago.

The penalty for Adam's sin was passed on to all his dominion, and now all living things die. Animals were created to eat plants for food, but some acquired the taste for meat after creation was cursed.

fill that prophecy.

Did he likewise turn his attention to the animal and plant kingdoms to mock all that a benevolent God had accomplished? Did he introduce mutant strains to degrade the genomes? Did he turn the animals against each other in a carnivorous frenzy? Did he twist helpful bacteria into pathogens? Did he genetically engineer plants to produce poisons? Obviously, Scripture relates none of this, but it would account for the current state of things.

This is the kind of ugly world often seen in the fossil record. We see evidence of violence and carnivorism, from offensive and defensive anatomical weaponry to meat remnants in fossilized dung or in the gut of fossilized animals. We see bones that bear scars of pre-death injuries and give eloquent testimony of a difficult and painful life and death. We find diseased animals with distorted bodies. We find plants with thorns. The earth was, as the Bible relates, "filled with violence," primarily human violence, but also animal violence. The fossilized world supports the record of Scripture that "all flesh had corrupted his way," and had decidedly earned God's disfavor and judgment. (Of course, animals don't sin and bear its moral penalty, but Adam did sin, and all in his dominion experienced the resulting pain, suffering, and death.)

Note that only a relatively few of these fossils are found in the Mesopotamian River Valley. Most are found buried in sedimentary strata laid down by energetic water action on every continent, including polar regions. Both local flood advocates and the supporters of a global flood believe that pre-Flood animals must have lived in all sectors of the globe. Local flood supporters may discount Scripture's inclusions of "all flesh, wherein is the breath of life" (Genesis 6:17), claiming that only local animals were included, but God mentioned that "clean beasts, and of beasts that are not clean, and of fowls and of every thing that creepeth upon the earth" (7:8) were on the Ark—everything that breathed air and lived on land. This demanded a global flood to judge and bury those not on board. The great Flood of Noah's day must have been global to accomplish its stated purpose.

PROMISE OF NO MORE FLOODS

The Flood year came to an end, and Noah, his family, and the animals left the Ark and entered a changed world. Sin had been punished, and a new day had dawned, but problems still remained. The earth was plagued by residual catastrophism, both weather-related and tectonically caused. It might have been severe enough that Noah's family needed assurance that the Flood was really over. To alleviate their fears, God promised there would never again be a similar convulsion of earth's systems. He said, "I will establish my covenant with you, neither shall all flesh be cut off any more by the waters of a flood; neither shall there any more be a flood to destroy the earth" (Genesis 9:11).

This could only be a comfort if the Flood was worldwide in scope, for there have been countless floods in the years since—major floods, even regional floods!

This is especially true in Mesopotamia, with known floods covering large portions of the valley. Some of Noah's descendants, if not Noah himself, surely experienced these floods, which wreaked local havoc for a while. But there was no cause for ultimate alarm, for God had promised there would never again be a worldwide flood like the one they had endured.

Such a promise would obviously be empty if the Genesis Flood was a local event. If that were the case, then God broke His promise, for there have been many major local floods since that time. Does God lie to us? Or did He not know? No, God's word is secure. Noah could trust Him, and we can trust Him as well.

In concert with the promise of no more worldwide floods, God gave a special sign to commemorate His covenant—a beautiful rainbow (Genesis 9:13). Since it is not mentioned in Scripture before this, we have reason to consider this the very first rainbow to adorn the sky. No doubt some individuals before the Flood had encountered a "rainbow" in the mist created by a waterfall, but did it ever fill the sky?

Rainbows require drops of liquid water in the air to split the light into its component wavelengths. Perhaps in pre-Flood times there was little liquid water in the atmosphere. It was probably not until after the Flood that earth had an atmosphere in which a rainbow could form.

MANY EXPRESSIONS OF THE GLOBAL NATURE OF THE FLOOD

While it is true that some seemingly all-inclusive words used in the Flood narrative can also be understood in a limited sense, proper interpretation depends on the context. For example, the word translated "all" in "*all* the high hills" (Genesis 7:19) is also used in Genesis 41:56-57: "And the famine was over *all* the face of the earth....And *all* countries came into Egypt to Joseph for to buy corn; because that the famine was so sore in *all* lands." In this passage, nations on other continents are probably not in view. The context in this passage suggests "all" is used in a limited sense, but what of Genesis 7:19 and the rest of the Flood narrative?

Consider that a double superlative precedes "all" in Genesis 7:19. The Flood is said to have "prevailed exceedingly" over the earth; it overwhelmingly conquered the land. By using powerful military imagery, Scripture

eliminates the possibility of a limited usage for "all" in this case. This sort of "overstatement" can be seen throughout the account. If we let the biblical context define its own words, we can come to no other interpretation than that gained from a plain-sense understanding. These normally all-encompassing terms are meant to be understood in a global sense.

In the Flood chapters, Genesis 6–9, numerous terms are used that normally imply a global extent. Together they provide the context for all the others. Reading them in list form provides a stunning awareness of Scripture's meaning, and demands a global interpretation of the whole.

- **Genesis 6**—"Multiply on the face of the earth" (v. 1). "Wickedness of man was great in the earth" (v. 5). "Made man on the earth" (v. 6). "Destroy man whom I have created from the face of the earth; both man, and beast, and the creeping thing, and the fowls of the air" (v. 7; not just herds of domesticated animals, as claimed). "The earth also was corrupt before God" (v. 11; how much can God observe?). "The earth was filled with violence" (v. 11). "God looked upon the earth" (v. 12). "All flesh...upon the earth" (not just humans) (v. 12). "The end of all flesh" (v. 13). "The earth is filled with violence" (v. 13). "Destroy them with the earth" (v. 13). "A flood of waters upon the earth" (v. 17). "To destroy all flesh" (v. 17). "Wherein is the breath of life" (v. 17; not just domesticated animals). "From under heaven" (v. 17; not just the atmosphere above Mesopotamia). "Every thing that is in the earth shall die" (v. 17; animals at a distance would have been unaffected by a local flood). "Every living thing of all flesh" (v. 19; this couldn't be just Noah's herds). "To keep them alive" (v. 19). "Fowls...to keep them alive" (v. 20; birds could certainly survive a local flood).

- **Genesis 7**—"To keep seed alive" (v. 3). "Upon the face of all the earth" (v. 3). "Every living substance that I have made" (v. 4). "Destroy from off the face of the earth" (v. 4). "The flood of waters was upon the earth" (v. 6). "Because of the waters of the flood" (v. 7). "The waters of the flood were upon the earth" (v. 10). "All the fountains" (v. 11; all, not limited to local geysers or volcanoes). "Of the great deep" (v. 11; the deep ocean). "Windows of heaven" (v. 11; a worldwide source implies a worldwide

Why Did God Give the Rainbow Sign?

Noah and his family had just come through an unimaginably frightening experience. Perhaps they had never even seen a storm, and certainly no one had ever seen one like this. It would have been indelibly impressed on their memories. During the Flood, the winds incessantly howled and the thunder pealed as the Ark pitched and rolled in the waves. Earthquakes shook the planet to its core, sending pulsating tsunamis in every direction. Underwater volcanoes and the spreading "fountains of the great deep" (Genesis 7:11) heated the water surrounding the Ark, making life on board almost unbearable. The windows of heaven remained open—it was like being under Niagara Falls.

This was not merely a modern Category 5 hurricane. Creationist researchers have begun to speculate on the nature of "hypercanes," storms dozens of times greater than present hurricanes, as best describing the Flood. Surely, the pre-Flood world fully "perished" (2 Peter 3:6) under the Flood's onslaught.

As Noah and his family stepped off the Ark, they entered a world totally unfamiliar to them. The geography had all changed. Plant and animal life had been devastated. Weather patterns were chaotic. Gone was the pre-Flood stability they were accustomed to.

Consider that the world was "broken." To the extent that we enjoy relative stability now, they had none then. It would perhaps have taken several centuries for earth to settle down to the pseudo-equilibrium in which we now live. Remember that the jet streams must be stabilized. The ocean currents must find their "paths of the seas" (Psalm 8:8). The continents must halt their rapid horizontal movements and cease their vertical rebounding. In particular, the oceans must give up their excess heat, which drove violent storms.

It was into this unstable world that Noah and his family were placed. No doubt, earthquakes were common. Of necessity they lived in tents, for buildings could not be made stable. Wood was in short supply, and rock structures are the least safe during earth tremors.

Calculations show that the ocean's excessive heat would have taken several hundred years or so to dissipate, and that during this period the Ice Age dominated. Intense rainfall continued, with swollen streams and violent storms. Job lived soon after the Flood, and his book contains many references to ice and snow. Up until perhaps the time of Abraham, the world was a dangerous place. Continual catastrophes dominated their lives.

No doubt they needed reassurance that there would never be another flood like the great Flood of Noah's day, for it must have seemed they were still in it. Thus, it was out of God's grace and mercy that He instituted this beautiful reminder of His protection. And every time they saw a majestic rainbow, it would remind them of the security they have in Him. And what a blessed thing it is to rest in that certain knowledge.

effect). "Rain was upon the earth" (v. 12). "Forty days and forty nights" (v. 12; no local flood would do this). "Every beast...all the cattle" (v. 14). "Every creeping thing that creepeth upon the earth" (v. 14; did Noah need to take rats and moles and snakes for them to survive a local flood?). "Every fowl...every bird of every sort" (v. 14). "Wherein is the breath of life" (v. 15; applies to animals worldwide). "The waters increased" (v. 17). "Bare up the ark" (v. 17). "Lift up above the earth" (v. 17). "Waters prevailed" (v. 18; similar to a military conquest). "Increased greatly" (v. 18). "Upon the earth" (v. 18; not just upon the valley). "The face of the waters" (v. 18; compare with the ocean in Genesis 1:2). "The waters prevailed exceedingly" (v. 19). "Upon the earth" (v. 19). "All the high hills" (v. 19). "That were under the whole heaven" (v. 19; all that were within God's sight). "Were covered" (v. 19). "Fifteen cubits upward" (v. 20; the draft of the 30-cubit Ark). "Did the waters prevail" (v. 20). "The mountains were covered" (v. 20; same word in Hebrew as high hills in v. 19). "All flesh died" (v. 21). "That moved upon the earth" (v. 21). "Fowl...cattle...beast...creeping things" (v. 21). "That creepeth upon the earth" (v. 21; most animals are small creeping things). "Upon the earth" (v. 21). "And every man" (v. 21). "In whose nostrils was the breath of life" (v. 22; all air-breathing animals). "All that was in the dry land" (v. 22). "Every living substance was destroyed" (v. 23). "Upon the face of the ground" (v. 23). "Man, and cattle, and the creeping things, and the fowl of the heaven" (v. 23). "They were destroyed from the earth" (v. 23). "Noah only remained alive" (v. 23). "They that were with him in the ark" (v. 23). "The waters prevailed" (v. 24).

• **Genesis 8**—"Every living thing" (v. 1). "All the cattle" (v. 1). "A wind to pass over the earth" (v. 1). "The waters assuaged" (v. 1). "The fountains also of the deep" (v. 2). "The windows of heaven" (v. 2). "Were stopped" (v. 2). "The rain from heaven was restrained" (v. 2; a special rain, not a local storm, for rains continue). "The waters returned" (v. 3). "From off the earth" (v. 3). "The waters were abated" (v. 3). "The mountains of Ararat" (v. 4; the entire Ararat region is about one mile in elevation, the headwaters of Mesopotamian rivers. Did the Ark float uphill in this "local" flood?). "The waters de-

creased continually" (v. 5). "The tops of the mountains [were] seen" (v. 5; three months later). "The waters were dried up" (v. 7). "From off the earth" (v. 7; after 40 more days). "To see if the waters were abated" (v. 8). "From off the face of the ground" (v. 8). "The dove found no rest" (v. 9). "The waters were on the face of the whole earth" (v. 9). "The waters were abated" (v. 11). "From off the earth" (v. 11). "The waters were dried up" (v. 13). "From off the earth" (v. 13). "The face of the ground" (v. 13). "Was the earth dried" (v. 14). "Every beast, every creeping thing, and every fowl" (v. 19; all of them, not some of them, left the Ark). "Curse the ground" (v. 21). "Every living thing" (v. 21; promise of no more such floods. It couldn't be a local flood). "While the earth remaineth" (v. 22).

• **Genesis 9**—"Be fruitful, and multiply, and replenish the earth" (v. 1). "Every beast of the earth" (v. 2; not just local farm animals). "Every fowl of the air" (v. 2). "That moveth upon the earth" (v. 2). "All the fishes of the sea" (v. 2). "Every moving thing that liveth" (v. 3). "Bring forth abundantly in the earth" (v. 7). "Establish my covenant" (v. 9). "With every living creature" (v. 10). "That is with you" (v. 10; there were no land-dwelling creatures not included in this covenant). "The fowl... the cattle...every beast of the earth" (v. 10). "To every beast of the earth" (v. 10). "All flesh be cut off" (v. 11). "By the waters of a flood" (v. 11). "A flood to destroy the earth" (v. 11). "Every living creature" (v. 12). "Perpetual generations" (v. 12). "Between me and the earth" (v. 13). "Every living creature" (v. 15). "Of all flesh" (v. 15). "Waters shall no more become a flood" (v. 15). "To destroy all flesh" (v. 15). "Every living creature" (v. 16). "Of all flesh" (v. 16). "That is upon the earth" (v. 16). "All flesh" (v. 17). "That is upon the earth" (v. 17). "The whole earth overspread" (v. 19; Noah's descendants are today worldwide. The same term was used to describe the Flood's extent).

The account makes no sense if the Flood was local, but reads naturally and logically if the Flood was global. How better could information regarding a global flood be described? It would seem that the Author of Genesis could hardly have been more explicit. Conversely, if the omniscient Author had intended to describe a local flood, He obscured the facts. If words can communicate truth, if God can express Himself clearly, then the

Flood was global.

It would seem that only a rank downgrading of Scripture, and/or an unhealthy desire for the approval of uniformitarian-minded men, could lead one to question this doctrine.

THE TESTIMONY OF JESUS CHRIST

Certainly Jesus Christ, the person of the Godhead intimately involved in accomplishing creation and the Flood, would know its extent. He referred to the Flood judgment event in terms best understood as implying its global nature. He even based His doctrine of the end times on it. While instructing His disciples regarding the last days, He said:

> As it was in the days of Noe, so shall it be also in the days of the Son of man. They did eat, they drank, they married wives, they were given in marriage, until the day that Noah entered into the ark, and the flood came, and destroyed them all. (Luke 17:26-27)

Jesus based His teaching of the coming worldwide judgment on the fact of the past worldwide judgment, and reminded His listeners that the great Flood of Noah's day was universal in scope in that it "destroyed them all." By comparing the two episodes, He implied that the coming judgment will destroy "all" who are not covered by Christ's sacrificial work on their behalf (i.e., in the Ark of safety, Jesus Christ), just as the past judgment destroyed "all" who refused God's protection in the Ark of Noah.

But what if the Flood was only local and only destroyed some of the world's inhabitants? Christ's teaching would be severely weakened. Thus, we see that a global flood implies a coming judgment upon all, while a local flood implies a partial judgment to come—which introduces theological chaos.

THE TESTIMONY OF THE APOSTLE PETER

In a very similar fashion, Peter reminds his readers of the past time when "the world that then was, being overflowed with water, perished" (2 Peter 3:6). On this he bases his teaching on the Lord's return, when the entire "heavens and the earth, which are now" will "pass away with a great noise, and the elements shall melt with fervent heat, and the earth…shall be burned up" (v. 7, 10). The coming destruction and renovation of the entire planet—indeed, the entire universe, producing "new heavens and a new earth" (v. 13)—is likened to the past destruction and renovation of the entire earth.

To those who advocate the local flood theory, we might ask: Will the coming re-creation of the new earth be just a local re-creation? Will only portions of earth "pass away with a great noise"? Which parts will melt with fervent heat? Will it only concern the portions of earth in which man sins? How does the local flood concept not imply that only part of the earth is "reserved unto fire" (v. 7)? Will sinners in some places escape God's coming wrath? What hope does this give the sinner? Some things cannot be. Obviously, the local flood proposal leads to doctrinal nonsense.

SUMMARY

Scripture unequivocally teaches the global, catastrophic Flood, and does so on many occasions and in many ways. The global Flood interpretation makes good exegetical and logical sense, as well as good theological sense, while unnatural renderings of the text to teach a local flood are illogical and unwarranted in the extreme. The coming chapters will demonstrate that local flood concepts are also unscientific.

CHAPTER 5

HISTORICAL REFERENCES TO CREATION AND THE FLOOD

The Bible speaks clearly. The great Flood of Noah's day was global in extent and dynamic in nature, forever altering the world. Only the eight people in Noah's family survived, and the entire world was repopulated from the families of Shem, Ham, and Japheth. God's confusion of the languages at Babel forced migration. As the language groups separated, particular traits sprang up that we now recognize as national and "racial" characteristics. Various people groups "remembered" the episode of the Flood, told to them by their forefathers, and kept it alive through tradition and tribal lore.

In all likelihood, written records had been kept of the days before the Flood and the horror of the Flood year. Survivors who remained close to Babel would have had access to them, but as migration continued, oral histories were eventually all they had. But the Flood could never be forgotten. It was indelibly impressed on their minds, for the Creator Himself had judged the wicked pre-Flood civilization. The story was kept alive and passed on to succeeding generations. Over the centuries of telling and retelling, the account may have shifted, but the essence of the story must have remained. Have any such "stories" survived to this day?

The stronger peoples would probably have stayed near Babel, preferring to simply drive the weaker groups away. Flood "legends" from this region might be expected to be closest to the true account, with fewer revisions. However, these peoples quickly embraced the rebellious spirit rampant at Babel, and soon adopted pagan thinking. Their oral and written "histo-

ries" might be purposively skewed, but might be more recognizable than others. Those whose journeys took them farther away might have lost some of the precision, or they may have gone to extraordinary lengths to preserve the truth. The final chapters of this book will focus on scientific evidence that confirms the biblical account, but let us first investigate the historical evidence.

DO WE HAVE A RECORD OF LIFE BEFORE THE FLOOD?

Interestingly, although the Bible doesn't tell us much about pre-Flood times, there are a few apocryphal writings that purport to do so. The Book of Enoch, which was likely written in Old Testament times in Israel, yet long after the true Enoch's time, makes such a claim in his name. Yet it contains numerous fascinating details not recorded elsewhere that have the ring of truth about them. One wonders if the story somehow survived orally and was later written down. Similarly, the Book of Jasher parallels the book of Genesis, with few incompatibilities. No claim is made here for inspiration, but reading either source today becomes a treasured experience.

Similar tales come down to us in the form of "historical" oral accounts from ancient cultures, designed as memory devices for those peoples. The ancient Miao tribe of China has a detailed history that is memorized by nearly everyone and sung at festivals. The "history" is very precise, and dates from a time long before Christian missionaries encountered the tribe and taught true biblical history. Yet the parallels are striking. Preserved in metrical form to encourage memorization, it bears a seeming similarity to Hebrew poetry. A portion of this lengthy poem is reproduced below, translated by a veteran worker among the tribe.[1]

On the day God created the heavens and earth.
On that day He opened the gateway of light.
In the earth He made heaps of earth and stone.
In the sky He made bodies, the sun and the moon.
In the earth He created the hawk and the kite.
In the water created the lobster and fish.
In the wilderness made He the tiger and bear,
Made verdure to cover the mountains,
Made forest extend with the ranges,
Made the light green cane,
Made the rank bamboo.

On the earth He created a man from the dirt.
Of the man thus created, a woman He formed.
Then the Patriarch Dirt made a balance of stones.
Estimated the weight of the earth to the bottom.
Calculated the bulk of the heavenly bodies.
And pondered the ways of the Deity, God.
The Patriarch Dirt begat Patriarch Se-teh.
The Patriarch Se-teh begat a son Lusu.
And Lusu had Gehlo and he begat Lama.
The Patriarch Lama Begat the man Nuah.
His wife was the Matriarch Gaw Bo-lu-en.
Their sons were Lo Han, Lo Shen and Jah-hu.

So the earth began filling with tribes and with families.
Creation was shared by the clans and the peoples.

These did not God's will nor returned His affection.
But fought with each other defying the Godhead.
Their leaders shook fists in the face of the Mighty.
Then the earth was convulsed to the depth of three strata.
Rending the air to the uttermost heaven.
God's anger arose till His Being was changed;
His wrath flaring up filled His eyes and His face.
Until He must come and demolish humanity.
Come and destroy a whole world full of people.

So it poured forty days in sheets and in torrents.
Then fifty-five days of misting and drizzle.
The waters surmounted the mountains and ranges.
The deluge ascending leapt valley and hollow.
An earth with no earth upon which to take refuge!

A world with no foothold where one might subsist!
The people were baffled, impotent and ruined,
Despairing, horror stricken, diminished and finished.
But the Patriarch Nuah was righteous.
The Matriarch Gaw Bo-lu-en upright.
Built a boat very wide.
Made a ship very vast.
Their household entire got aboard and were floated,
The family complete rode the deluge in safety.
The animals with him were female and male.
The birds went along and were mated in pairs.
When the time was fulfilled, God commanded the waters.
The day had arrived, the flood waters receded.
Then Nuah liberated a dove from their refuge,
Sent a bird to go forth and bring again tidings.
The flood had gone down into lake and to ocean;
The mud was confined to the pools and the hollows.
There was land once again where a man might reside;
There was a place in the earth now to rear habitations.
Buffalo then were brought, an oblation to God,
Fatter cattle became sacrifice to the Mighty.
The Divine One then gave them His blessing;
Their God then bestowed His good graces.

Lo-han then begat Cusah and Mesay.
Lo-shan begat Elan and Nga-shur.
Their offspring begotten became tribes and peoples;
Their descendants established encampments and cities.
Their singing was all with the same tunes and music;
Their speaking was all with the same words and language.
Then they said let us build us a very big city;
Let us raise unto heaven a very high tower.
This was wrong, but they reached this decision;
Not right, but they rashly persisted.
God struck at them then, changed their language and accent.
Descending in wrath, He confused tones and voices.
One's speech to the others who hear him has no meaning;
He's speaking in words, but they can't understand him.
So the city they built was never completed;
The tower they wrought has to stand thus unfinished.
In despair then they separate under all heaven,
They part from each other the globe to encircle.
They arrive at six corners and speak the six languages.

The similarities between Genesis and Miao history are unmistakable. To the founders and leaders of this people group, keeping the memory of the Flood's reasons and devastation was so important that they kept it alive in a way that could hardly be forgotten. Remember, this "history" dates from long before the influence of missionaries, who have been few and far between in this isolated and remote tribe. A list of identical details would be lengthy.

Note in particular the similarity of some of these names to those in the Bible account: Seth, Lamech, Noah, Ham, Shem, and Japheth come down to us from the Miao as Se-teh, Lama, Nuah, Lo Han, Lo Shen, and Jah-hu. Ham's descendants Cush and Mizram become Cusah and Mesay. Shem's descendants Elam and Asshur are recorded as Elan and Nga-shur. One can only conclude that an accurate historical (and valued) record is being transmitted.

The history also transmitted accurate scientific information regarding the spherical shape of the earth. A literal translation of one line is: "They parted and live encircle world-ball." The Miao knew nothing of the world being round. This passage seems to indicate the more complete knowledge of an ancient civilization.

Easily recognized are clear references to the creation, the Fall due to man's sin, the great Flood of Noah's day, and the Tower of Babel incident with the dispersion of nations and languages. The Miao culture dates to the extreme past. The best understanding ascribes the poem to remote history, preserving tribal traditions and origins, and as such forms a strong witness to biblical history.

Do Other Ancient Sources Mention the Flood?

No humans besides Noah and his family survived the Flood, so there was no one else to report it. But everyone since then has descended from Noah, and without a doubt each generation would have passed on the story. Noah and his family had lived through a most memorable event, and it would be prominent in family traditions from then on. The father would tell his children, and they would tell their children. Several generations later, Noah would be almost legendary, but the story had made an unforgettable impression, never to leave his descendants' oral histories. Through the telling and retelling, the account might be embellished and grow bigger with blurred details, but the essence would remain.

In the oral histories of nearly every tribe and ethnic group, a flood story survives to this day in their body of folklore and tribal heritage. Anthropologists have cataloged hundreds of these "universal flood traditions." Is it credible to ascribe, as secular uniformitarians do, each separate account to tribal myth? It causes naturalists and uniformitarians great concern that all people groups have manufactured the same "untrue" story. Secularists often claim that early missionaries taught the story, but that doesn't hold, especially when you recognize that more essential truths need telling but are still lacking. Often hitherto unreached tribal groups already have such a story upon first contact, and it is collected by the missionaries. The flood legends could not have been taught by the same missionaries.

All relate the same basic tale, how that, due to the wickedness of man, the supreme God was angry and

Engraving of a Babylonian king.

planned to send a flood of judgment. One man was faithful and received warning, and built a boat to save his family. All the rest of humanity perished. In many accounts, animals played a part, either as passengers or by affecting the end. As the flood ceased, the boat landed on a mountain, and the survivors repopulated the earth.

Mythologists know that when similar myths exist in separate cultures that have had no obvious recent contact, there is either a historical common source for the cultures, or the two groups historically experienced a common event. The biblical answer is that all people groups descended from Noah and his family, who all survived the same event. Their descendants have since separated and migrated to all parts of the earth.

The story seems to have changed somewhat with the telling and retelling, and with migration over multiple generations, but the original essence can still be recognized. A set of standard questions asked of over 200 such "stories" yields the following statistics.[2]

1. Was the flood global?   95%
2. Was wickedness of man the cause?   66%
3. Was there a favored family or individual?   88%
4. Was the remnant forewarned?   66%
5. Was survival due to a boat?   70%
6. Were animals also saved?   67%
7. Did animals play any part?   73%
8. Did survivors end up on a mountain?   57%
9. Were birds sent out?   35%
10. Did survivors sacrifice afterward?   13%
11. Was the rainbow mentioned?   7%
12. Was geography local?   82%

Likewise, we should not be surprised to find that a compilation of similar "histories" mirrors the biblical teaching of a primordial golden age of prosperity and ease, where man had direct access to God, foodstuffs were plentiful, animals were unafraid of man, the woman was created from and for the man while he slept, and man was immortal. This time of "paradise" lasted until man offended God or the gods, and this "heaven on earth" was withdrawn. Such worldwide traditions are well-known among anthropologists who, dominated by uniformitarian thinking, attribute them either to a common dream, a common heritage, or universal human psychology.

As with flood legends, these far-flung human peoples, originally having had no recent contact with each other

or any teaching from Christian missionaries, yet holding the same unlikely origins view, can best be understood in biblical terms. All have descended from Adam and Noah. All have the same unforgettable milestones in their history, memories to be retained as best they can. Migration and time may have blurred the details, in some cultures more than others, but almost all retain some memory of creation, a golden age, the Fall due to sin, the great Flood, and the dispersion at Babel. These stories are more memory than myth.

THE EPIC OF GILGAMESH

Similar "histories" come from ancient tablets, of which the best known is the Epic of Gilgamesh. In many ways it mirrors Genesis, reinforcing some details and introducing others, yet infusing rank, pagan spiritism in such a way that no thinking person would consider it "true." It mentions the wickedness of man as the cause of God's wrath against man, for which He sent the Flood to judge the earth. The Ark, the water, the landing place, the animals, the sacrifice afterward are mentioned, although details are obscured with non-credible additions, implying the Epic is really a twisted copy of an original, factual account. We can surmise that the biblical Genesis is the pure source. The tablet comes in both Babylonian and Assyrian versions, both quite ancient, likely dating to the time soon after the rebellion at Babel. Could people in open disobedience to God

Epic of Gilgamesh cuneiform tablet.

have been the first to rewrite history to justify their rebellion?

The Epic of Gilgamesh is surely an astonishing document, found on several broken clay tablets in the Assyrian city of Nineveh in the ancient library of King Ashurbanipal. From archaeological constraints, it was determined to have been written only in the 7th century B.C. during the Babylonian Empire (Moses lived around 1300 B.C.), having been copied from prior pagan documents that no longer exist. Based on linguistic analysis, the original text from which Gilgamesh was copied could have been composed no earlier than 1800 B.C. For reference, Abraham lived during the 22nd century B.C., long before any of the documents and only about 300 years after the Flood (according to a strict reading of the Masoretic Text). Thus, none of the writings existed until long after the Flood.

For over a century now, the standard view among "higher critics" of the Bible and their liberal followers has been that the Genesis Flood account was written long after Moses. They claim an unknown group of Jewish priests or scribes wrote this morality story by revising an older Babylonian myth. The Gilgamesh Epic is their original of choice. Could such an inferior and cartoonish tale have been the source document for the straightforward narrative style of Genesis, complete with such beauty and believability? Not without extensive rewriting. Perhaps the so-called "higher critics" should be more critical of their own writings.

The Gilgamesh Epic contains the flood story, but it is so full of fanciful and unbelievable details that probably no one ever considered it true. Even ancient pagans were not that gullible. The Babylonian flood story may have been the politically correct story of the time, but how could anyone believe a cubical Ark could have been seaworthy, or that the gods gathered like flies to receive sacrifices? The similarities between the Epic and Genesis are striking, but Genesis is written in a clear fashion as a historical narrative, with an obvious intent that it be believed. The stupendous facts given in Genesis may be wholly out of our experience, but the account is understandable and believable. Yet the assigned early date of the undiscovered Gilgamesh sources from which it was claimed to have been compiled predates the assigned late date of Genesis written by the liberal's mythical scribes. Therfore, in their view Genesis is the copy and thus non-historical.

WHO WROTE GENESIS?

Traditionally Moses is credited with writing Genesis, but it covers events far predating his lifetime. If he wrote it, even under the inspiration of the Holy Spirit, it stands unique in Scripture. Some hold that Genesis was actually written as eyewitness accounts by the patriarchs Adam through Joseph. In this view, the pre-Flood portion of Genesis was penned by Noah, while the Flood details came through the sons of Noah. Moses collected and compiled the ancient eyewitness accounts handed down from Noah through Abraham.[1]

Note that each section is "signed" at its end by the relevant observer, from Adam through Joseph, using the same formula, "these are the generations of…." The Creator Himself wrote the first section, creation from God's perspective (Genesis 1:1–2:4). Adam wrote the next section, creation from Adam's perspective (2:4b–5:1). Next is Noah's section, covering events of his life and pre-Flood times (5:1b–6:9). The sons of Noah wrote the Flood narrative (6:9b–10:1).

Shem tells us of the Tower of Babel incident and the formation of the new nations (10b–11:10). Terah recorded details of the Semitic line, forefathers of Israel (11:10b–11:27). Isaac documented the life of Abraham and a brief section on Ishmael (11:27b–25:19). Jacob relates his life story and a brief inclusion regarding Esau (25:19b–37:2). The sons of Jacob tell of Joseph and the Israel in Egypt (37b–50:26).[2]

1. Bill Cooper, 2012, *The Authenticity of the Book of Genesis,* Portsmouth, UK: Creation Science Movement, 28-32.

2. Henry Morris, 1976, *The Genesis Record*, Grand Rapids, MI: Baker Book House, 26-30.

AN EVEN EARLIER ACCOUNT

Unknown to most archaeologists is an even earlier Flood tablet. It was discovered in the ancient Babylonian city of Nippur in the 1890s. The tablet was so encrusted, its value was not immediately recognized. It had to be treated and restored. By 1909, Dr. Hermann Hilprecht had discerned the figures and translated the text. Given the catalogue designation CBM 13532, the tablet dates from about 2200 B.C., rather soon after the Flood itself. More importantly, while the differences between Genesis and Gilgamesh are striking, the similarities between Genesis and this tablet are obvious. There is no detail that differs from Genesis, and nothing extra is added.

Hilprecht's translation reads as follows, with unreadable portions of the text noted.

> The springs of the deep will I open. A flood will I send which will affect all of mankind at once. But seek thou deliverance before the flood breaks forth, for over all living beings, however many there are, will I bring annihilation, destruction, ruin. Take wood and pitch and build a large ship!…cubits be its complete height….a houseboat shall it be, containing those who preserve their life….with a strong roofing cover it….the ship which thou makest, take into it….the animals of the field, the birds of the air and the reptiles, two of each, instead of (their whole number)….and the family of the….[3]

This clear text stands as both a confirmation of Scripture and a condemnation of liberal "scholarship." Furthermore, it exposes the foolishness of such scholars' total fascination with the later and inferior Gilgamesh Epic. It evidently so clearly undermines the "critical" view and supports Genesis that it never receives any mention among these "scholars." Professor Hilprecht himself was hardly a defender of Scripture, yet he was a recognized expert in ancient languages. His translation originally caused quite a storm of controversy among academics, for it undercut their position that Genesis carries no authority. Interestingly, no challenge was ever levied against his translation, but he was reprimanded (and exonerated) for a violation of a minor publishing protocol. Perhaps this was the "scholars'" justification for burying his work, but it remains buried today. Few know of the tablet and of its strong testimony.[4]

Yet another ancient tablet has been found, this one from the Akkadian culture, which was contemporaneous with the Sumerians. The Akkadian culture also thrived soon after the Flood, and was prominently involved in the Tower of Babel language confusion. It continued as a recognizable culture at least up until Abraham's day. Some portions are missing from the partial and broken tablets, but we can gain insights into the understanding and memories of these early post-Flood peoples. Their Flood account was also rather similar to both Genesis and Gilgamesh, but included additional, interesting comments regarding the times immediately prior to the Flood.[5]

It included the sin of man as the ultimate cause of the Flood, the waters and the animals, and the mountainous landing place. It also related that there was a drought and associated famine in the preceding few years. The land is described as well-watered and lush until the last seven years before waters from below erupted, the skies opened up, and the Flood arrived. It lists the difficulties each year brought, including excessive hostility among the people in the third year of the seven. The fourth year, the people felt hemmed in by calamities and overcrowding. In the fifth heartbreaking year, grown children returned to their parents for relief from the famine, but were turned away. Infants seeking milk were denied by their mothers. The sixth year was worse, as parents cannibalized their children. Neighbors turned on neighbors for food. Described as walking dead people, with wasted bodies, they all soon succumbed to the floodwaters. Crops are described as withering away. The rain dried up and rivers ceased to flow. Dried ground produced salt. A pestilence overran the people. Neither human nor animal could bear young.

What can we learn from this record of the seven years before the Flood, when the beautiful "paradise-like" conditions of the pre-Flood world were beginning to break up? Was nature turning against the inhabitants as they were turning against each other? Is this account a faded memory through Noah's sons that harbingers of the Flood were evident? From Scripture, we learn that if God hadn't intervened, all mankind would have perished, a concept supported by this pagan source.

YET ANOTHER "DOCUMENT"

A different sort of account comes from the fossil record of life before the Flood—not in written words, of course, but fossils do contain a record of life and living conditions. For instance, the history of a tree is "written" in its rings. Not all trees produce rings; in fact,

TREE RING DATING

Several species of trees live almost indefinitely. The giant sequoia trees of California are known to live over 3,000 years. This is determined by counting their tree rings. There are two parts to a ring: a lighter-colored growth portion, and a darker-colored stabilization season. Under normal circumstances, woody trees add one ring per year. Many trees do not produce annual rings, especially those in temperate or tropical regions.

Living trees can be sampled for their tree ring "record" without harming them by extracting a very thin cylinder (core) of wood. A well-known study involved bristlecone pine trees in California's White Mountains, while others have employed oak trees in south Germany and pine trees from Northern Ireland. Linear sequences of rings are obtained by cross-matching tree ring patterns from living trees and those from dead wood. Most chronologies only go back a few centuries, but a few give longer ages than the Bible implies, supposedly up to 10,000 years or so.

Tree rings are more than a record of years. Year-to-year variation in ring width reveals information about the growth conditions in a particular year. Insect infestation clearly manifests itself, as does disease or fire damage. Each of these interrupts the normal growth cycle. Day length, amount of sunshine, water potential, nutrients, the tree's age, temperature, rainfall, height above ground, proximity to a branch—all impact tree growth and tree ring production. By assuming that the outer ring records the most recent year and that each ring signals one year, a researcher can determine the "date" of a particular ring simply by counting rings.

How valid is the assumption of one ring per year in a climate where tree-growing conditions are variable? This has been put to the test by research foresters employed by the government of Australia. Their task was to investigate how a tree grows, how and when it adds a new ring, the effect of nutrients, rainfall, etc., over a range of related studies.[1]

By attaching sensitive probes onto actively growing trees, tree growth could be monitored as it occurred. This was not merely a ring counting effort, but an observation of living trees and how they react to ambient conditions—how and when they make a ring. Measurements were taken every 15 minutes throughout the years of study!

It was found that all trees, even slow-growing ones, respond dynamically to even tiny environmental changes. It was concluded that numerous "normal" conditions can produce an extra ring, or no ring at all. Weather was fingered as the most significant culprit. Unusual storms with abundant rainfall interspersed with dry periods can produce multiple rings, essentially one per major storm. The basic assumption of tree ring dating is demonstrably in error. Can we trust the overlapping calibration curves?

Petrified wood showing tree rings.

As it pertains to Flood model considerations, remember that the centuries immediately following the Flood witnessed the coming of the Ice Age. As the Flood ended, trees sprouted and entered an active growth stage. The still-warm oceans were rapidly evaporating, thus providing raw material for major monsoon-type storms. Earth was ravaged by frequent and wide-ranging atmospheric disturbances, dumping excessive snowfall in northern regions and rainfall to the south. If ever there was a time when multiple rings could develop in trees, this was it. Those centuries probably produced tree ring growth that was anything but annual.

1. Geoff Downes, 2010, *Tree Rings, Dating and Changing Climate*, DVD, Creation Ministries International.

the dominant trees before the Flood were more pithy than woody, and thus produced no rings. But many trees that lived before the Flood are well-preserved in numerous geologic layers, petrified with rings intact. Rings usually relate to growth in one year, with winter and summer growth periods visible. A year with lots of rain would produce a thicker ring than one from a dry year. Trees living through the same time period would likely have a recognizable tree ring pattern. From the study of tree rings, living or dead, the environment for that year can be discerned. Was it well-watered? Was there an insect infestation? Did fires or frost ravage the forest?

As is discussed throughout this book, virtually all geologic layers of sedimentary rock were deposited as sediments during the great Flood. Thus, the trees trapped in those sediments lived before the Flood and were buried by it. The tree rings record the environment throughout the tree's life. What can they tell us about pre-Flood times?

Rings of petrified trees from numerous layers, representing several different geologic Periods (thought by uniformitarians to have been separated by tens of millions of years or more), have now been studied. The tree rings tell us that in general, every year before the Flood was a good growth year, with sufficient water and abundant nutrition. A somewhat monotonous regularity testifies to an apparent subtropical "paradise" on all continents and in each "time" period.

Until, that is, the time just before the trees died, as recorded by the rings just under the petrified bark. The research often shows that the outer seven rings of trees preserved in numerous layers thought by uniformitarians to have lived at different ages—the rings produced during the last seven years before the trees died (during the Flood catastrophe)—indicate that the environment began to break up and show less regularity. Even though the trees are not normally thought to have lived at the

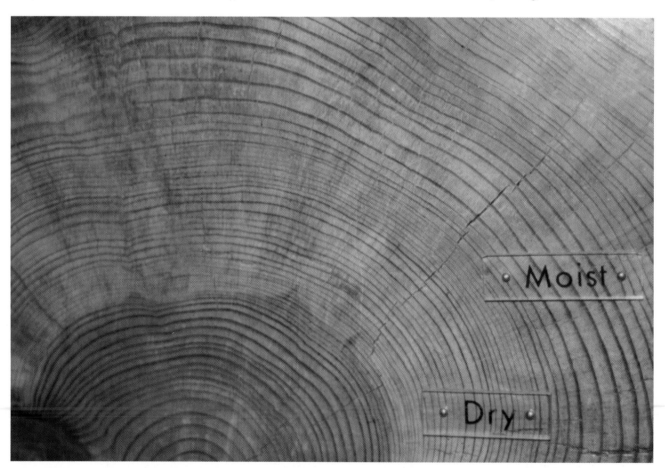

Tree rings record much about the environment in which they were formed. Lengthy chronologies based on the assumption of one ring per year may be inaccurate, since they ignore the effect of special conditions. The unstable weather and storms in the centuries following the great Flood were ideal for forming multiple rings. Lengthy chronologies based on the assumption of one ring per year may be inaccurate, since they ignore the effect of special conditions. Extra rings were quite possible in the chaotic years immediately following the Flood.

same time (or died in the same tragedy), exactly seven years before their last ring, the rings from many trees in all layers are irregular. Abnormal weather patterns show up in the unusual deviation in the rings. Perhaps these are hints that the "fountains" were becoming unstable.

Throughout the time he was building the Ark, Noah was "a preacher of righteousness" (2 Peter 2:5), proclaiming a coming storm/calamity to a generation to whom such storms were unknown. As Noah neared the end of his construction project, there were hints the people could see that their perfect world and easy life were falling apart. They had every reason to believe and board the Ark, yet they rejected God's gracious offer of salvation.

Hurricane Katrina from space. Major hurricanes termed hypercanes punctuated the great Flood of Noah's day.

CHAPTER 6

QUESTIONS AND ISSUES CONCERNING THE GLOBAL FLOOD

Recognizing and believing that Scripture teaches that the great Flood of Noah's day was global in extent is only the start. This brings up numerous questions and issues for which we must find answers. The same questions that plagued church leaders in Charles Lyell's day are echoed today. Those questions pummeled theologians into abandoning the doctrines of special creation and the young earth, and ultimately to jettisoning the inerrancy of scriptural doctrine. The questions deserve answers. Some of the most persistent ones that still bother believers are listed below, each with a brief answer.[1]

WHERE DID ALL THE WATER COME FROM?

As 19th-century explorers mapped the dimensions of the world's continents, and surveyors determined the height of the world's mountain chains, a shocking truth emerged: There isn't enough water on the planet to cover it today—certainly not for the better part of a year. The Himalaya Mountains are much too high for water to inundate them at all, let alone for the span of time required by Scripture. The critics concluded that the Bible must be in error, and that the Flood was merely local.

Let us remember the sources of water for the Flood. There was, of course, a violent upwelling in the pre-Flood oceans. There were also the "fountains of the great deep," which sent huge volumes of sub-surface fluids onto the land, and the "windows of heaven"

pouring down rain from above. Tectonic forces pulsated, pushing ocean water landward again and again, maintaining a bulge in sea level. Together, the sources of water resulted in a worldwide flood.

Let us also remember that earth is "the water planet," with water covering about 71 percent of its surface. A view of earth from space reveals primarily water. Moreover, scientists now know that more water resides underground nestled within the pores and molecular structure of rocks than is present on the surface. Make no mistake—there is plenty of water to cover the earth, but that's not a complete answer.

Today, the oceans are much wider than the continents, and on average they are much deeper than the continents are high. The average elevation of earth's solid surface is quite a distance below sea level. Phrased another way, if all the water, liquid and solid, were removed from the planet and the solid material smoothed off to a completely smooth sphere and then the water replaced, water would cover the earth to a depth of over 3 kilometers, or about 10,000 feet.

Suppose a large meteorite or asteroid were to fall into the oceans of today. It could conceivably generate such a tsunami that it would wash completely over most continents. The problem is that the mountains are too high to allow it to remain there, for the water would immediately drain to lower elevations.

If the mountains are too high and the oceans too deep to allow for a worldwide flood today, was the relative to-

DID NOAH'S FLOOD COVER THE HIMALAYA MOUNTAINS?

Few doctrines in Scripture are as clearly taught as the global nature of the great Flood of Noah's day. Genesis clearly teaches that "the waters...increased greatly...and the mountains were covered" (Genesis 7:18-20).

Through the centuries, few Christians questioned this doctrine. The Bible said it, and that was enough—until the late 1700s, that is. For the first time, the globe was being explored. The extremely lofty Himalaya Mountains were surveyed, capped by Mount Everest at 29,029 feet in elevation. Did the waters cover them? Is there enough water on the planet to do so? The questions seemed so far-fetched that many European churchmen dismissed the idea that the Flood was global, adopting the local flood concept that still dominates Christian colleges and seminaries today. Like dominos, other doctrines soon began to fall—the young age for the earth, the special creation of plants and animals, and the inerrancy of Scripture.

We now know, of course, that earth has plenty of water to launch a global flood. It has been calculated that if the earth's surface were completely flat, with no high mountains and no deep ocean basins, that water would cover the earth to a depth of about 10,000 feet. But is there enough water to cover a 29,029-foot mountain?

The key is to remember that the Flood didn't have to cover the present earth, but it did have to cover the pre-Flood earth, and the Bible teaches that the Flood fully restructured the earth. "The world that then was, being overflowed with water, perished" (2 Peter 3:6). It is gone forever. The earth of today was radically altered by that global event.

That Flood accomplished abundant geologic work, eroding sediments here, redepositing them there, pushing up continents, elevating plateaus, denuding terrains, etc., so that the earth today is quite different from before. Today, mountain ranges that didn't exist before rise high above the sea.

Mount Everest and the Himalayan range, along with the Alps, the Rockies, the Appalachians, the Andes, and most of the world's other mountains, are flanked with ocean-bottom sediments, full of marine fossils laid down by the Flood. Mount Everest itself has marine fossils at its summit. These rock layers containing so many marine fossils cover an extensive area, including much of Asia and beyond. They give every indication of resulting from cataclysmic water processes. These are the kinds of deposits we would expect to result from the worldwide, world-destroying Flood of Noah's day.

At the end of the Flood, after thick sequences of sediments had accumulated under water, the continental plates began to move and the Indian subcontinent collided with Asia. This caused a rapid crumpling of the sediments and a doubling of the roughly 20-mile thickness of the crust there to form the highest mountains in the world, and they continue to slowly grow. Today, they stand as giants—folded and fractured, with layers of ocean-bottom sediments at their summits. Noah's Flood didn't cover the Himalayas; it formed them!

Thus, we find the biblical account not only possible, but also supported by the evidence. A pre-Flood world with lessened topographic extremes could have been covered by the great Flood. That Flood caused today's high mountains and deep oceans, making such a flood impossible to repeat. This is just as God promised, back in Genesis.

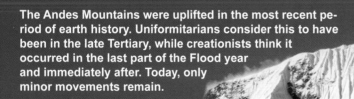

The Andes Mountains were uplifted in the most recent period of earth history. Uniformitarians consider this to have been in the late Tertiary, while creationists think it occurred in the last part of the Flood year and immediately after. Today, only minor movements remain.

pography ever different enough to allow it in the past? It appears that there was such a time—in pre-Flood days. As discussed earlier, there is scant evidence that pre-Flood mountains were very high. In fact, geologists have determined that nearly all of today's mountain ranges arose late in the planet's history; or in biblical terms, at the end of the Flood and afterward. There is also evidence that marine plants and animals, whose fossils are found in great abundance all around the earth, lived near the coast in relatively shallow seas, not under great depths of water. Plate tectonics, which wreaked havoc throughout the Flood, formed the ocean basins and pushed up the mountains. They are features caused by the Flood and didn't exist beforehand.

WHEN DID THE MOUNTAINS RISE?

Uniformitarianism maintains that tectonic forces have always acted, and thus there should be mountains of every age. Catastrophists/creationists, however, consider mountains to be largely the result of Noah's Flood, which first deposited strata, then later uplifted them into our modern mountain chains. Intense geological processes were operating at rates, scales, and intensities far in excess of today's "uniform" norms. Creationists believe some mountains may have risen during the Flood (for example, the Appalachian Mountains), but most mountains (Sierra Nevada, Rocky Mountains, etc.) were elevated in the latest Flood or earliest post-Flood times. Scripture affirms that the waters once "stood above the mountains" (Psalm 104:6), then retreated (v. 7), and then the mountains rose and the valleys sank (v. 8). Thus, creationists would expect the world's mountain chains to be among its most recent geologic features.[2]

As can be seen from the following list of data collected from numerous investigators and abridged from a similar chart by evolutionists,[3] this expectation has been confirmed. Keep in mind that in uniformitarian thinking, which involves billions of years, a few million years is no time at all. Thus, even evolutionists admit nearly all the world's mountains rose just "yesterday" in earth history.

MOUNTAIN CHAIN/ PLATEAU/RIFT	YEARS SINCE MAIN UPLIFT
EUROPE	
Swiss Alps	<2 million
Apennines Mountains	1–2 million
Pyrenees Mountains	2–5 million
Baetic Cordillera	2–5 million
Carpathian Mountains	2–5 million
Caucasus Mountains	<2 million
Ural Mountains	1–2 million
Sudeten Mountains	1–5 million
ASIA	
Tibetan Plateau	<3.4 million
Himalaya Mountains	<3.4 million
Kunlun Mountains	<4 million
Tien Shan Mountains	<2 million
Shanxi Mountains	<3 million
Japanese Mountains	<5 million
Taiwan Mountains	<5 million
NORTH AMERICA	
Sierra Nevada Mountains	<2 million
Main Colorado Plateau	<3 million
Bighorn Mountains	<3 million
Later Rocky Mountains	<5 million
Canadian Cordillera	2–5 million
Cascade Range	4–5 million
SOUTH AMERICA	
Chilean Andes	<5 million
Bolivian Andes	<5 million
Ecuadorian Andes	<5 million
AFRICA	
Ethiopian Rift	<2.9 million
Western Rift	<3 million
Ruwenzori Mountains	<3 million
OTHER	
New Guinea Mountains	2 million
New Zealand Mountains	<5 million

Virtually all the mountains of the entire world rose up in the last episode of earth's geologic history, just as expected from creation thinking. While some fine points may await resolution, the big picture favors the reality of a recent global cataclysm.

WHERE DID THE WATER GO?

The waters of the Flood have obviously left the land and returned to the ocean basins, and that is where we find them today. A view of earth from space confirms this expectation. From above the South Pacific, one can hardly see anything but water. Water covers over two thirds of the globe. An immense reservoir of water was aggressively built up during the initial 40-day period of the Flood, which maintained that onslaught for months. At the five-month point, the "ark rested…

upon the mountains of Ararat" (Genesis 8:4), today an interior range on the Anatolian Plateau, at which time water levels began to wane. For the next seven months, water drained off the land, giving Noah opportunity to test its level with the raven and dove. Finally, when it was determined that the ground surface at the base of the mountain was dry enough to support life, the Ark's occupants disembarked and descended.

Note that it took seven months for the floodwaters to drain. Studies show that water takes a significant amount of time to drain by gravity alone. The rainwater molecules or snowflakes that fall in the watershed of the Mississippi River enter the river in Minnesota and sometimes take a month or more to reach New Orleans. Yet, some of the continents are even larger than this area, thousands of miles in width, and it would take similar time periods for water to travel from the interior to the ocean.

One of the most important research successes in creation thinking was the development of the concept of Catastrophic Plate Tectonics by five of the leading creation science theorists from several fields. They recognized the evidence for plate tectonics was quite strong, but that it was interpreted wrongly by uniformitarians. The data fit better into the short chronology of Scripture. Rightly considered, it constitutes the primary mechanism for not only causing the great Flood, but also ending it and redistributing earth's land mass to its present configuration, including the formation of mountain ranges and deep ocean basins.[4]

At the height of the Flood, water stood above the mountains, but at its end the waters rushed off into deep ocean basins, where they are now. Some global tectonic mechanism must have been involved to deepen the oceans and raise the continents (as implied in Psalm 104:6-8). Plate tectonics no doubt played the major role, but not at the modern miniscule rates of movement. The continents "sprinted" rather than "drifted" to their new locations as new oceanic plates were formed by rising basaltic magma along the mid-ocean rifts. Evidence has been found that the oceanic plates subducted under adjacent continents quite rapidly. This possibility has been understood as more

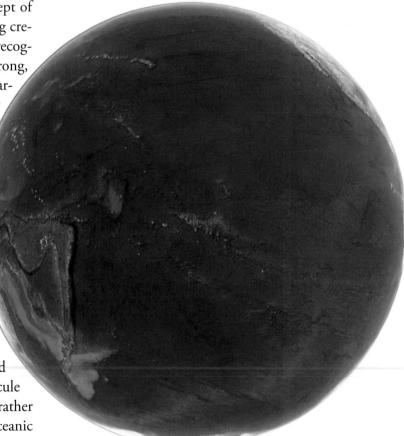

At the end of the Flood, the waters rushed off the continents into the newly enlarged ocean basins. Looking at earth over the South Pacific, there can be no doubt where the floodwater went. It's still here.

THE GLOBAL FLOOD

A Providential Wind

The Bible tells us that "God remembered Noah… and God made a wind to pass over the earth, and the waters assuaged" (Genesis 8:1), commencing a cascade of events that ended the Flood. We know about wind and its effect, but such a supernaturally caused wind is beyond our experience.

Such a wind would have several implications. For one thing, it would have played a part in draining the land. The continents today are, in places, several thousand miles in width. To get the water from the continents' interior to the shores and into the ocean would normally have taken some time. This wind would have aided its movement.

Remember also that the land surface was fully saturated at the Flood's end, and a strong, prolonged wind would have helped dry it out. By sending out the raven and the dove, Noah was testing to see how far this evaporation had progressed. Eventually, "the face of the ground was dry" (Genesis 8:13), but not yet able to support life. A month later "was the earth dried" (v. 14) and Noah was able to free the animals.

It was God's gracious providence to send the "wind" as He did. The great Flood of Noah's day employed recognizable geological processes throughout, but they operated at rates, scales, and intensities far beyond their modern counterparts. God's sovereign grace pervaded it all. "The LORD sitteth upon the flood; yea, the LORD sitteth King for ever" (Psalm 29:10).

---

has been learned of the properties of rock under intense heat, temperature, and stress. Today, we see the evidence of past movement at much greater rates. The plate tectonic model and reconstruction of continents in catastrophism resembles that of the standard view, except for the rate of plate movements. There are several unexplained enigmas in uniformitarian plate tectonics that Catastrophic Plate Tectonics explains quite plausibly.[5]

Scripture tells us of another factor that helped facilitate draining—God sent a driving force to assist. We are told in Genesis 8:1 that a special "wind passed over the land," both "pushing" the water toward the deepening ocean basins and helping evaporate water from the soggy ground. Today's waves are primarily caused by wind, not by tides. These waves, generated by the uplifting continents, were propelled along by a mighty and persistent "wind." Gradually, the land dried and the water table lowered.

How Could All the Animals Be Housed on Board the Ark?

The next big problem for our theological forefathers concerned the animals on the Ark. Continuing worldwide exploration discovered numerous large animals

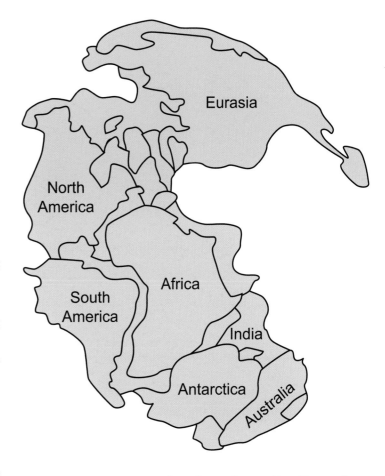

When the waters were gathered together on Day Three of creation, the land may have emerged as one supercontinent that later divided into separate land masses.

that were previously unknown in Europe, and multitudes of previously unknown small animals as well. Fossil discoveries compiled a similar list of extinct animals. The number and volume of these animals are staggering. It seemed to skeptical Bible students that there was simply not enough room on the Ark to transport and care for all of these species. Their reaction was that Scripture must be wrong, and that the writer(s) of Genesis simply didn't know the implications of what science had recently discovered.

We are told in Scripture that Noah was to take two of each land-dwelling, air-breathing "kind," male and female, onto the Ark for the purpose of survival (Genesis 6:17-19). This provision didn't apply to fish and other marine organisms, for they could survive, at least in representative numbers, outside the Ark. He was told to take seven (or seven pairs) of the clean animals. Perhaps this was because clean animals would soon be permissible as food for humans, or, more likely, because clean animals were fit to serve as sacrificial animals in worship while on the Ark and afterward. But how many kinds needed to be on board?

A kind differs from a modern species, which usually represents a separate breeding population. However, many species can hybridize (when similar but somewhat different species mate) and produce fertile offspring, and thus should be classed in the same species. A kind may be better approximated by our modern designation genus or family. All taxonomic categories are somewhat arbitrary and do not necessarily reflect separate creations. Depending on many factors, each one may contain many species. Obviously, the num-

HOW COULD FISH SURVIVE NOAH'S FLOOD?

If such a flood took place, it would have laid down multiple layers of mud full of the remains of plants and animals that died in the Flood. These layers would be widespread (since the Flood was global) and give evidence of having been laid down rapidly.

The Flood was not only an episode of judgment; it was also a time of God's grace and salvation. Noah and his family, and two representatives of each "kind" of land-dwelling, air-breathing animal (seven of each "clean" kind), were protected and preserved on board Noah's Ark. Outside, "all in whose nostrils was the breath of life, of all that was in the dry land, died" (Genesis 7:22).

But what about the fish and other marine creatures? Obviously, they weren't taken on board the Ark. How could they survive, particularly both fresh and saltwater forms? As a matter of fact, most of them didn't survive. Over 95 percent of all fossils are marine creatures. They died, and were fossilized by the trillions. Many are buried in great fossil graveyards, tightly packed together, choked with sediments, buried before they had time to decay. Obviously, they didn't live in the environment in which they died. But how could any have survived?

In the complex of events and conditions that made up the Flood, certainly there were pockets of fresh and/or clean water at any one time. Remember, it was raining in torrents, and we can expect that the rain was fairly fresh water. Many studies have shown that waters of various temperatures, chemistries, and sediment loads do not tend to mix; they tend to remain segregated into zones. It would be unlikely for any one area to retain such zones for very long during the tumult of the Flood, but on a worldwide scale, some such segregated zones would have existed at any given time. Furthermore, we don't know the tolerance levels of pre-Flood fish for sediment, salt, and temperature. Modern fish have a great variety of responses to different environments. Perhaps before the Flood, fish were even more adaptable.

There is also the possibility that great amounts of vegetation were dislodged from their pre-Flood locations and remained intertwined during the Flood as floating mats. Many creationists suggest that the decay and abrasion of these mats are responsible for many of our major coal seams, but underneath these mats, the turbulence of the surface would have been lessened. Perhaps many fish found shelter and nutrition under them, as insects may have on the mats themselves.

Even though there is much we don't know about what went on during the Flood, we can see that there is at least a plausible answer that can be proposed to such questions.

ber of species far exceeds the number of kinds. For instance, several species of dog, including domestic dogs, wolves, coyotes, etc. (which are labeled as separate species in the modern classification scheme), can and readily do interbreed. Thus, all are obviously one kind. The same could be said of bear, cat, deer, cattle, or rodent species, and many other groups. There are hundreds of species of hummingbird, for example, many of which are known to be interfertile, but there is probably just one hummingbird kind.

Research may one day determine just how many kinds there really are and thus how many needed to be on the Ark, but in lieu of that knowledge it might be helpful to construct a "worst case scenario" and ask if the Ark was large enough to house today's known number of species. To do so, we need to know much about the various animal types, their number, their average size, their transport on ships, their food needs, etc. This is inexact speculation, but working with what we know, we wonder: Could the Ark hold two of each species? If so, it certainly could handle two of each kind, a far lower, and more likely, number.

There are well over one million species of animals on earth today (some speculate up to six million), but only some of the animals must be accounted for on the Ark. "All in whose nostrils was the breath of life, of all that was in the dry land" (Genesis 7:22) needed to be protected from the floodwaters. Representatives of various fish types would survive outside, and so would corals, whales, clams, and marine arthropods, like lobsters. They died by the trillions, and we have their fossils, but some survived and perpetuated their kind after the Flood. Those kinds had no need to be on the Ark, and were not required biblically to be protected.

Insects, which make up the majority of arthropod species, would not have to be on board either. Even land-based insects can survive extended periods in water, some on floating debris, and others in egg or larval stages. Possessing neither "the breath of life" (insects absorb oxygen through their abdomen, not by using lungs) nor blood (their bodily fluids are quite different from blood), their presence on the Ark was not mandated, and we can surmise they were omitted. The turbulent, sediment-filled floodwaters were devastating to life in the sea, as evidenced by the abundant marine fossil record, but pockets of all kinds would have survived to continue the kind.

Furthermore, certain mammals could have survived outside, such as whales and dolphins. Floodwaters were deadly and many individuals died, but at least two of each kind survived somewhere, somehow. Among the birds, perhaps penguins could have made it outside the Ark, but most birds would have required the safety provided on the Ark. Survival outside could also be possible for some reptiles such as sea turtles and sea snakes, and certain of the amphibians, as well. Some could perhaps survive outside, but most needed the Ark.

An approximate listing of Ark travelers could be pared down to:

CLASSIFICATION	NUMBER OF KNOWN SPECIES[6]	PROBABLE NUMBER ON ARK
Mammals	3,700	<3,700
Birds	8,600	<8,600
Reptiles	6,300	<6,300
Amphibians	2,500	<2,500
Fishes	20,600	0
Tunicates	1,400	0
Echinoderms	6,000	0
Arthropods	838,500	0
Mollusks	107,250	0
Worms	34,700	0
Coelenterates et al	9,600	0
Sponges	4,800	0
Protozoans	28,350	0
Total # of Species	1,072,300	21,100

For fairness, in this hypothetical worst-case scenario of species on the Ark, we should add extinct species, bringing the (generous) rough approximation to 25,000 or so. Double this number to account for both genders and you arrive at only about 50,000 animals for the Ark's passenger list. (Allowing for seven of the few "clean" kinds doesn't add much.) This number represents the outside maximum number of individual animals that needed to be on board. Working with the number of "kinds" as we should be (i.e., groupings of related species) instead of species themselves, the number decreases dramatically. Creationist researcher John Woodmorappe concludes the outside maximum number of animals aboard the Ark was on the order of 16,000 (but more likely just a few thousand, equating kind with the modern family), not 50,000.[7]

New species are regularly discovered, but these are mostly bacteria or insects or marine invertebrates, thus not required to have been on the Ark. All of these are

DINOSAURS ACCORDING TO THEIR CREATOR

Dinosaurs have long been an effective tool for teaching evolutionary dogma. However, since all things were created by the God of the Bible during the creation week not long ago, and He didn't use evolution to do so, there must be a better understanding of them. Let's go to His account and adopt His view.

The dinosaurs were (by definition based on hip structure) land animals, and thus were created on Day Six, probably within the category "beast of the earth" and/or "creeping things" (Genesis 1:24-25). There were also large marine reptiles and flying reptiles created on Day Five (v. 21), but these were technically not dinosaurs, not having the right hip structure. Along with all animals and mankind, they were created to be plant eaters (vs. 29-30), for there was no death of conscious life before Adam and Eve rebelled against God.

Of the many dinosaur fossils found, almost all give evidence of having been plant eaters. Several of the dinosaur fossil types, however, do possess serrated teeth, sharp claws, spikes, armor plates, etc., perhaps used for a variety of offensive or defensive purposes. Of course, scientists can never be certain about a creature's life habits when they only have bits of dead ones to study, and most dinosaur fossils are extremely fragmentary, usually consisting of part of a single bone. And many animals alive today that have sharp teeth and claws use them for strictly non-predatory means. But some dinosaur fossils are found with partially digested animals in their stomachs and dung, leading to the conclusion that some of them ate meat.

The Bible doesn't give details of how some of them gained carnivorous habits, but it does give us a clue. When Adam and Eve rebelled, God pronounced the awful curse of death on all creation. In doing so, He not only fulfilled His promise that they would begin to die (Genesis 2:17), but perhaps changed the genetic makeup of many "kinds" so that all their descendants would forever be different. He changed Eve's body so that childbirth was more difficult (3:16), and the plants (v. 18) and the animals, as well (v. 14). Perhaps at this time some dinosaurs and other animals acquired or began to develop a taste for meat, and either adapted or acquired specialized body parts for aggression or protection. This may be over-speculation, but sin ruins everything, and before long the entire planet was corrupt (6:11-12).

God told Noah to bring pairs of each kind of unclean, air-breathing land animal on board the Ark, including, evidently, the dinosaurs (Genesis 7:15). Not all dinosaurs were giants; most were rather small. An average size might be comparable to a pony; a big animal, but not huge. Many species were quite similar to other species. Probably all named species could be lumped into several dozen kinds.

Popular treatments portray dinosaurs as fearsome killer giants, but in fact most were rather small plant eaters.

As do most modern reptiles, dinosaurs might have continued to grow throughout life; the largest of a kind would likely be the oldest. Thus, the dinosaurs on the Ark probably would have been young adults, no bigger than a cow perhaps. There was plenty of room.

The world after the Flood was much different than before, with much less vegetation and a colder, harsher climate. Evidently, the dinosaurs gradually died out. Perhaps the last of them were even hunted to extinction by humans, as would be indicated by the many legends of people slaying dragons, the descriptions of which closely resemble modern reconstructions of dinosaurs.

At any rate, biblical history has an explanation for dinosaurs, their creation, lifestyle, and extinction. Christian parents are encouraged to use these qualities to teach biblical truth.

quite small and usually similar to known species, thus probably fall within one of the biblical kinds already considered. Rarely does a new land mammal or bird or reptile turn up. Adding a small number to the total doesn't alter the implications of the study.

IS HOUSING 50,000+/- ANIMALS ON A HUGE SHIP WITHIN THE REALM OF POSSIBILITY?

To answer this question, we must first answer several other questions. To begin with, we must calculate the volume of the Ark. The Bible's description of the Ark's size is given in cubits—approximately the distance between a man's elbow and fingertip, about eighteen inches—and was specified as 300 cubits long, 50 cubits wide, and 30 cubits high. Thus, the Ark calculates as about 450 feet long by 75 feet wide by 45 feet high, and yields a volume for the Ark of 1,518,750 cubic feet.

For comparison, this volume is equivalent to about 569 double-deck railroad stock cars used for transporting animals. How many animals that many stock cars or that size ship could hold can be answered by knowing the average size of the animals and how much space

each needed.

Most animals are rather tiny. Only a familiar few are large: cows, horses, giraffes, and elephants. The dinosaurs that were alive when the Flood occurred could have been represented by young adults, not necessarily the largest specimen of each type. Most of them were rather small and don't change the average size. An exhaustive study demonstrated that the average size of the animals on the Ark approximates that of a rat.[8] For ease of comparison, John Whitcomb and Henry Morris earlier assumed an average size estimate as that of a sheep, for it is known how much space it takes to transport sheep. A railroad stock car can comfortably transport 240 sheep on a long trip. Thus:

$$\frac{50,000 \text{ "sheep"}}{240 \text{ "sheep"/car}} = 208 \text{ stock cars needed}$$

$$\frac{208 \text{ stock cars needed}}{569 \text{ stock car equivalency}} = 36\% \text{ of the Ark's capacity}$$

Thus, the Ark was at least two times bigger than it needed to be, given these reasonable assumptions. Remember, this is the worst-case scenario. We have assumed a number of animals on board much greater than it probably was. And we have generously estimated the average size of the animals and found the Ark was still big enough. The Ark was certainly large enough to do the job!

Animals that were not able to survive outside were safely housed on board the Ark. This included most (but not all) mammals, birds, and reptiles. Pairs genetically representative for each kind were safely transported in their "rooms," or literally "nests" (see page 89). There was plenty of space for all.

How Could Noah Build the Ark?

Once again, we are supplied with only scanty information and must make reasonable assumptions to proceed. The Genesis creation account culminates with Adam and Eve in close fellowship with their Creator. Obviously, if they were able to converse and think clearly with the Creator of all, they must have possessed significant intelligence. Talking and walking with God Himself would probably require mental abilities we can hardly comprehend. In some not-insignificant way, they bore His image, and He is omniscient.

They at least had sufficient intelligence to perform the tasks God commanded them to address, such as tending the Garden of Eden and naming the animals. Adam was given the responsibility to "subdue" creation by understanding its intricacies and to have "dominion" over it by managing it wisely. We can be sure Adam and his descendants were able to accomplish great things. The Curse interrupted Adam's discovery progress, but even after the Curse he and his descendants lived for over 900 years on average, and these years prior to the Flood were marked by abundant and easy food supply and minimal mutation buildup. Even a person of meager intelligence can learn to function over time, and Adam (and by extension Noah) was probably smart at the start. No doubt, Noah was able to comprehend God's instructions and begin the construction project.[9]

If the entire pre-Flood civilization was intelligent and spoke the same language, think of what could be accomplished, for good or evil. At the time of the Curse, God had promised both Adam and Satan that a Redeemer who would fully conquer Satan would come through the seed of the woman. Ever since that time, Satan has tried to destroy humankind, distort it, and recruit followers in his rebellion against God. Little wonder that to preserve the race and keep the promise alive, God eventually sent the Flood to punish rebellion and give creation a fresh start.

For the question at hand, we can assume Noah was an intelligent and godly person. He had been educated in the patriarchal line through Seth. We know he was at least 480 years old when he started, for he was 600 when the Flood came 120 years after God had announced His intention to judge the earth and its inhabitants. Perhaps Noah had all that time to build, perhaps less.

For much the same reasons, we can surmise that Noah was able to hire other workers to help. Noah was a faithful man who worshipped God, and God often blesses His faithful followers. Maybe he was a shipbuilder already. Whatever his profession, Noah was substantially able to ignore it while the Ark was in preparation, so he must have been financially secure. These things we cannot know, of course, but they do seem reasonable.

At the very least, Noah had three sons to help, for they were also believers who chose to board the Ark when the time came. Perhaps Noah's father, Lamech, and his grandfather, Methuselah, helped also. They were alive in this period. No mention is made of their help, but it seems reasonable. Interestingly, Methuselah's name was prophetic, meaning "when he dies, it (judgment) shall be sent."[10] A study of the years and ages shows that Lamech died a few years before the Flood, and that Methuselah died in the year of the Flood. Did he die in the outpouring of God's wrath? Not likely. Was his death at 969 years old natural and long overdue? Or did he die as a result of the "violence" of those days? Was he a martyr? Did God's timing of the Flood rescue Noah and his family from certain martyrdom as well? We'll never know this side of heaven.

Let us again assume the worst case and consider that only Noah and his sons worked on the Ark. Could four men accomplish such a job in the time allotted, or in any amount of time? Let's also assume they weren't shipbuilders by trade. However, even untrained builders will gain all the skills needed in a few years of frantic practice, knowing that if they don't succeed, they will perish. After a year or so, they would have been "professionals"!

Remember, the Ark was not necessarily a show boat, with ornate surfaces, or a racing vessel. All it needed to be was big enough, strong enough, and watertight. It had no specific destination, it just had to float and carry a heavy but precious cargo. Design engineers know that any useful structure is mostly open space. Probably less than 5 percent of the total volume has to be worked lumber, stone, metal, or other material. Can we assume, in this worst-case study, that 25 percent of the Ark's total volume was actually wood, shaped and installed? Noah and his sons had to fell the trees, transport the logs, shape the wood into lumber, and install it according to plan. We can assume that while God revealed the overall design, the rest was up to them. It seems reasonable that four experienced and motivated builders could acquire, work, and install at least an average of 15 cubic feet of rough lumber per day, perhaps much more.

We already know the volume of the Ark—approximately 1,518,750 cubic feet. The amount of worked lumber needed:

(25%) x (vol. of Ark) = (.25) x (1,518,750 cu. ft.) = 379,688 cu. ft. lumber

How much could be installed per year, assuming 52 weeks per year, six days of work per week, and 15 cubic feet installed per day?

(15 cu. ft. per day) x (6 days per week) x (52 weeks per year) = 4,680 cu. ft. installed per year

At that rate, how many years would it take?

379,688 cu. ft. needed = 81 years max. construction time

Remember, Noah probably had 120 years to prepare. So we see in the worst-case scenario that there was plenty of time to build the Ark. No doubt it was a most difficult task, but thankfully Noah was a faithful man and accomplished the job.

How Could Noah Gather All the Animals?

In old earth thinking, the world of Noah's day was identical to the world we know. Things have always been "uniform," and four to five thousand years ago life was essentially identical to that in the modern world. The animals and their habitats were no different from the ones we know, and a world-restructuring flood could not happen. But to one who believes the Bible contains true history,

Noah's world was quite different.

Evidence from Flood-deposited fossils and associated strata suggests that habitats were quite different, for nearly all the major fossils are types that live in temperate climates, and they are found on all continents, including the polar regions. Even evolutionists acknowledge that essentially all fossils speak of warmer, wetter conditions throughout time and all around the globe. The continents may have all been connected at that time, with few impassable barriers to migration. Representatives of each animal group probably lived in all areas. In short, it was a very different world, and getting all the animal types on the Ark would not have been as difficult as today.

The Bible does not say Noah needed to gather the animals himself. He was simply commanded to build the Ark, and the animals would come in on their own. "And they went in unto Noah into the ark, two and two of all flesh" (Genesis 7:15). This is no minor point. No matter where the animals lived previously, God saw to it that two representatives of each kind were present when the time came. They entered the Ark, "and the Lord shut him in" (v. 16).

Students of animal behavior have documented a certain behavior in many animals. They seem to have a mysterious ability to sense impending danger. They

Nearly every animal type possesses the ability to migrate to avoid danger or survive climate change. Perhaps this instinct was originally supplied by the Creator to chosen pairs as the great Flood neared to facilitate their survival on the Ark.

"know" when a calamity is about to strike. Before an earthquake, many animals are seen to be restless and fearful. Predicting earthquakes by observing animal behavior is often no less unsuccessful than by other, more technical methods. How do the animals do it? Do they sense tiny vibrations that sensitive seismic instruments miss? Or do they just "know"?

When the catastrophic tsunami hit Indonesia in December 2004, few animals died. Instead, in the preceding few hours, many animals were observed running inland toward higher ground. They survived, but the "smarter" humans got closer to see and were overwhelmed.

From a naturalistic, evolutionary standpoint, there is no explanation for the origin of this premonition instinct in animals. What random mutation could have instituted it? How could a learned but seldom-used behavior be transmitted to offspring? To be sure, there is a survival advantage in having it, but what is it, where did it come from, and how can it be passed on?

Another equally mysterious instinct involves migration. From birds to insects to herds of caribou, many animals migrate long distances. Some migration is multigenerational. The monarch butterfly breeds in Mexico, migrates to Canada, and dies. Its offspring migrate back to Mexico, where they've never been, to start another cycle. Again, there is a survival advantage, but what is its source? In what part of the brain is this

SELECTED BY NATURE, OR DESIGNED TO FILL?

Mutation and natural selection surround the concept of evolution. These are the claimed mechanisms by which evolution works. Mutations randomly alter existing genes, and natural selection supposedly selects the most beneficial mutant genes and favors them for survival, allowing them to enter the gene pool and be passed on to succeeding generations. But are these mechanisms sufficient to account for the amazing design and complexity we see around us?

Everyone sees the unmistakable design. Christians ascribe it to the supernatural Creator God of Scripture. Intelligent design advocates only claim that life is too well-designed to arise without intelligence. Naturalists lay it at the feet of unthinking natural selection. Which is more credible?

Genes, made up of myriads of nucleic acid base pairs arranged in precise order, are amazingly complex. Mutations occur when one or more of the base pairs is altered or relocated. But random changes in a complex system always cause deterioration, not the increasing complexity evolution needs. Scientists have searched for random mutations that confer an advantage to the organism and/or its offspring, but they have little to show for their efforts. Usually, the mutation only alters the gene in an insignificant way and its impact is not advantageous. Such mutations slowly accumulate, causing long-term harm. Others allow the organism to survive some particular physiological stress, but none

benefit the organism as a whole. A mutation might eliminate some trait that is normally useful, but mutations add nothing new. None have been observed to add to the genome's complexity. Thus, most are neutral, some are harmful, and others are deadly. Is this the "stuff" of evolution?

All too often, natural selection is spoken of as if it were a living, thinking, all-powerful being, able to make provision for the future—able to provide the innovative traits and new body parts an organism needs. Often it is attributed godlike powers. However, what goes by the term natural selection actually involves the outworking of a creature's innate design. Natural selection has no brain and cannot divine the future. It is, after all, only "natural." It can neither plan nor provide. The omniscient, omnipotent God of creation can do what random changes cannot. He designed and created each "kind" of plant and animal during the creation week, and then commanded them at the end of the creation week and after the great Flood of Noah's day to "be fruitful and fill the earth" (Genesis 1:28; 8:17). His design empowers animals to survive, vary, adapt, reproduce, and fill the earth. Each "kind" can shift its capabilities, but not evolve into different kinds. All of this was ordained by a wise, loving, planning Provider.

For further information, see Randy Guliuzza, 2011, Darwin's Sacred Imposter: Recognizing Missed Warning Signs, *Acts & Facts*, 40 (5): 12-15; and Randy Guliuzza, 2012, Darwin's Sacred Imposter: Answering Questions about the Fallacy of Natural Selection, *Acts & Facts*, 41 (2): 12-15.

information stored, and how can it be inherited? Why do so many "unrelated" animals possess it?

Creation has a plausible explanation, although a supernatural one. Perhaps God in His sovereignty chose a particular pair of animals from each kind and instilled in them knowledge of the impending disaster and the location of safety. On instruction, they migrated to the Ark and went aboard. They, and they alone, survived. Their descendants, alive today, still possess premonition and migration instincts modified by today's conditions.

Naturalists disallow any supernatural solution and reject this. But they have no better solution. Usually they speak of it being imparted by natural selection, as if natural selection were alive and volitionally planning for the future. They ascribe godlike qualities to this inanimate, unthinking attribute, which certainly can't do anything on its own. Many, if not most, animals have versions of these instincts. In an evolutionary sense, animals only distantly related (i.e., from butterflies to caribou) have such instincts, and thus the instincts must have arisen separately, for they appear after the lines are supposed to have split. Thus, they could not have had a common source, and certainly did not arrive at such a brilliant solution from a blind source.

HOW COULD NOAH CARE FOR THE ANIMALS?

Caring for an unruly conglomeration of diverse animals poses another huge problem for Noah and his family. Feeding, exercise, cleaning up after, and keeping the peace for an entire year may seem to some people to be too big a job for such a small crew.

Authorities have noticed yet another behavior pattern in many animals. In the face of overwhelming danger over which they have no control and from which they cannot escape, animals often undergo personality changes and forget former relationships. Aggression and fear between them ceases. Predator and prey share a common foe, and thus mingle together in relative harmony until it passes.

Some animals enter a state of hibernation, almost like a deep sleep. When in hibernation, or winter sleep, food and exercise needs are greatly reduced. Others go into a state of estivation, a summer version of hibernation, but one in which physical desires are also greatly reduced. Other animals, such as the domestic dog, sim-

ply hunker down and wait until the danger is gone. This period of dormancy may last for weeks.

Scripture may hint at this. God instructed Noah to build the Ark with "nests" (the literal translation of "rooms," Genesis 6:14), perhaps implying a safe place to lie still.

There would have been little use for such behavior in the peaceful and homogeneous pre-Flood environment, but on the Ark the animals were faced with a prolonged period of terror over which they had no control. The noises, the motion, the smells, the small quarters, the first-time experience, the crowded environment, the lack of exercise, the lengthy voyage, and other factors no doubt shocked the animal's physiology in ways they had never previously experienced. It seems reasonable to propose that God in His grace acted to alleviate the plight of the animals and the workload of Noah and his family by bringing peace to the Ark's animal cargo. One possible way to do so would be to instill this ability to those on board, minimizing their needs for a time. Certainly, they did not merely lie down and sleep the whole time, but it seems reasonable that their bodies temporarily adapted to survive the months of confinement. Their descendants still retain these tendencies.

HOW COULD THE ARK SURVIVE THE FLOOD?

The Flood involved forces and processes outside of our experience. Simultaneously, "the fountains of the great deep" broke open, and volcanoes, earthquakes, asteroid impacts, colliding tsunamis, underwater gravity slides, etc., all contributed a great tectonic convulsion that permanently altered the planet. Yet the Ark rode through this cataclysm, safe and sound. How could it do so? Wouldn't it have capsized, sending its passengers to a watery grave? If it had, it would have spelled doom for all land-dwelling animals and the image of God in man, as well. Satan would have won the war. So, how could the Ark have survived?

Remember, the Ark was not designed to go anywhere. In fact, once the whole earth was flooded, there was nowhere to go. It only had to float and keep the occupants alive. Obviously, the whole account of the Flood involves supernatural oversight. God was in full control. When we investigate how He exercised that control, we stand amazed.

Note the ratio of length to width of the Ark's design: 300 cubits to 50 cubits, or approximately 450 feet long to 75 feet wide. This ratio of 6 to 1 is well known in shipbuilding as an optimum design for stability. Many modern naval engineers, when designing vessels from cargo ships to battleships, utilize this same basic design ratio.

The Ark's long, slender shape would have maximized cargo space while keeping it safe. The length would have tended to keep the Ark facing into wave trends, thereby minimizing chances it would be broadsided by a wave that could capsize it. A cross-section view shows that the pair of forces operating on the Ark, consisting of the Ark's weight (acting downward) and the buoyancy force (acting upward), form what naval engineers term a "righting couple." A pair (a couple) of forces act in opposite but parallel directions that would tend to force the vessel to "right" itself when tilted. As shown below, for any degree of tilt up to 90 degrees, the couple would act to right the Ark and return it to an upright orientation.

Several engineering studies of Ark models have compared the Ark's design as given in Scripture to several other potential design ratios. The most elaborate and extensive comparison was carried out by the Korea Institute of Ship and Ocean Engineering.[11] Once again,

the Ark's design was shown to be optimum for its task and circumstances. The whole account has "the ring of truth" to it.

One final note—God instructed Noah to pitch the Ark "within and without with pitch" (Genesis 6:14). Pitch can be an oil-based material or a resinous substance derived from trees. Today's oil deposits reside in Flood-deposited strata, eliminating them as a potential source for the Ark, but tree pitch can be easily produced from wood. Perhaps Noah was to actually inject the wood with a resinous substance, much like creosote is injected into railroad ties to keep them from rotting. This resin would tend to waterproof the wood, minimize attack by insects, and preserve it from rotting.

HOW DID ALL THE ANIMALS GET TO THEIR PRESENT LOCATIONS?

The human and animal passengers on board the Ark were the only land-dwelling, air-breathing survivors of the Flood—the only representatives of their respective "kinds."

Upon disembarking, Noah and his family were commanded to "be fruitful, and multiply, and replenish the earth" (Genesis 9:1). A similar command had long before been given to Adam and Eve (1:28). The use

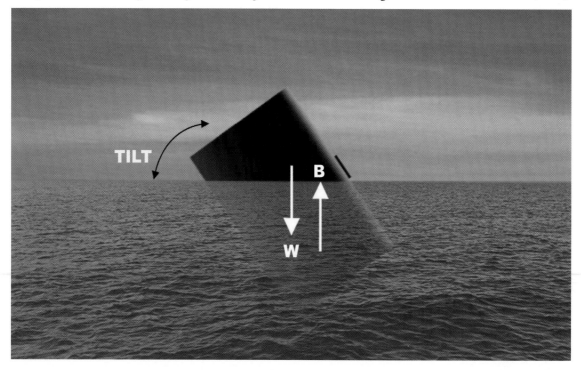

A cross-section of the floating Ark showing its weight pulling downward while the water's buoyant force pushes upward. The two forces acting together (termed a "righting couple") would tend to keep the Ark from capsizing in rough seas.

WHY DON'T WE FIND MORE HUMAN FOSSILS?

The fossil record abounds with the remains of past life, most of which were deposited during the Flood of Noah's day, as "the world that then was, being overflowed with water, perished" (2 Peter 3:6). These organisms were trapped and buried in ocean-bottom mud, which later hardened into sedimentary rock, fossilizing the organic remains.

But where are the pre-Flood human remains? According to Scripture, the patriarchs lived long ages, and had large families and many years of childbearing potential. There may have been a large population. Where are all their fossils?

First, we must recognize the nature of the fossil record. Over 95 percent of all fossils are marine creatures, such as clams, corals, and trilobites—mostly invertebrates with a hard outer surface. Of the remaining 5 percent, most are plants. Much less than 1 percent of all fossils are land animals. This encompasses reptiles (including dinosaurs), amphibians, mammals, birds, and humans.

Land creatures have what could be called a "low fossilization potential." As land animals die in water, they bloat, float, and come apart. It is very difficult to trap a bloated animal under water in order for it to be buried. Furthermore, scavengers readily devour both flesh and bone. Seawater and bacterial action destroy everything. The scouring ability of underwater mudflows, common during the Flood, would grind bone to powder.

But the purpose of Noah's Flood was to destroy the land communities—not preserve them—especially humans. In any scenario, what land fossils were preserved in Flood sediments would have been buried late in the Flood, near the surface, and would have been subject to erosion and destruction once again as the floodwaters rushed off the rising continents.

Myriads of people lived before the Flood, considering the patriarchal families as typical. They weren't necessarily all alive when the Flood came, for "the earth [was] filled with violence" (Genesis 6:13). Bloodshed would no doubt have terminated many family lines, but you would suspect some would have been fossilized.

For purposes of discussion, let us (generously) assume 300,000,000 people did get fossilized, distributed in the sedimentary record, which consists of about 300,000,000 cubic miles. The chances of such a fossil intersecting the earth's surface, being found by someone, and then being properly and honestly identified is vanishingly small.

On the other hand, if evolution is true and humans have lived on earth for three million years, many trillions have lived and died. Where are *their* fossils? This is the more vexing question.

Neandertal skeleton found in La grotte de Clamouse. Human and animal bodies would rarely be fossilized in the great Flood sediments. They would bloat and float on the water's surface, while sediments were deposited at the bottom. Most fossils are of marine shellfish, with a hard outer shell and rather spherical shape.

of the word "replenish" in both instances has caused some misunderstanding, for superficially it appears to imply they were to "refill" earth with inhabitants. That works for the Flood, but it has been used by advocates of the gap theory to suggest that just as the pre-Flood civilization had died in the Flood judgment and the earth needed "refilling," so a population of humans had existed prior to Adam's creation who had all died when Satan fell. In both cases, the world would have been quite barren and needed filling. But the two instances are not equivalent. Actually, the Hebrew word from which "replenish" is translated would more accurately be rendered "fill" rather than to imply "refill," and is translated to communicate this nearly every time it is used in the King James Bible. Furthermore, in the days of King James, the English word "replenish" simply meant "fill." There is no word "plenish" and thus no "re-plenishing." In any case, Noah and his family were to be the progenitors of the entire human race to follow.

After the Flood, the animals were given a slightly differ-ent command. They were told to "breed abundantly in the earth, and be fruitful, and multiply upon the earth" (Genesis 8:17). A balanced ecology helps produce a healthy animal food chain, as well as encourage proper plant growth and soil stability. But until animals mi-grated from the Ark, there were scarcely any creatures of any sort. Eventually, animals arrived in each loca-tion.

Usually, once an animal population increases to "fill its ecological niche," it ceases increasing and maintains a stable population. Some poorly understood capping mechanism encourages them to lower their birthrate. But when a catastrophic event causes imbalance, ani-mals have been noticed to suddenly increase their nor-mal reproduction rate to fill the niche.

In the days prior to the 1980 northward-directed erup-tion of Mount St. Helens, the local elk herd was ob-served to migrate from the north side around to the south. They seemed to know it was coming their way and moved to safety. They survived the catastrophe, and

THE GEOGRAPHIC CENTER

A research project conducted by ICR asso-ciate Andrew J. Woods, M.S, speaks to the migration issue.[1] The geographic center of earth's land mass was calculated, con-sidered to be the optimum location from which to begin migration. All of earth's land area was divided into *pixels*, and the surface distance to every other pixel was calculated. The least average distance be-tween each pixel and every other pixel was computed and defined as the geographic center of earth's land mass—the optimal migration starting point.

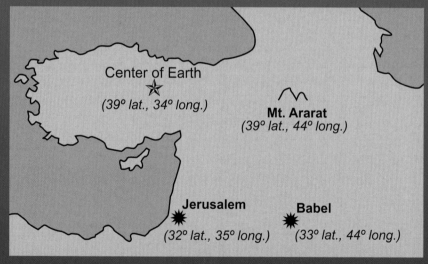

The geographic center of earth's land surface is somewhere near both the "mountains of Ararat" and Babel. This would be the optimum starting place for migration to "fill the earth."

A biblicist might suspect the center would be at Jerusalem, the center of God's atten-tion, where His Son came to live and then die for the sins of the world, and where His millennial Kingdom will one day be set up. Alternatively, another possible "center" is at one of the two true spreading centers mentioned in the Bible, the mountains of Ara-rat or the Tower of Babel.

Actually, these three locations are in the same geograph-ic region, and the calculations reveal all fairly close to the actual center, which turned out to be near Ankara, Turkey, known as Galatia in the New Testament. Once again, we see the biblical account has "the ring of truth" about it. For what it's worth, the anti-center, the spot that is on average the farthest from every other point, is off the southern tip of New Zealand.

1. See Henry M. Morris, 1973, The Center of the Earth, *Acts & Facts*, 2 (4).

Glaciers are made of frozen water, evaporated from seawater and precipitated on land. The larger the glaciers, the less water is in the ocean. During the Ice Age, ocean levels dropped some 500 feet or so, but rose as the Ice Age ended.

days later they returned to the devastated landscape. Usually an elk cow births one calf every two years or so. But in this unfilled niche, their birthing numbers were seen to increase rapidly, and it was common for cows to birth twins every year. Can we conclude that the Creator of elk had given their ancestors this ability in a previous catastrophe, and that it normally lies dormant? Might it restart only when needed, according to plan? Did the same tendency kick in after the Flood for many animals when the world was so devastated and empty? From this tiny beginning, the whole earth was repopulated.

As the animals multiplied, they migrated into unoccupied areas in their daily search for food. There was no need for the herbivores to antagonistically compete, for plants were sprouting everywhere. If access to a particular morsel was denied, they simply moved to the next site.

The olive leaf collected by the dove that Noah released was growing, probably from a branch or leaf germinated in the drying mud. One of the hardiest plants in this situation, a sprig had likely floated until grounded, and had subsequently sprouted. Seeds, seed pods, cones, etc., would have taken longer to grow, but there were plenty of sprigs sprouting for food. Stronger animal groups and individual animals would have claimed the most advantageous resources, while weaker ones would have simply migrated to less competitive areas.

The command to fill the earth rings hollow without the ability to accomplish it, but in the aftermath of the great Flood it became possible. The Ice Age, as it is known, followed hard on the heels of the Flood, in essence spawned by the instability caused by that Flood. It was a time of excessive snowfall that accumulated on the continents, even lasting through the summer periods.[12]

Two obvious necessary requirements for an ice buildup are more snowfall and less snowmelt. Snow was packed into solid ice due to the weight of the deepening snow above it, which flowed outward across the continents as glaciers. At the height of the Ice Age, the polar ice caps extended far beyond their present locations. Ice covered Europe and much of Canada and the northerly United States, as well as Antarctica and southern South America.

Polar ice caps during the Ice Age were many thousands of feet thick in places. Some people have criticized creationist speculations of a short Ice Age by noting that it would take too long to build up such thicknesses. But thick ice can build up rapidly. When Mount St. Helens erupted in 1980, there was no ice left near the summit. However, in the years following, ice rapidly built up such that today's summit glacier is hundreds of feet thick. No great time was needed.[13]

The existence of a past Ice Age doesn't imply that the

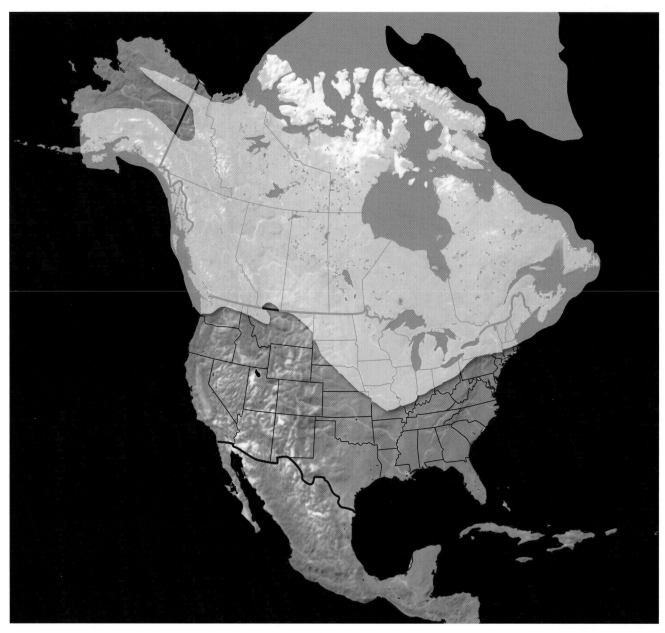

The Ice Age came after the great Flood, essentially caused by the Flood's warm waters. Enhanced evaporation resulted in excessive snowfall in polar regions that packed into ice and flowed toward lower latitudes. This map shows the glaciers' maximum extent in North America.

entire earth was frozen. While glaciers blanketed northern and southern regions, much of the rest of the globe enjoyed moderate weather, with comfortable temperatures and abundant rainfall even in equatorial regions. For instance, Egypt was once well-watered and temperate where now there is desert. Pleasant zones in the northern hemisphere were farther south than now, and comfortable regions flanked the ice caps. This lasted until the end of the Ice Age when the glaciers melted, shifting the better climatic conditions up into Europe and North America, leaving once-pleasant southerly zones less favorable.

Scores of possible causes for the Ice Age have been pro-

posed, focusing on a planet-wide decrease in temperature. Minor alterations in normal parameters, such as the amount of incoming sunlight, are considered by uniformitarians to cause a planetary cool-down and thus glaciation. But cold weather will not increase snowfall. The colder the temperature, the less moisture the air can hold, and thus the less snow will fall. Northern Canada today sees bitter cold, but it doesn't snow much there. Similar limitations apply to a decrease in solar radiation. The principle of uniformity limits the extent of proposed changes, and as a result none of the proposed uniformitarian causes are capable of much change, nor are they well accepted. It may be that the

Flood provides the key.

That key, surprisingly, is heat—specifically, hot oceans. During the Flood, as the "fountains of the great deep" broke open, spewing superheated magma, water, and brine into the ocean, immense amounts of evaporation took place. In places above spreading centers where hot magma was extruded, the oceans probably even boiled. This heating was exacerbated by intense friction caused by tectonic plate movements, faulting, and mountain building. As the Flood ended, the ocean water temperature was likely many degrees hotter than it is now, resulting in excessive evaporation. This moisture initially contributed to the continual rain from the "windows of heaven," and added to the water for the Flood.

But once the Flood was over, the oceans remained very warm for centuries, leading to the ice buildup. Water cools slowly, and as we know, the warmer the water, the more the evaporation. On a planetary scale, the very warm ocean provided abundant water for Ice Age precipitation.

The temperature difference between the ocean and the now-barren continents set up storm patterns that drove moisture inland, where cooler temperatures caused it to condense and fall as snow. Meanwhile, the latter stages of the Flood and early post-Flood times were marked by large volcanic eruptions, which threw vast amounts of volcanic dust and aerosols into the atmosphere, partially blocking the sunlight and prohibiting the snow

WAS THERE REALLY AN ICE AGE?

The Ice Age has always been a problem for science. While abundant evidence has been found for continental glaciation, the cause has remained enigmatic. Scores of scenarios have been proposed: global cooling, decrease in the sun's intensity, rampant volcanic activity, etc., but none are truly able to bring about such profound changes—none except the creation proposal, that is.

The ice sheets never covered more than a minor portion of the globe—perhaps about 50 percent of the continents. In North America, ice covered much of central Canada and as far south as Kansas. Weather in the rest of the world was affected, but the areas were not under ice.

The obvious requirements for ice buildup are more snowfall and less snowmelt. But how does this happen? No scheme shackled by the constraints of uniformitarianism can alter earth's conditions to that extent. And besides, if things get too cold, the air can't contain much moisture and it doesn't snow much. And so the puzzle remains.

A key to more snowfall is more evaporation, and the best way to achieve that is to have warmer oceans. We would also need somewhat warmer winters in polar latitudes to allow for more snowfall, and intense weather patterns to transport the evaporated moisture from the ocean to the continents. And then we need colder summers to allow the snow to accumulate over the years.

Everyone agrees that these conditions would cause an ice age, but uniformitarian ideas can't allow the earth's systems to change that much. Many creationists think the Flood of Noah's day provides the key.

As the Flood ended, the oceans were warmer than today. The pre-Flood world had been uniformly warmer, and during the Flood the "fountains of the great deep" (Genesis 7:11) would have added much heat. This warmth would have continually pumped warm moisture into the atmosphere—and thus resulted in warm, wet winters.

Furthermore, the land surface at the end of the Flood was little more than a mud slick, and would have reflected solar radiation without absorbing much heat. The large temperature difference between ocean and land, coupled with strong polar cooling, would cause intense and prolonged storms.

Finally, the post-Flood times witnessed extensive volcanism, as the earth struggled to regain crustal equilibrium. This would fill the atmosphere with volcanic aerosols, bouncing incoming solar radiation back into space—thus, there would be colder summers.

More evaporation, warmer winters, more intense storms, and colder summers: The result? An "ice age" that would last until the oceans gave up their excess heat, the volcanism lessened, and vegetation was reestablished. This likely would take less than 1,000 years following the biblical Flood.

from melting.

Thus, the period immediately following the Flood was characterized by greater evaporation, more precipitation, and less snowmelt, meeting the requirements for an Ice Age. Calculations show that this would continue until the oceans gave up their excess heat and the atmosphere cleared, ending the Ice Age. Several hundred years were involved, extending the glacial period into and past the time of Abraham and Job.

This episode also affected human and animal migration. During the time when the glaciers were spreading out, vast amounts of ocean water had evaporated, fallen to earth, and were trapped on the continents as ice and not allowed to return to the sea. Studies of various indicators show that so much water was temporarily removed from the oceans that sea level may have dropped up to 500 feet. This would permit migration on foot to every continent.

Continents today are fringed by their continental shelf, which typically protrudes out into the ocean for many miles, eventually dropping into the ocean depths. The shelf is actually part of the continent and made up of the same rock strata as found inland, as evidenced by the presence of oil being produced by offshore drilling. If the oceans were 500 feet lower, the shelf of each continent would be exposed and connected by land bridges. Asia and Alaska would be connected by a land bridge 1,000 miles wide, and even Australia would be nearly connected to southeast Asia. Migration could occur without crossing the ocean. Thus, God's command to fill the earth could be obeyed.

WASN'T EVIDENCE FOR THE LOCAL FLOOD DISCOVERED?

It has been taught in many "Christian" circles that local flood ideas have been proven by discovery. In 1929, the eminent archaeologist Sir Leonard Woolley pronounced from his excavation in the city of Ur: "I have found the Flood." Among the ruins of the ancient homeland of Abraham, he had found an eight-foot layer of clay, with artifacts above and below, but nothing within it. As was common in the 20th century, he held a uniformitarian mindset in higher regard than the Bible, yet he still claimed to retain a modified orthodox faith. The local flood concept was prominent then, especially among scholars. His discovery claimed to support the flood in Mesopotamia, but only a minor, local

one. Soon, a similar discovery was made at the city of Kish, several hundred miles to the north. This was a major flood indeed, but not a global one.

Additional studies, however, showed that these two flood layers were not contemporaneous, so they didn't even represent the same flood. It certainly wasn't the great Flood, for the layer at Ur didn't even cover the whole city. This may have been a major flood to the people along the banks of the Euphrates near the Persian Gulf (where there have been many floods over the years, some quite large), but this was not the biblical Flood. Evidence for that Flood can readily be appreciated by noting that below the city's excavated ruins are many thousands of feet of true Flood-deposited strata, full of multiplied millions of fossilized plants and animals, as revealed by extensive oil exploration drilling and production. Oil is produced in abundance from these strata, which cover much of today's Middle East, far more area than the local flood evidence Woolley found. Local flood advocates are looking in the wrong place for the wrong markers.

The Black Sea "Local" Flood

Similar claims for major flooding were made in November 1999 regarding studies along the Black Sea, north of Turkey, by geologists Bill Ryan and Walter Pitman, based on their discovery of ancient ruins in the lake-bottom sediments. Their study was followed up by Robert Ballard, who had earlier gained fame by discovering the long-lost *Titanic* ocean liner remains. When the murky depths of the Black Sea were scanned with scientific instruments, possible archaeological remains of a long-ago civilization appeared. They found, among other things, questionable remains of structures and walls, buried in unconsolidated flood debris. Not adhering to biblical precision and understanding, the researchers misinterpreted the evidence and claimed this may have been the stimulus for ancient flood legends, as well as the biblical account of the great Flood of Noah's day.

Archaeologists concluded years ago that evidence points to a Mesopotamian origin for agriculture, writing, animal husbandry and domestication, urban life, and many other aspects of modern culture. Thus, the Black Sea proposal has some support. But this also conforms to biblical history. The Ark of Noah landed somewhere in the nearby "mountains of Ararat," and the Tower of Babel incident took place not far away, from which

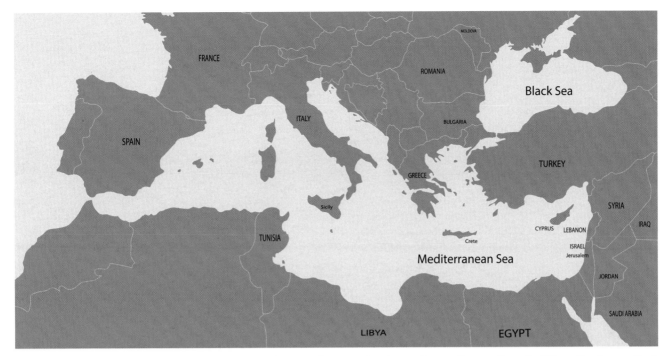

The great Ice Age followed the Flood, trapping huge volumes of water as ice on the continents. When the ice melted, ocean levels rose, refilling the Mediterranean Sea and eventually flooding the Black Sea area.

modern civilization spread out over the globe. Christians would expect mankind to have "re-started" here, but does a drowned (although controversial) city in today's Black Sea point unequivocally to a local Noahic flood? Is there another interpretation more consistent with a literal understanding of Genesis?

Once again, these ruins rested on top of several thousand feet of fossil-bearing strata. This local (but major) flood, if real, probably occurred sometime after the migration from the Tower of Babel, near the end of the Ice Age or even later. Several hundred years after the great Flood, as melting glaciers began to return their trapped, frozen waters to the ocean, sea level began to rise dramatically and rapidly. Waters may have poured into the Mediterranean basin through the Straits of Gibraltar and eventually overtopped the Bosporus Strait near Istanbul, Turkey, another natural barrier, and then entered the Black Sea.

It probably happened as it does today. When an embankment begins to fail, a notch is eroded that quickly deepens and widens until the whole natural dam fails catastrophically. Such a sudden influx would have spilled vast amounts of water into the Black Sea basin, which probably held just a comparatively small fresh-

water lake at that time, turning a freshwater environment into a marine environment.

The Black Sea discovery made international news, and was readily accepted by an unwary public, including Christian leaders. Many felt the Scripture was vindicated. Secularists considered it evidence that Scripture is nothing more than uneducated attempts to record and understand local history in a pre-scientific fashion.

Now that some time for reflection has passed, however, the whole claim is in question.[14] The relics recovered match archaeological remains of recent civilizations on the nearby land. The researchers had speculated that the survivors of this local flood might have migrated in all directions, taking with them the seed-thought that, when embellished, became the biblical flood. In reality, this was at most just a minor post-Flood readjustment.

SUMMARY

We can say that even seemingly insurmountable questions about the great Flood of Noah's day have good answers, and claims of local flood advocates do not measure up to scientific scrutiny or biblical revelation. Difficult questions always have good answers, if we are willing to study and believe.

CHAPTER 7

SCIENTIFIC EVIDENCE THAT THE FLOOD WAS CATASTROPHIC IN NATURE

The great Flood of Noah's day as described in Genesis can only be understood as catastrophic in nature and global in extent, with individual processes operating on at least a regional scale. Scripture leaves no room for any other interpretation. We cannot travel back in time to observe the Flood and study its processes, but we are able to study present evidence—the "damage" done by processes in the past—and discern the nature and the level of energy that must have been involved. And so we ask, does the geological evidence agree with Scripture? Were past geologic events actually catastrophic, or were they equivalent to processes operating today—i.e., "uniform" in nature?

For the last several generations, geology has been locked in uniformitarian thinking, refusing even to consider possible major events. More recently, this stranglehold has loosened somewhat as geological evidence has continued to mount in opposition to what uniformitarianism processes could produce, thus forcing geologists to consider major events. For instance, it's now commonplace to hear mainstream geologists speak of asteroid impacts killing off the dinosaurs, gigantic Ice Age floods, magnetic field reversals, continental plates moving about, underwater gravity flows of sediments, etc.—all concepts that were anathema to earth scientists just a few decades ago. This new day of "neo-catastrophism" has revitalized earth science and returned it to being a more data-driven science, with professionals responding more honestly to the data rather than forcing interpretations into strict Lyellian uniformitarianism.[1]

Geologists now openly speculate concerning long ago episodes in which things happened rapidly.[2] Numerous summary papers espousing catastrophism appear in the literature and professional conferences. This information has trickled down into industrial application, but despite this new way of thinking, uniformitarianism still reigns as an underlying theme in classroom teaching. Creationists have always been "catastrophists," and creationist/catastrophist research often leads the way in this new understanding. Much has been accomplished, but much still remains to be done. This chapter will document several major catastrophic "victories" and demonstrate how known catastrophic events in the recent past can be applied as analogies to help interpret unobserved occurrences in the more remote past. Furthermore, catastrophic thinking answers many questions in geology, providing a better reconstruction of the unseen past.

ACCEPTED CATASTROPHES

Undeniable catastrophes have occurred in the present day and in the recent past that were observed by scientists or reliable witnesses and are thus without controversy. These include "normal" catastrophes like river floods, hurricanes, earthquakes, tsunamis, etc. Others are not so normal. Some that occurred to our present (i.e., post-Flood) world may not have been directly observed, yet their record is on the surface, fairly easy to interpret. Study of rare modern catastrophes has taught us much about earth's potential for major events, and helped us identify more ancient catastrophes. Let us consider several recent devastating geologic episodes.

The Channeled Scablands

Perhaps the most well-known triumph of catastrophic thinking over strict uniformitarianism is that of Dr. J. Harlen Bretz and the Channeled Scablands. Beginning in the 1920s, Bretz studied a spate of deep gorges in eastern Washington that are oriented in the same general direction. He noted they were cut into hard basaltic rock and that the stream beds entering the deep eroded canyons were nearly dry. But when water was flowing, there must have been waterfalls up to 400 feet high entering the gorges. Great boulders had been tossed about and now lay in boulder fields. Standard thinking insisted slow-moving water operating over long ages was the only agent that could so deeply erode through hard rock. But responding to the data, Bretz concluded that unknown high-energy events must have been responsible. He speculated that the Scablands must have been sculptured by some huge flood—not the biblical Flood, but one of near biblical proportions must have been responsible.

For decades, Bretz presented his findings in professional geology meetings and in university settings, but his conviction that a single but mysterious great volume of water had rapidly carved these parallel canyons fell on deaf ears. He was treated shamefully by his peers.

In their thinking, no such catastrophe had occurred. It sounded too much like biblical catastrophism. Thankfully, Bretz persevered and eventually was vindicated.

Field investigation determined that if a dammed-up Ice Age meltwater lake comparable in size to today's Lake Michigan had broken through its temporary icy barrier and released torrents of water across southern Idaho

Scattered throughout the Pacific Northwest are deep canyons in hard basaltic rock, called "coulees," obviously eroded by more water than is now flowing. The remaining falls are either much reduced or "dry." The coulees are oriented in the same general direction, indicating rapid water flow over the area. The Missoula Flood, occurring at the end of the Ice Age, is now understood as the cause.

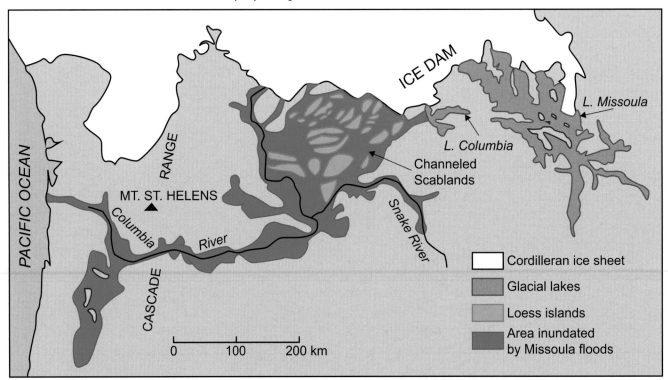

The Missoula Flood, which left coulees and dry falls behind, not only altered the countryside, it forever changed geology. This once-controversial flood reintroduced the concept of catastrophism to geology.

THE GLOBAL FLOOD

and eastern Washington in a short period of time, that could have accomplished the job. Evidence of just such a lake was discovered near Missoula, Montana. An unusual deposit consisting of extensive glacial lake sediments (where today there is no lake) confirmed that a huge lake had been at this spot during the Ice Age. Somehow the lake had drained away.

Bretz proposed that an enclosing dam of ice and/or glacial moraine had catastrophically failed, and the spillage had raced across Idaho and eastern Washington. As it did so, it carved through the hard rock in its path and left deep canyons reminiscent of Grand Canyon behind, along with immense gravel ripples and boulder fields strewn across the landscape. When the waters had been forced to temporarily pond behind obstructions, they deposited extensive sedimentary layers of recently eroded material. The waters quickly made their way via the Columbia River drainage basin to the Pacific Ocean. Now the water is gone, but the meager trickles of water in huge riverbeds and "dry falls" entering the canyons—or "coulees," as they are known—testify to greater water volumes in the past.

By 1960, Bretz had won the day and convinced geologists that, at least on this occasion, catastrophic processes had ruled. If this much damage resulted from a large but local failed lake flowing over a corner of the continent, what damage could we expect from the great Flood?[3]

Rapidly moving water can erode great volumes of rock. When enormous quantities of water were released from Glen Canyon Dam, an underground cavern was carved through reinforced concrete within minutes.

Nothing of the magnitude of that flood happens today on a regular basis. No modern-day "uniformitarian" or even neo-catastrophic counterpart can be observed on such a regional scale. Erosion happens, but it usually isn't observed carving deeply into solid rock. However, engineers have discovered that water flowing over a rock surface at a rapid rate can quickly erode even hard rock through a process called cavitation.

Cavitation

As water molecules move quickly over a rough surface, they create vacuum bubbles behind them that actually "implode" with such a great force they fracture the adjacent rock, thereby accelerating erosion. Such erosion requires a major event, one that involves great volumes of water with a high velocity.

Cavitation, a process well-studied by engineers and geologists, is known to be quite capable of eroding huge volumes of concrete or rock quickly. The U.S. Army Corps of Engineers reckons that cavitation was the culprit that eroded an enormous volume of reinforced concrete and the surrounding rock under a spillway draining Glen Canyon Dam in 1983. The dam had been constructed to protect the Colorado River and Grand Canyon below from intermittent water floods. But spring runoff was threatening to overtop the dam and send dangerous volumes of water downstream, possibly inflicting much damage to the dam and to in-

The Touchet Beds formed quickly as water released by a burst ice dam flooded eastern Washington.

habitants below.

To minimize the damage, the overflow spillways were opened, draining the excess water in a controlled way. Immediately, clear lake water was seen gushing from the concrete tunnels as if it came from a giant hose. Seismographs sensed, however, that something substantial was happening underground. Suddenly, the exiting water turned muddy red, the color of the underlying rock. Before they could close the spillway, the water's rapid velocity had quickly eaten through the spillway's thick reinforced concrete casing and opened a huge chasm in the rock beneath. Within minutes, a cavern 32 by 40 by 150 feet had been excavated.

Never again can we doubt that dynamic floodwaters can do extensive geologic work in a hurry. We are still left to ponder the effects of the great Flood, which involved erosion on a grander scale with waters flowing at much greater sustained volumes and velocities. Think of the sedimentary deposits that would accrue.[4]

The Touchet Beds in Burlingame Canyon

Many other examples of large-scale erosion have occurred in recent history and are well-documented. One such devastating event occurred in 1926 in a small corner of the Scablands area. Unusually heavy rainfall caused local streams to swell, and a small irrigation ditch near Walla Walla, Washington, became choked with debris. Water, flowing at an abnormally high 80 cubic feet per second, was temporarily diverted into an emergency canal while the ditch was cleared.

No one knew at the time, but the surrounding hills through which the diversion canal flowed consisted of poorly consolidated debris carried in by the long-ago Missoula Flood. Evidently, at one point along the flood's path, a chain of small mountains acted like the sides of a giant basin that briefly captured some of the released water. The sediment-choked water sloshed back and forth until finally working its way out through a gap in the mountains, the Wallula Gap. With each "slosh," some of the sediments carried by the turbid water collected as distinct layers, each up to three feet thick. This continued dozens of times until a thick covering of scores of nearly identical layers blanketed the area, now known as the Touchet Beds. No one really knew much about these interesting, poorly consolidated underground layers until the irrigation ditch became clogged and the water was redirected over them.

The diverted water ran down a slope leading into nearby Pine Creek through a small, usually dry ditch. The abnormally high flow that was suddenly introduced into the narrow ditch careened along and cascaded down the mesa in an impressive waterfall. Suddenly, under this extreme water volume and velocity, the underlying strata gave way and headward erosion began in earnest. What once was an insignificant drainage ditch became a gully. The gully became a gulch. The gulch became a miniature Grand Canyon. It took six days to stabilize the irrigation canal and drainage ditch. It was then observed that these six days of runaway ditch erosion removed around 150,000 m³ (five million cubic feet) of silt, sand, and rock. Today, Burlingame Canyon measures 1,500 feet long, and averages 120 feet wide and about 120 feet deep—an impressive canyon.

Remember, this canyon was observed to form in a few days by extreme erosion due to an unusual downpour. Comparable to numerous local floods, the runoff was observed to accomplish much geologic work quickly on a local scale. Similar devastation is often wrought by "normal" floods, such as is often seen on the Mississippi River. Our minds can hardly comprehend the potential of much greater volumes of water moving at much greater rates, scales, and intensities. We can only extrapolate present catastrophic processes onto past events about which we have limited knowledge.

Mount St. Helens Eruption

Other recent well-observed events have taught us much about the potential of the great Flood of Noah's day. Perhaps the greatest learning tool was the eruption of Mount St. Helens in 1980. This volcanic event was not the same as the great Flood, but in some ways it is analogous. Keep in mind that while the great Flood was primarily a hydraulic cataclysm, it involved a tectonic restructuring of the entire planet as well, as the "fountains of the great deep" broke open. Associated with this were devastating tsunamis, major faulting, mega-earthquakes, and mountain building, as well as rapid erosion of rocks, deposition of sediments, volcanic eruptions, etc.[5]

Similarly, when Mount St. Helens erupted in 1980, it was not only a tectonic incident with predictable volcanic results, it spawned numerous water-related processes and products. Before the eruption, the mountain had been capped by a thick glacier. Sudden heating melted the glacier, and water raced down the mountain's northern slope. Water avalanching with tsunami-like intensity savaged the forest and hillsides below, combining with ashfall and pyroclastic flows from the eruption itself. Some rock strata in vulnerable areas

were quickly eroded, and sediments were instantly deposited on other areas in layers looking much the same as those to which geologists normally attach great age.[6]

At the mountain's base, layers of sediment up to 600 feet thick were deposited that in a few years hardened into rather solid rock. Over the next few years, canyons were gouged into these layers, producing in one location a scale model of Grand Canyon in just one afternoon. Elsewhere, wood is petrifying, coal is forming, etc., all in the few years since the eruption. The igneous rock (dacite) in the new lava dome that should date "too young to measure" by radioisotope dating instead gives an anomalous date of 2.4 million years old when the proper isotopic dating method (potassium-argon) is used.[7] Modern local catastrophes such as the eruption of Mount St. Helens provide us a glimpse into earth's past.[8]

ICR has found that there is no better "first dose" of creation information than the lessons learned at Mount St. Helens. It has often been an individual's introduction to creation thinking and research, made all the more powerful because the eruption was so well observed and studied. The Mount St. Helens catastrophe becomes a model for the great Flood. It teaches us about volcanism, erosion, deposition, solidification, fossilization, etc., all acting in a short time. A catchy slogan helps illustrate this: To form geologic features, *it either takes a little bit of water and a long time, or a lot of water and a short time.* Even though we didn't witness the great Flood, we do see modern catastrophes, and they rapidly accomplish things the Flood did on an even grander scale. In a short, biblically compatible timescale, such a flood can account for all the features we see on earth's surface, features that many geologists normally misinterpret as evidence for great age. Earth doesn't really look old, but it does look flooded.

The Flood has always been the key to understanding earth's geologic history. One cannot rightly interpret any place on earth without the Flood for, on the authority of the Word of God, where could you go on earth and not encounter a flooded terrain? The great Flood of Noah's day was global and changed everything. To eliminate the Flood from one's geologic thinking is to guarantee an incorrect geologic interpretation. To include Flood thinking doesn't guarantee right interpretations, but at least it puts you in the right ballpark.

LESSONS LEARNED AT MOUNT ST. HELENS INCLUDE:

- Up to 600 feet of sediments were rapidly deposited, virtually identical to those found worldwide in the greater geologic record.

- A deep, eroded canyon through those sediments that has been dubbed the Little Grand Canyon was carved in one afternoon.

- Fresh volcanic rocks called dacites are dated by radiometric means to be over a million years old, yet are only decades old.

- A log mat of about four million trees, remains of a forest that was catastrophically scoured from the ground, now floats in a nearby lake.

- A thick peat layer is accumulating under the mat and is poised to become a coal deposit if buried by another eruption.

- Upright floating logs that look like they grew in place have the signature appearance of the petrified "forest" at Yellowstone National Park.

THE YOUNG EARTH

Obviously, the research at Mount St. Helens speaks to the issue of the age of the earth and how we determine it. Uniformitarianism extrapolates present processes, which seem to be operating quite slowly, back into the past. But past processes often give evidence of having operated at much greater rates than they do now, and in fact Scripture insists things were quite different in the past, particularly during the creation and Flood periods. If Scripture is correct and things were different, then assuming they were always the same guarantees a wrong interpretation.

Scripture describes the Flood in no uncertain terms as global and earth-changing. No place on earth could have escaped its fury, and thus every location's history is punctuated by the Flood's effects. Reconstructing the history of any location depends on acknowledging the Flood and discerning its local impact. In reality, the biblical doctrine of the global Flood works out to be synonymous with the young earth doctrine. If the Flood was global, the earth is young.

Ask a uniformitarian, "Where is the evidence for millions of years?" For that matter, ask an evolutionist, "Where is the evidence for evolution?" Traditionally, the answer to both questions has always been, "In the rock and fossil records." The fossils document evolutionary transitions and the rocks document millions and millions of years—or so we are taught.

ALL ROCK TYPES REQUIRE CATASTROPHIC DEPOSITION

In the world of today—the "uniform" world—various rock types are sometimes being formed in various local situations, but the strata of the rock record require more than uniform processes can accomplish. Available for our study are sedimentary rock strata, including sandstone, shale, and limestone, and many varieties of each. All start out as sediments and harden into rock. There are igneous rocks, sometimes spewed out in volcanic eruptions, which once were molten but have cooled. And there are metamorphic rocks, which before were another rock type but have been altered into their present forms.

Some rocks come from sediments of biological origin. Others have crystallized due to changing temperature. But many rocks that are formed today differ markedly in character and scale from their counterparts in the rock record. Apparently, processes other than those we observe today were responsible for their origin. This book is not the place to fully explain lithologic processes, but a brief description of how rocks are formed and how they are found will prove instructive.[9]

SEDIMENTARY ROCK

Rocks of sedimentary origin divide into several categories—clastic rocks that consist of pieces of a previous rock (such as sandstone, made up of sand grains cemented together); rocks that were chemically precipitated; and rocks that consist primarily of organic debris and/or fossils. Each requires conditions and scales seldom observed today. Uniformitarians may point to similar sediments being deposited in local high-energy events today, but those of the past reflect strikingly different rates, scales, and intensities. We can learn much from them.

Clastic rocks are catalogued according the dominant particle size. Conglomerates contain the larger "grain" sizes, from boulders to cobbles to pebbles to granules, with the larger sizes often imbedded within a matrix of smaller grains. Nearly all clastic rock was deposited as sediments by moving fluid, either water or air. Extensive engineering tests have determined the necessary water velocity and viscosity to move the variously sized particles. Obviously, it takes more energy to move a boulder than it does to move a grain of sand, as it does to move a coarse sand grain than a fine sand grain (or a smaller silt-size particle, or an even smaller clay-size one).

Sandstone

Most sandstones are understood to have been water-deposited, and the geometry of the beds provides evidence of the water depth and velocity. Prominent sandstones seen in the American West frequently exhibit cross-bedding, with sand deposited at an angle to the dominant layering. Sometimes these are considered to be fossilized desert sand dunes, but the angle of cross-bedding and the presence of animal tracks require the sand to have been saturated when it was deposited. The average grain size coupled with the height of the "dunes" sometimes necessitates water velocities at depth to have been several meters per second. Such velocities are only observed today during hurricanes or when the geometry of an estuary restricts water flow

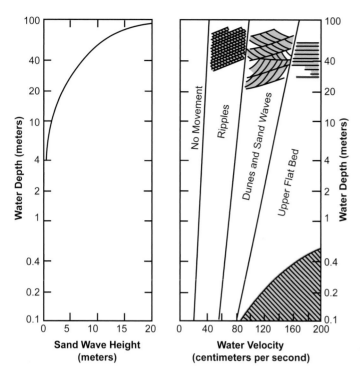

Bed form stability diagram. Water depth and velocity determine sediment characteristics.[10]

into a channel, something impossible on the large scale implied by the deposits. Uniformity of geological processes and rates does not address this.

The enormous quantities of sand comprising such deposits likewise stymie uniformitarians. Sand, transported by either water or air, must come from somewhere. It may come from the erosion of a previous deposit or from the open ocean, but often no local source has been identified that satisfies the conditions. So, the sand must come from a far distant source, transported by rapidly moving water.

Granite contains abundant quartz grains, which decompose into sand grains. The granitic interior of Canada is a possible source of sand, but it is far to the north of the American West deposits. Major water currents must have been involved, to erode and/or transport. Uniformitarian thinking relies on hypothetical slow-moving streams to erode and transport the grains, but no such migrating stream bed could possibly have flowed across wide areas for the length of time required and covered such immense areas. The catastrophic conditions needed would nullify uniformitarianism.

Another problem for uniformity of process involves the vast expenditure of energy required to move such massive quantities of sand for a long distance. Merely claiming small energy levels were active over millions of years, coupled with local albeit migrating geometry, doesn't satisfy the vast scales involved. Extensive, dynamic water flows generated by major tectonic episodes could get the job done, however.

Shale

The majority of the sedimentary rock record consists of fine-grain shale and similar rocks, like mudstone and siltstone. Today, fine sediments originate by the weathering of various rocks on the continents (including volcanic rocks), and then transportation by rivers to floodplains, deltas, lakes, and the ocean, where they accumulate. But the particles are so fine that they settle out slowly even when the water is still. Shale deposits are embarrassingly thick, requiring a constant supply of sediments and a continually calm environment. There must be some means present to flocculate the clay into larger "clumps" and allow them to settle more rapidly. Certain chemicals can cause the particles to do this when introduced, but what natural, large-scale process provides for this?

Shale, siltstone, and other "mudrocks" can often be seen in mountains and road cuts, with layers extending for long distances. Do thin, widespread layers of almost monotonous repetition speak of tidal and wave action? Waves might provide a continuous repetition of conditions, but not necessarily a continual supply of sediments, and certainly not calm water. The lateral scale implied by the strata further belies water action on a stationary beach.

A recent flume study demonstrated how tiny clay particles can flocculate, or clump together, at flow velocities great enough to transport sand.[11] The study authors report that clay beds quickly accumulate under fast-moving currents, a range similar to the velocities experienced in devastating floods. It seems the very large and thick expanses of clay-rich rocks can best be explained by flooding conditions. Perhaps the great Flood of Noah's day provided the sediments through erosion and abrasion, and its dynamics provided the mechanism to explain the deposits we see—all quite unlike any process observed today.

Modern deltaic deposits are well-studied, but many shales and siltstones thought by uniformitarians to have originated in past deltas are so different that it seems they could not have come from similar processes. Modern deltaic sediment layers undulate as the water

SEDIMENTARY STRUCTURE SHOWS A YOUNG EARTH

Sedimentary rock, which makes up most of the surface cover of the continents, is by definition deposited by moving fluids. Normally, the sediments contain evidence of their fluid-borne history in what is called *sedimentary structures*. These features include cross-bedding, graded-bedding paleocurrent markers, laminations, ripple marks, etc. If the hardening conditions are met (i.e., the presence of a cementing agent and pressure to drive water from the matrix), the sediments soon harden into sedimentary rock, making the "structure" permanent.

Geologists have traditionally surmised that most deposits are the results of the calm and gradual uniformitarian processes currently in operation. Conversely, more recent geologic models recognize that processes of the past may have acted at rates and intensities exceeding those of today, while catastrophists look to processes far exceeding those. Although they may have been the same basic processes, they were acting at catastrophic levels, accomplishing much depositional work in a short time. Continuing catastrophic action would quickly deposit a second layer, and then more. The question remains: How long ago did a particular depositional sequence of events take place?

We know that life proliferates in every near-surface layer of soft sediment. This is true on land, and especially true underwater. Plant roots penetrate the soil. Animals such as worms, moles, clams, etc., burrow through the sediment, churning it up and turning it over through a process called *bioturbation*. While muddy sediments are still fresh and soft, the ephemeral sedimentary structures within the deposits are in jeopardy of being obliterated by the action of plant and animal life. This obviously destroys the sedimentary structure. But how long does it take?

A 2008 study undertook to determine just how much time was required to destroy all such structures.[1] Numerous recent storm deposits, dominated by sedimentary structure, were investigated in their natural setting. It was observed that the bioturbation in the soft sediments was so intense that within months all sedimentary structure was destroyed. As long as sediments are still soft, they will be bioturbated until all structure

Chattanooga Shale stratification.

is lost. Yet the geologic record of earth history abounds with such structural features.

This comprises a good geologic age indicator, and in fact points to a young earth. The total picture must be considered when considering sedimentary rocks.[2] Within a relatively short time after deposition (months or years), all sedimentary structure would disappear through the rapid, destructive action of plant and animal life alone. The sediments would be exposed to bioturbation until the next layer covered them and until hardening was complete. Uniformitarianism insists that many, if not most, strata surfaces were at or near the living biozomes for long periods of time. If so, they would have been thoroughly reworked by living plant and animal action, yet they appear to have been isolated from destructive bioturbation. Thus, the length of time between the layers could not have been great. The total time involved for the entire sequence must therefore have been short.

Scripture specifies that the time elapsed for all of creation and earth history has not been very long. Geology confirms it.

1. Murray K. Gingras et al, 2008, How fast do marine invertebrates burrow?, *Palaeogeography, Palaeoclimatology, Palaeoecology,* 270 (3-4): 280-286.

2. Miles O. Hayes, 1967, Hurricanes as Geologic Agents: Case Studies of Hurricane Carla, 1961, and Cindy, 1963, Austin, TX: University of Texas Bureau of Economic Geology, Report of Investigation 61: 56.

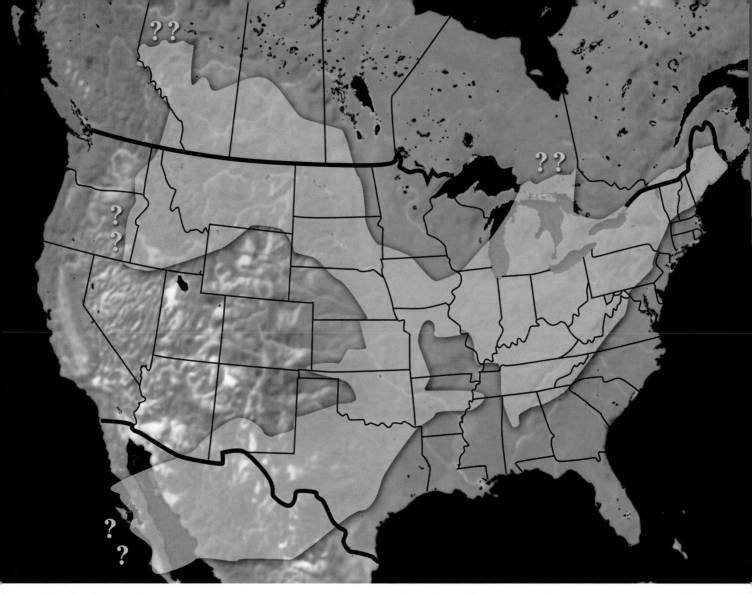

The Chattanooga Black Shale covers a large fraction of the continental United States (at least as much as shown in this map) and is underlain by a flat, featureless erosional surface. Consisting of tiny clay-size particles, and seldom more than 20 feet thick, it baffles uniformitarians, who propose slow settling of particles out of standing water. There is no modern analogy for this type of deposition.

is distributed and individual beds don't extend very far, but geologic layers interpreted as deltaic may extend for hundreds or thousands of miles. Some process altogether larger and more dynamic is required.

The Chattanooga Shale: An Evolutionary Enigma

Some shales are black in color, loaded with organic material. The classic North American example of black shale is the Chattanooga Shale, traditionally thought to have been deposited in deep and stagnant ocean water. But that may be too simple, for other evolutionists perceive a problem they call "The Chattanooga Black Shale Enigma."[12]

Flood geology places essentially all strata during the great Flood of Noah's day, a depositional situation that is quite different from deep and stagnant water. Sel-

dom more than 20 feet thick, the Chattanooga Shale is underlain by an amazingly flat, featureless erosional surface, with no significant high or low areas where deposition took place. Such flat erosion usually speaks of rapid sheet erosion. This shale deposit is often presented as classic evidence for uniformitarian deposition in a "calm and placid sea," but could there be another interpretation? A closer look at the details provides a catastrophic depositional model, instead.

The shale consists of innumerable fine layers or laminations, which can be easily separated. Often between the layers are fossils, both marine creatures such as brachiopods and land plants like lepidodendrons. Also present are animal escape burrows, formed as rapidly buried sea creatures attempted to burrow out of an underwater grave. The mix of environments seems to speak against a calm environment.

The laminations are also problematic, for instead of being uniformly flat, they are graded and tilted up at an angle, and in some places form cross-beds, requiring a rapid current environment. An overall look at the strata leads to a diagnosis of hummocky cross-stratification, also indicative of rapid water current and continual deposition of particles. The clay particles themselves are uniformly aligned, as revealed by an AMS study (anisotropy of magnetic susceptibility), a prime indicator of current.

Most importantly, the layer is enormous in areal extent. It was first identified in Tennessee (where it received its name), but now is widely recognized from Alabama to Canada on the east coast, to Iowa and Texas, to Oregon on the west coast, and into northern Mexico and even offshore.[13] No modern analogy exists for such a deposit.

The Flood account in Genesis specifically informs us that the Flood was catastrophic in nature (Genesis 7:11-12, 17-20, 24, etc.) and global in extent (e.g., 6:13, 17; 7:10, 21-23; 8:3, 5, 11; 9:15). We would expect its damage to give evidence of this catastrophic cause and extent, and indeed the Chattanooga Shale surely provides such evidence. It provides no such support for the uniformitarian worldview.

Limestone

Limestone ($CaCO_3$) can be derived from both organic and inorganic sources. Organic limestone deposition occurs today, and these deposits are often cited as evidence for uniformitarian origins for all limestones. For example, modern lime (aragonite) collects in the Caribbean Sea and is the favorite example, but its extent is far more limited than limestones in the rock record. Again, uniformitarianism doesn't speak to this.

There are major differences between past and present limestones that must be noted. Modern limey sediments are of extremely fine texture and consist of a mineral called aragonite (particles approximately 20 microns in diameter, or silt-size). Where limey sediments of the past have hardened into solid limestone, the texture is an even finer-grain, clay-size mineral called calcite (particles typically less than 4 microns in diameter). The two types seem to have had a different history. Both consist of $CaCO_3$, but separate origins are implicated for their extent and makeup.

The fascinating swirls seen here are due not to swirling deposition, but to uneven erosion of a cross-bedded sandstone. A flat surface would show intersecting bedding lines. The dimensions of the cross-beds reveal the depth of water involved, and the sizes of sand grains show its velocity.

Fossils are often found in limestone, but not in every one or in each location. An offshore reef hosts abundant lime-secreting organisms and many with carbonate shells. Together they live and die, and their remains merge into solid rock. It depends on waves, tides, storms, etc., but the general shape of a living reef is known. Beds interpreted as ancient or fossil reefs are quite different. They are instead best understood as destroyed and transported reef material, not an in-place reef. Usually only a small percentage of the "ancient" so-called reef consists of broken fragments of reef creatures, while the majority is a matrix of inorganic limey sediments.

The best-known limestone bed in Grand Canyon, the Redwall Limestone, has become the prime uniformitarian example of "slow and gradual" accumulation in hypothetical calm and placid seas. Limestone beds often cover immense areas, sometimes semi-continental in scope. This example is no exception, for it covers several states, unlike any living reef. Creationists and evolutionists have both spent considerable time studying this important bed. A study by creationist Dr. Steve Austin found firm evidence that this deposition required catastrophic conditions. Cross-beds preserved in the limestone—evidence of large, rapidly moving currents of mud and water—speak of dynamic moving water.[14]

The cross-beds surround a remarkable 7-foot-thick deposit of large nautiloid fossils, implicating a major kill event. Fossils are rarely seen in Grand Canyon rocks, and uniformitarians hadn't expected significant fossils here. Earlier, a geologist had discovered a few dozen two-foot-long nautiloids (a free-swimming marine creature something like a squid with a straight shell) in an obscure side canyon. Uniformity might conclude they were buried by a local disturbance, and none were expected in other areas. Dr. Steve Austin's catastrophist thinking led him to investigate other relatively unexplored side canyons. In every one, he discovered more two-foot-long nautiloids where they had been trapped and buried alive by rapid deposition. His search led him to an estimated four billion of these remarkable creatures preserved as fossils in this bed, over several states, most in pristine condition, with no scavenging or decay.

Nautiloids were a marine predator. Similar animals live in the ocean today, but they don't live in enormous schools, such as indicated by the billions of fossils. Evidently this records a stage during the great Flood when conditions were suddenly intolerable for these creatures, and they all got trapped in suffocating, sediment-laden water.

Furthermore, their bodies are aligned in a preferred orientation, demonstrating flowing currents of water saturated with limey mud. The mud had collected so rapidly that these free-swimming creatures had not been able to escape. Austin traced the deposit into neighboring areas, up into Utah and Nevada. This was truly an extensive kill site, a major discovery in Grand Canyon, and one that demonstrates the inability of uniformitarian thinking to explain what we see.

Over half of the sedimentary layers found on the conti-

nents are marine sediments, having been derived from marine sources and containing marine fossils. They result from oceanic invasion of the land. Each displays geometry and character unlike modern deposits and requires a catastrophic explanation on a large scale. Consider these few examples.

St. Peter Sandstone: This major Ordovician deposit of cross-bedded sandstone drapes over the North American continent, covering more than 1.5 million square miles in area, with a thickness of 100 to 300 feet, extending from the Rocky Mountains to the East Coast (about 2,000 miles), and from Mexico to Canada.

The height of the imbedded cross-beds implies rapid movement of deep water and an unimaginable quantity of sand. The thinness of the sand blanket requires that prior to deposition, erosion had scoured the continent down to a vast featureless plain, with less than 300 feet difference in elevation everywhere. Compared to its vast area, its thickness is reminiscent of a piece of onion-skin paper draped across a flat area the size of Chicago. How could this be? Proposing the existence of a continent-wide flat plane with no hills or mountains and a thin covering deposit strains credibility. Nothing even remotely like this is happening today.

Uniformitarians refer to this deposit as an ancient beachfront and/or shallow offshore deposit that migrated across the continent, even though coastlines today have pronounced topography and cover only local areas. Is not the proposed incursion of the great Flood, at times both eroding and depositing, a better explanation?

Providence Limestone: Traced from Kentucky to Colorado, this thin Pennsylvanian limestone is rarely over ten feet thick. Often above and below are coal seams, thought to be the metamorphosed remains of terrestrial swamp peats altered by heat and pressure. This type of limestone is thought by uniformitarians to have been deposited in deeper water as single-cell organisms died and settled to the bottom. The combination of deposits necessitates the area bobbing up and down like a cork. How could this happen in a uniformitarian world? How could an underlying continent-wide surface be so flat and featureless, with less than ten feet of relief? At the very least, non-uniformitarian conditions are on display.

Blanket Chert: Remnants of a blanket chert deposit in the Devonian system are found from Texas to New

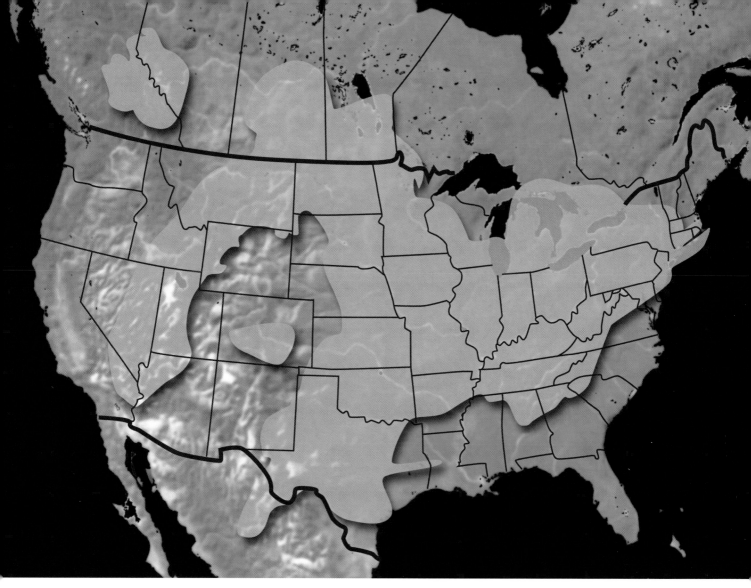

Area covered by the St. Peter Sandstone and correlating strata, the basal sandstone deposited at the beginning of the Tippecanoe Megasequence.

York to Georgia. Chert consists of silica nodules cemented together. Chert can be made in laboratory settings using elevated temperature and pressure, but little if any is being formed in nature today. This chert deposit averages 300 feet thick and covers a subcontinental region. Surely this deposit requires dynamic conditions quite unlike those we observe today. Once again, uniformitarianism, the dominant mindset in science today, fails to satisfy.

Strata designated as terrestrial require conditions and geologic episodes entirely different from those observed today in land environments. Present terrestrial environments include lakebed sedimentation, deltaic deposits, beachfronts, glacial moraines, and riverbeds, all typically water-deposited. Desert sand deposits are wind-blown, but need saturation to solidify into rock. Modern non-marine deposits consist of land-derived

sediments and fossils, and are of small areal extent and thickness. Conversely, non-marine deposits of the past, while also primarily consisting of water-laid deposits of land-derived sediments and creatures, are of regional extent and contain features best explained by a cataclysm. Sometimes a vague comparison can be made, but such comparisons only point out the uniqueness of past processes. Consider a few examples.

Morrison Deposit: The dinosaur fossil-bearing Morrison Formation consists of a relatively thin layer averaging about 100 feet thick that covers an area of 600,000 square miles. Contained within are thousands of partial dinosaur carcasses, and tens of thousands of shattered dinosaur bones. Obviously, the articulated skeletons required rapid burial, for scavengers and bacteria are normally ever-present to devour any unprotected remains. Interestingly, the most common fossil at Dino-

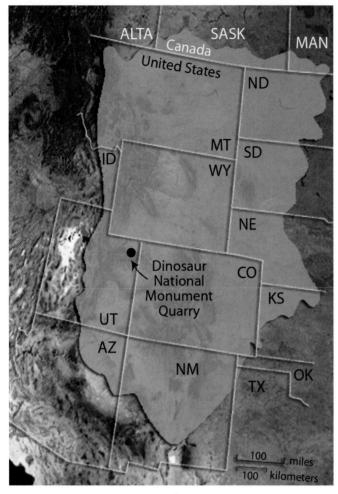

The Morrison Formation exhibits volcanic ash flowing along as mud. Animals and plants from varied environments—marine, terrestrial, mountainous, coastal—are mixed together in its well-known dinosaur fossil sites. This deposit is not a snapshot of life, but a record of violent death and transportation.[15]

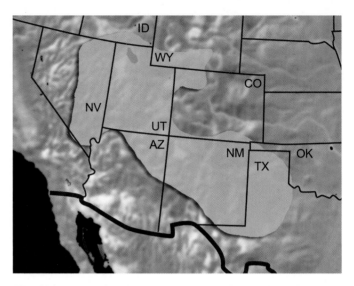

The Shinarump Conglomerate covers about 125,000 square miles and averages 50 feet thick. Large boulders and coarse grains require rapid water flow, following extensive erosion. Abundant petrified wood is present. No modern process can account for this.

saur National Monument in the Morrison Formation is that of an articulated clam. The encasing rock was water-deposited, sometimes interpreted by uniformitarians as due to sporadic river floods, each one trapping and burying land-dwelling dinosaurs along with animals and plants from a wide variety of habitats. But no river today covers as much of the American West. At the time of deposition, the mud was saturated with great volumes of volcanic ash from a distant source, most likely from central California. This remarkable deposit not only speaks of major water movement on the continents, but of terrifying tectonism and extinction as well.

Shinarump Conglomerate: Known for its abundant petrified wood, this extensive deposit covers about 125,000 square miles and averages 50 feet thick. Dated to the Triassic system, it too requires conditions of

erosion and deposition wholly unlike any we currently experience. Water movement carried along remains of an extensive forest, along with large cobbles. The size of the boulders and cobbles contained within would take rapid water movement on a regional scale to move them. What process operating today can do this?

Exotic Blocks Moved by Debris Flow: Landslides and slumps occur today on a local scale and are well-studied, but past events require regional forces that take one's breath away. In numerous places worldwide, large blocks of rock that were transported long distances are found. Geologists have measured the dimensions of some of these blocks in terms of miles in each direction. Some were rapidly moved many miles.[16] In the Mojave Desert, huge boulders up to a mile in diameter were catastrophically deposited in giant submarine landslides near the former edge of the continent. Associated debris flows can be observed an astounding 100 miles from the source area. These weren't simply boulders that rolled down a hill. Admittedly, these deposits are neither global nor semi-continental, but they are much larger than modern processes address. What uniformitarian process could accomplish this? The most viable explanation involves large and dynamic mudflow, quite unlike anything uniformitarianism can offer. Remember, the Flood model predicts catastrophic geological processes acting on a wide scale, and this is what we find. The evidence confirms the biblical teaching.

Worldwide Stratigraphic Trends: In addition to re-

MUDROCKS

Mudrock is a general term for a variety of rocks made up of tiny silt-size or clay-size particles. Often they are uninteresting rocks, with an abundance of monotonous flat-looking layers less than 1 cm thick. Yet even though they make up about two-thirds of the sedimentary record, their origin is quite mysterious. The rocks are obviously water-deposited, but small particles resist settling out of water. Instead, the tiny grains are whisked away by even minor currents. In completely calm water, where there is no current, they typically fall by gravity at the rate of about one foot every three days. How did such a huge volume of uncooperative sediments accumulate? Uniformitarians have long taught that the individual grains required extremely calm and placid seas to slowly sink to the bottom, where they are thought to have collected into thick, extensive beds. But having a story to tell is not the same as having a good explanation.

Mudstones or mudrocks include shale, easily comprising the largest percentage of sedimentary rock types. The category of mudrocks also includes limestone and the mudflows entombing so many dinosaur fossils. Predictably, siltstone belongs in the classification of mudrock as well. Most of the rocks in coal regions are mudrocks, and oil-bearing rocks are often mudrocks. The pyroclastic deposits of Mount St. Helens also fall into this category. Rocks of this type have been exceptionally well-studied and their nature is understood, but they are an enigma as to origin. How could they form? In sedimentology labs, small grains can be made to sink in completely still water only after having been treated with slippery chemicals, both wholly unnatural conditions. Under what circumstances do they sink and build up?[1]

Note that if these particles are able to flocculate into larger agglomerations first, they can then sink even in the presence of moving water. Another possibility involves particles rapidly sliding "en masse" down a gentle slope rather than in vertical free fall. These conditions may seem reasonable, but remember that uniformitarianism fully depends on the long-term, large-scale "calm and placid seas" concept. If uniformitarians admit that such non-uniform conditions are necessary to account for the majority of rocks, they will have forfeited the entire "game."

Careful observation of these rocks reveals that more than simple planar laminations are present. Cross-laminations due to horizontal flow are there too. These are less pronounced than cross-bedding in sandstone and consist simply of planar laminations with minor tilts to them. This makes all the difference, for cross-beds cannot be formed by free fall, but only in the presence of rapid currents. Wave tank studies have discovered the requirements for these features to form— they result from what is termed "upper-stage plane bed." These

Deposits of fine-grain sediments, like these near Las Vegas, Nevada, can be seen almost anywhere. Called mudrocks, they make up the majority of sedimentary rock and are usually deposited by water. Uniformitarians propose that tiny grains simply settled out of water and collected on the bottom, but this would take an impossibly long time. Research shows that rapid grain flocculation and underwater mudflows better explain the evidence.

conditions are illustrated on the bed form stability diagram on page 106, which plots mean grain size versus critical current velocity. Deposition requires a flow velocity on the order of a meter per second, hardly calm conditions for small particles to collect. Only under these dynamic conditions can the majority of rocks form.

1. Juergen Schieber, John Southard and Kevin Thaisen, 2007, Accretion of Mudstone Beds from Migrating Floccule Ripples, *Science*, 318 (5857): 1760-1763; Steven A. Austin, Understanding the Mudrock Revolution and the Global Flood as Described in Scripture, presented August 4, 2008, at the Sixth International Conference on Creationism in Pittsburgh, Pennsylvania.

Debris flow of large boulders in Death Valley.

gional patterns in both marine and non-marine strata, scientists have recognized worldwide trends in the geologic strata. As the prominent catastrophic evolutionist Dr. Derek Ager has noted, "At certain times in earth history, particular types of sedimentary environments were prevalent over vast areas of the earth's surface."[17] He and many others have noted that at particular "times" in supposed geologic history, deposition of a particular rock type was common, a type that may not have been deposited before or since. This makes little sense in a uniformitarian world.

It may be that at specific times during the great Flood of Noah's day, the ever-changing conditions hit on one set of conditions that spread to global dimensions. It might have involved chemistry or temperature, turbulence, etc. Likely the conditions involved catastrophic plate movements or planet-wide disturbances. Only when those conditions prevailed could a certain rock type be deposited. While other rock and fossil types may have been deposited at those times in various locations, these persist on a worldwide scale and demand a global cause.

Examples of global deposition trends and "times":

Greenstone Belts	Precambrian
Banded Iron Formations	Precambrian
Quartz Sandstone	Cambrian
Dolomite	Ordovician
Shales	Devonian
Red Beds	Triassic
Limestone	Mississippian
Coal	Carboniferous
Chalk	Cretaceous

IGNEOUS ROCK

The world's vast deposits of igneous rock also give eloquent testimony of earth's catastrophic history. The sheer volume of past volcanic episodes should convince any unbiased observer that things were different in the past, not at all similar to the uniformity of today. There are, of course, igneous bodies solidifying on earth now, both above ground (extrusive, i.e., volcanoes) and underground (intrusive, i.e., plutons), but these are hardly comparable to those of yesteryear in geometry, volume, or the amount of energy required.

The accompanying diagram of past volcanic episodes, some erupting following the great Flood and some inferred from their products, will prove instructive. Note that the volume of material extruded and the energies involved have declined many-fold over the centuries since the great Flood. The time right before and soon after the end of the Flood was a time of immense volcanism marked by extensive eruptions as the continents were spreading apart, the mountain chains were rising, and the ocean floor was dropping. The volcanic aerosols pumped into the atmosphere contributed to the Ice Age that followed the Flood, as solar radiation was prevented from entering. As did many natural processes, they tapered off in the centuries following, and are rather quiescent now.

Consider the Columbia River Basalts, where volcanic deposits cover over 100,000 square miles in the states of Washington and Oregon, with basalt up to one mile thick! Compare that with the largest volcanic eruption in recent history on American soil, that of Mount St. Helens in 1980. It's almost trivial by comparison.

It seems that earth must have been in relative equilibrium before the Flood, but all its processes were so destabilized that it took several hundred years to settle back down to the relative "uniformity" we now enjoy. Fortunately, we experience only a faint whisper of past conflagrations.

METAMORPHIC ROCK

When sedimentary or igneous rock undergoes intense heat and pressure, it metamorphoses into rock of a different sort, often altering and recrystallizing. Metamorphic rock sometimes forms today when friction from significant faulting bakes the adjacent rock, or perhaps when a hot, semi-molten granite body intrudes into the sediment. This contact metamorphism extends only for short distances, perhaps just a few inches or feet into the rock, which is permanently altered. But

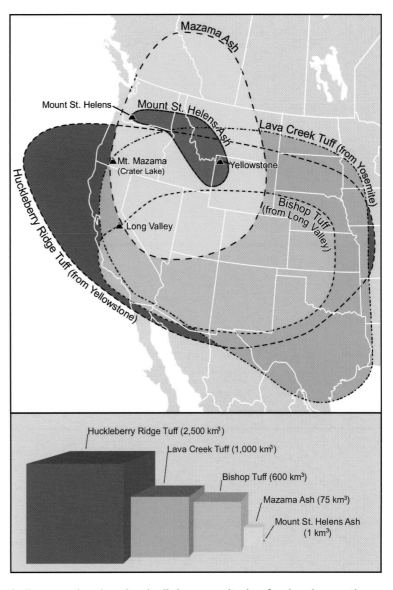

A diagram showing the declining magnitude of volcanic eruptions. Those occurring during and soon after the great Flood were immense compared to more recent ones.[18]

Pillar basalts at Giant's Causeway in Northern Ireland. Immense volcanism resulted in a regional deposit that cracked into pillars as it cooled. There is no modern analog for an igneous deposit of this size. Evidence of catastrophic processes operating on a regional scale would be an expected result of a global flood.

WERE THE HUGE COLUMBIA RIVER BASALTS FORMED DURING THE FLOOD?

Often skeptics of creation/Flood/young earth thinking scoffingly claim that no evidence for the Flood exists. Even though most geologists have abandoned old-style uniformitarianism in favor of a grudging acceptance of neo-catastrophism, they still deny the global, year-long cataclysm of Noah's day described in Scripture. They should be asked, "What sort of evidence would you be prepared to accept? Obviously, we can't observe past events, but if such a world-restructuring flood occurred, what would you expect to result from it? What evidence would you expect to find?" For most skeptics, no evidence would persuade them. Their rejection of the Noahic Flood, as an out-working of God's holy wrath on sinful men, is for philosophical reasons—"religious" reasons—irrespective of scientific evidence.

When considering non-repeatable events of the past, we are limited to scientific "predictions"—not predictions of the future, but predictions of the evidence. Reasoning from the scriptural record, we can "predict" that when we examine the geological results of the Flood, we will see regionally extensive geologic strata, deposited by catastrophic processes, which must have been operating on at least a regional scale, and that these large-scale results will dominate the rock record. My uniformitarian colleagues would predict the record would be dominated by the rather slow and gradual geological processes possible today, operating on local scales. Once both sides have made their predictions, the evidence can be evaluated as to which one is the better fit.

The Columbia River Basalt group of lava flows in Washington, Oregon, and Idaho illustrate this. A thick series of lava flows was stacked one on top of another in rapid succession until it covered an area of some 100,000 square miles and with a volume of about 40,000 cubic miles. This dwarfs the largest historic lava flow, which occurred in Iceland in 1783 and covered an area of about 200 square miles with a volume of less than 3 cubic miles. One can scarcely envision such eruptions, producing a veritable "lake of lava" thousands of times larger than anything witnessed by modern men. The molten material of the Columbia River eruptions flowed from several locations along linear cracks in the earth's surface, but even this deposit is dwarfed by past, much larger basalt deposits that have been recognized.

Occurring in layers stratigraphically below the Columbia River Basalts are thick layers of water-deposited,

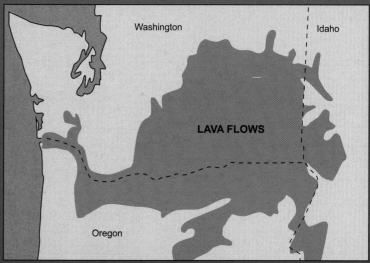

The area covered by Columbia River basaltic lava flows. This series of eruptions formed a veritable lake of lava 100,000 square miles and one mile thick.

fossil-bearing sedimentary rock, obviously deposited by the Flood itself. Thus, Flood advocates interpret these mega-eruptions of basalt as likely occurring during the very last stages of the Flood or in the years of readjustment that followed, as earth's systems regained the relative equilibrium in which we now find them. Surely this was a fearful time.

Obviously such large-scale volcanism does not match uniformitarian predictions regarding the past. Yet it does match the creation/Flood/young earth prediction of catastrophic processes operating on a regional scale during and immediately following the Flood. While neither side can directly observe the past, the biblical model is the one that best predicts the evidence, and is thus, from a scientific perspective, more likely correct.

metamorphic rocks formed in the past are immense, sometimes as wide as an entire mountain range. Uniformitarianism holds that it takes eons of time for the minerals to realign themselves into the new crystalline forms or into a preferred direction, too much time for the creation model to handle.

How, then, did the vast volumes of metamorphic rock found in the geologic record form? A sizable percentage of many continents consists of metamorphic rock, so surely some mechanism other than contact metamorphism accomplished it. Uniformitarian geologists call this "regional metamorphism," and so it is. But merely naming a condition is not the same as explaining it. How could the necessary forces be applied so widely? Laboratory studies have shown that each metamorphic mineral can form rapidly under certain conditions, at even low or moderate temperatures. Time is certainly not the determinative factor. For a larger volume to metamorphose, one prerequisite is the presence of interstitial water that disburses temperature and diffuses minerals, sometimes even transforming crystal structures into a different structure. Under these conditions, metamorphism can quickly produce rock features that are normally misunderstood by uniformitarians as evidence of great age.[19]

Research will continue to enlighten us, but we would do well to see how the creation model handles the data. Remember, God created the earth on Day One of the creation week (Genesis 1:1), implying that solid material sprang into existence from nothing. It was as yet "without form," or in an incomplete state, not yet ready to accomplish its intended task. It was in some mysterious way suspended in a worldwide watery matrix (v. 2). The semi-solid material may have been the partial precursor to some of the metamorphic rocks we know.

On Day Three, God called the waters "into one place, and let the dry land appear" (v. 9). Again we have only meager information, but perhaps the original creation involved the formation of only one continent uplifted out of the one ocean. It does not seem that God simply spoke and things appeared. Instead, He used a process or processes that took some (short) period of time to accomplish the work. Gravity and other laws of physics with which we are familiar were probably already acting to facilitate the spinning of the earth on its axis,

The typically flat-lying or slightly tilted rock strata in Grand Canyon overlie metamorphic Vishnu Schist, which covers a large area. Exceptional forces are required to metamorphose rock, which only occurs today in tiny zones.

and were there to act on the rock. Under any circumstances, we can surmise it would take some amount of time for water to drain off an uplifting continent. Were newly formed sediments eroded and redeposited? Perhaps God operated within natural laws that He had just put in place, but vastly accelerated their rate of operation. However He did it, the relative uniformity of today is not capable of doing the job; it was superseded by God's creative power and activity.

Intense, unimaginable forces may have been in action. There was ample power—creation power—to metamorphose soft, saturated sediments and rock into other forms at God's command. No great time was needed, as the laws that matter obeyed were being miraculously manipulated to do the Creator's bidding. We are specifically told that the creation week was marked by non-uniform activity. Day Three no doubt saw much of the newly formed "rock" eroded and redeposited as sediments, and the alteration of much Day One and/or Day Three sediment into what we now call metamorphic rock.

We need not consider erosion and metamorphism in a negative light and thus assign them to the time period after the Curse. Metamorphic rock can be and evidently was "very good" for God's purposes, for today it provides a stable mass on which much of the continental mass rests. In a similar vein, sedimentary rock can be considered "very good" too, for today's aquifers that supply so much of man's water needs come from them. On Day Three, such rock would have been completely fossil-free, for life had not yet been created.

A similar evaluation of God's plan might also be made regarding the Flood period, a time when great hydraulic and tectonic power was unleashed. From our perspective, the judgment God unleashed was terrifying, but He had an overriding purpose. All processes were under God's sovereign control, designed to accomplish His greater goals. As the Flood commenced and continued, unthinkable forces impacted earth's entire crust. Sediments deposited on continents were soon deeply buried and heated intensely. Continents were crushed and subducted; mountains were uplifted, faulted, and folded. Volcanoes erupted. The spewing forth of the "fountains" brought minerals, metals, nutrients, etc., to the surface that were not there before. He thus used this tragic Flood to provide for mankind. The opportunity was plentiful for much metamorphism of rocks.

What uniformitarianism cannot afford, Flood catastrophism pays in full.[20]

CATASTROPHIC EROSION

All sediment, especially recently deposited sediment, is subject to erosion. So is hardened sedimentary rock. Igneous and metamorphic rocks are often more resistant to erosion, but they are not invulnerable. As we look at past erosion episodes, we see erosion on a scale and intensity that demand a dynamic and wide-ranging cause.

Grand Canyon becomes "Exhibit A" for erosion. Uniformity tells us that the Colorado River eroded and removed all the material from the entire canyon grain by grain over millions of years. The reasoning is elegant—erosion proceeds very slowly today, and at present rates it would take long ages to form the canyon. Can river scouring and side canyon erosion account for what we see?

Each year, millions of school kids are taught this story about the unseen past. It may come as a surprise, but geologists who study Grand Canyon are less certain. Frequent professional conferences address this question, and as yet consensus answers elude researchers. Problems with the long-held ancestral river theory include the enormous quantity of sediments that was eroded and what happened to it. This quantity includes not just the canyon's sediments, but also much greater volumes from the upriver Colorado drainage system. The sediments are not found at the mouth of the canyon where the river slows down and should drop its sediment load. Perhaps they should be in the Gulf of California in Mexico, where the river enters the ocean, but they aren't there. Some feel they are found in the low-lying desert near the Salton Sea or offshore San Diego, but this would require water velocities and volumes much greater than normal.

Perhaps we would do better to question the assumption of uniformitarianism and look elsewhere. Perhaps there was a time before scientists could observe when water volumes and velocities were higher and could erode things at greater rates. Maybe it happened when the sediments were little more than unconsolidated mud and thus more susceptible to erosion. Maybe erosive processes of the past differed from or exceeded those of today. Some researchers have proposed that a major inland lake once filled the area just upriver from the canyon, held in place by what is now the Kaibab Upwarp acting as a natural dam. Eventually, water overtopped the dam and broke through and carved Grand Canyon rapidly.

Creationists would put this erosion period after most of the floodwaters had drained back into the ocean, either in the very last phases of the Flood year or soon after. The sediments were only a few months or years old and more easily eroded. Downwarping of the ocean basins and uplift of the continents had trapped numerous bodies of water on land, without outlets. For instance, the Great Salt Lake of Utah

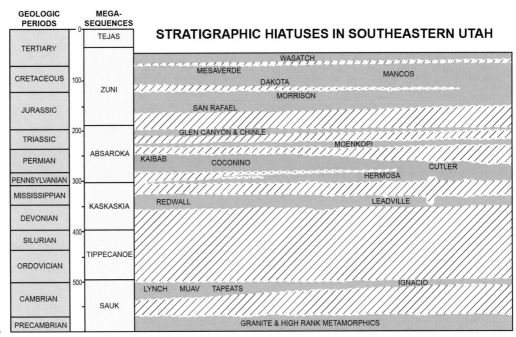

The sedimentary layers in southeastern Utah shown in proper time relationship (listed in millions of years, per uniformitarian thinking). The brown areas represent strata, while the areas with diagonal lines are assumed time gaps. The standard geologic column is given on the left. The horizontal distance represents about 200 km, while the total thickness of the actual strata is about 3½ km. Actually, the strata are resting on top of each other with no gaps between. The time gaps are required by standard thinking regarding the geologic "ages." Note that in this classic area, most of the strata are "missing."[22]

is but a remnant of the much larger Lake Bonneville. The Ice Age followed the Flood, with excessive rainfall coupled with glacial melt. With all that excess water, such lakes would have been unstable. The geological evidence for a lake of this nature is recognized by many, and the erosional forms and remnants seem to fit this general model. The Colorado River provides but a shadow of the erosional power needed to breach and erode this "grand" canyon.[21]

Similarly, most rivers in the world are much smaller than their present canyons require. Evidently, much more water was flowing in the past. Geologists call them "underfit" rivers. They speak of a time in the recent past when much more water was on the surface, much more rain fell, and the sediments were much more saturated. What a good description of the time of the Flood.

The accompanying chart illustrates sedimentary layers (shown as brown), the erosional unconformities (wavy lines), and the space for strata missing either through erosion or non-deposition (shown as zones with diagonal lines). Such charts could be drawn anywhere, but the well-studied and well-represented layers in eastern Utah serve as an illustrative model. Tourists know

it as the Grand Staircase, of which the lower section represents Grand Canyon. Shown are the many pancake-like layers in sequence and the erosional gaps between them. Note that more of the total geologic column is missing than is present.

But the evidence for erosion is missing as well. There are a number of environments in which no sediments are deposited, but in reality, the fact that layers are missing *is* considered to be the evidence for erosion. Note that the assigned "time" between two layers might be tens of millions of years, but the contacts are typically flat and featureless. There are no stream beds in the surfaces and no valleys. Erosion should quickly produce irregular terrain, but there is none. In the next chapter, more will be discussed on this important point.

Step back and take a look. The flat and featureless contacts between strata can easily be seen in road cuts or eroded terrains. They often extend for many miles. The big-picture stratigraphic sections reveal flat gaps sometimes spanning the continent. These types of discussions were never held a generation ago, but expanding geological knowledge has made regional maps and other data available. No longer is it legitimate for geologists to restrict their focus to a single outcrop or hand specimen while ignoring larger implications.

Sharp Contacts and Earth's Rotation

A research project begun by geophysicist Dr. John Baumgardner during his tenure at the Institute for Creation Research may shed some light on the nature of these contacts. The contacts are so precise, one sedimentary rock type immediately follows a different type, often with a knife-edge contact. This should cause any observer to wonder how depositional conditions could have changed so rapidly. Wouldn't there have been a gradational change between one formation and the next, especially if it took long ages? Certainly, some rock layer types do grade into the next. For example, sandstone may grade into a sandy limestone, and then into a limestone, etc., but often the contact between sandstone and limestone is abrupt. What could cause this? The answer may partially lie in Catastrophic Plate Tectonics, for the parameters are in place for things to happen rapidly during this tumultuous time.[23]

Continental plates, consisting primarily of granite and its sedimentary derivatives, have a different density than oceanic plates, which have a more dense basaltic makeup. As the plates shifted during the Flood year, earth's center of gravity was changing. This has striking implications. The action of a rotating sphere like planet earth can be mathematically described by a set of sophisticated equations called Euler's equations. From them, we can reliably predict what would have happened.

The same equations govern the workings of a spinning top or gyroscope. Its spin is stable until some force or added weight nudges it out of equilibrium. Then it may wobble off center until it restabilizes. If it gets far out of balance, it begins to gyrate violently. It might even flip its rotating axis. After a few wild gyrations, things calm down and return to normal.

The earth spinning on its axis can be compared to a spinning top. A sphere spins stably around its axis unless the center of gravity changes. If a spinning top is "nudged," it gyrates wildly until equilibrium is reestablished. During the Flood, the shifting continents would have temporarily destabilized earth, leading to "instantly" changing wave directions and velocities, each changing bring different sediment and fossil content. This partially accounts for abrupt changes in strata.

The whitish Coconino Sandstone, thought by uniformitarians to be solidified desert sand dunes, here overlies the reddish Hermit Shale, a "deltaic" deposit dated as 20 million years older. If the delta was uplifted to host a desert, it would have undergone extensive erosion, but the flatness of contact between the strata belies this interpretation.

SURFACE FEATURES REQUIRE RAPID DEPOSITION

A growing number of geologists now accept that catastrophic processes are necessary for the deposition of nearly all rock types. Only a short time may have been needed to form each bed of sediments that eventually hardened into sedimentary rock. But how much time elapsed between the deposition of one bed and the deposition of an overlying bed? One clue is that the various features present on the top surface of each bed (either soft sediments or hardened sedimentary rock) would not last very long if exposed to the elements. These features had to be covered rather quickly, before they had a chance to erode or be destroyed.

One very common feature is the presence of ripple marks, which form as water moves over a surface. These can frequently be seen on a beach after the tide has receded, and can also be seen on the ocean bottom where a particular current direction dominates. Animal tracks are also common. In any case, these surface features, which had to be formed in soft sediment, are very fragile, and if present on any surface—whether soft unconsolidated material or hard rock—will not last very long.

Keep in mind that almost every sedimentary rock layer was deposited by moving water. Every geologist agrees with this. Unless erosion dominates locally, sediments normally accumulate on an ocean bottom, lakebed, delta, lagoon, stream bank, etc. If subsequent events lift the deposit up out of the water, erosion and/or non-deposition will result. But if a zone stays under water, it will continue to be subjected to water action and will either receive more sediment or be eroded. In such an active environment, ripple marks in soft sediments can be preserved only if they are quickly buried by overlying materials so that they are protected and thus have time to harden into rock.

These conditions are rarely met in a uniformitarian

Ripple marks in Grand Canyon's Hakatai Shale. Such fragile surface features could not long escape erosion, yet this rock "dates" as nearly a billion years old.

world, but ripple marks and other surface features are readily seen in many locations, "frozen" into solid rock. Sometimes several thin layers of rock are stacked on top of one another, each displaying obvious ripple marks. There must have been a continued supply of sediments, but how could all the ripple marks have been preserved? The marks in different layers may be in varied orientations, indicating that the water currents responsible for deposition shifted rapidly and erratically while deposition continued.

There is no possibility that fragile features will last if unprotected for millions of years, waiting to be re-submerged and buried and thus protected from destructive forces. We cannot determine exactly how much time passed between the deposition of two adjacent layers simply by looking at ripple marks, raindrop impressions, animal footprints, etc., but we can conclude that much less time passed than it takes for surface features to be eroded and disappear.

Since almost every layer gives demonstrable evidence of having been laid down rapidly and catastrophically, and since nearly all such catastrophic layers have surface features that were not eroded, one can reasonably conclude that the whole sequence of rocks was deposited in a short time by a dynamic, water-charged, sediment-laden event—such as the one described in Genesis 7 and 8.

The line of contact between two layers bears comment. Often it is perfectly flat—a knife-edge contact. Uniformitarian thinking might assign a long interval, even millions of years, to the time between the deposition of one layer and the next. But in any environment, even during a short time period something will mar the surface, making it uneven. It might be the activity of plants or animals, or perhaps uplift and erosion, or freezing and thawing. Precise stratigraphic contacts assure us that the hiatus between the layers was insignificant.

If the continents were rapidly splitting—continental "sprint" rather than slow, uniform continental "drift," creationists like to say—the same sort of gyrations would evidently have happened during the Flood. Shifting continents and the upwelling of vast volumes of outer core and mantle material via the rupturing "fountains of the great deep" would have caused rotational instability in earth's "gyroscope," abruptly altering its rotation at the very time sediments were being deposited. This would cause sedimentary patterns to shift dramatically. A wobble or flip-flop of this huge gyroscope would generate large-scale, directional currents of water over the continents that were able to transport and deposit the vast quantity of sediments seen in the stratigraphic record. A different current direction would suddenly dominate in a particular location with a different sediment source. We can envision how sedimentary conditions and their products could have immediately changed, producing sequential layers that radically differed from each other.

Earth's spinning axis is different from its magnetic axis, but such movements would affect that too, able to cause "polar wandering" and even rapid flipping of the poles. We might also suspect from this that the ride on board the Ark was a wild one. No one, even the occupants of the well-designed Ark of Noah, could have survived without God's direct supernatural aid.

FOSSILS

Just as the rocks and rock types testify to the six-day creation and worldwide Flood, the fossils they contain are remains of God-created plants and animals, usually buried by dynamic water deposition. First, it is good to remember that every fossil type—from molds and casts, to silicified and calcified fossils, to coal—requires rapid burial away from scavengers, bacterial action, and oxygen to be preserved. Organic materials decay rapidly and are an essential part of the food supply for many other animals. Within a few weeks of death (or, at the most, years in special cases) most plant or animal remains are gone. Yet fossil remains are abundant and extensive, some showing exquisite detail of preservation. Often, fossils show signs that the creatures died in

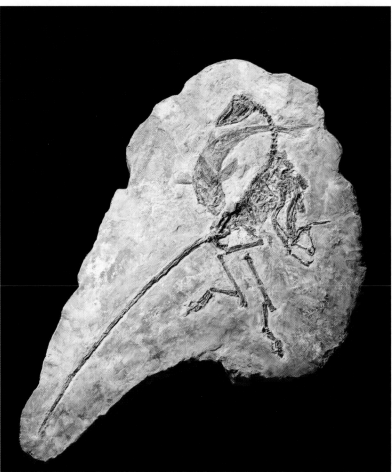

A crow-size dinosaur in the throes of death, suffocating while being rapidly buried in sediments.

agony, being asphyxiated or buried alive.

Students are incessantly taught that when an animal dies, it lies on the ground or at the bottom of the sea for long ages until sediment covers and then fossilizes it as the sediments slowly harden into rock. Tectonic forces eventually lift the now fossil-bearing layer up where erosion exposes the fossil. This oft-repeated and published "story" has just as often been refuted. Left to the ravages of nature, dead plants or animals do not normally fossilize. How many dead animals beside the highway remain after a week or two? Of the animals that died in recent floods or tsunamis and were swept into the ocean, how many escaped being eaten by scavengers? The answer, as we all know, is zero. Why, then, must each generation of students be indoctrinated with this "scientific fairy tale"?

Often uniformitarians claim to be able to divine the lives and habits of a fossilized creature from the depositional environment and other fossils from the area in which it is found. But we must remember that the fossils aren't necessarily found where the plant or animal

The Message of the Fossil Record

1. Sudden appearance of basic types
2. Basic types show stasis
3. Complexity at the start
4. Extinction, not evolution
5. No ancestor / descendant relationships
6. The fossil record is complete
7. All phyla present at the start
8. Many fossils found throughout the column
9. Most fossils are marine invertebrates
10. Fossils found in catastrophic deposits
11. Indications of violent death
12. No complete ecosystem
13. Animals and plants from mixed habitats
14. Fossils found mostly on continents

lived. The fossil bed is not a snapshot of life. It's not even the place of death, in many cases. No life habitat is preserved. Usually, no adequate food supply is nearby. Instead, a fossil is found in the place to which it was transported by moving water, and buried in the sediments also carried along by the water. Many times, fossils from vastly different environments are found jumbled together, from sea and land, from swamp and mountain, marine invertebrate and land mammal.

Thus, the fossil location is not a slice of life; it is, instead, a fossil graveyard—a place of violent death and burial.

The fossil record certainly doesn't point toward evolution, documenting the steady transformation of some organism into another type through uniform transi-

tions, but it does indicate that each basic type appeared abruptly, without the needed "missing links." Once a type appeared, it remained that type—no evolutionary changes. There is variety, but no new types. Each type was complex at the start, not simple as would be expected by evolution. If something was ever alive, it was complex. No ancestral lineage can be traced, and there is no use looking for needed missing forms, for the fossil record is rich and complete. Myriads of fossils have been discovered and the missing links are still missing.

According to the evolutionary timetable, all basic body styles appeared abruptly at the "Cambrian explosion" of life in the Cambrian Period, near the bottom of the fossil-bearing geologic column. Each basic phylum sprang into existence without known ancestors. Fossil types found throughout the geologic column by and large don't undergo change, they exhibit "stasis." They stay the same; they don't evolve. Almost all fossils are marine invertebrates, just like they should be if the great Flood was responsible for depositing them. And these marine fossils are found inland.[24]

Some fossils give ready evidence of catastrophic deposition. Great fossil graveyards containing billions of fossils are spread across the globe. It takes such unusual conditions to bury and preserve any living remains; surely, huge deposits indicating quick burial directly speak to flood conditions.

Think of the Morrison Formation of the American West, containing innumerable dinosaur remains ripped apart and quickly buried in a slurry of mud and volcanic ash. The dinosaurs appear to have lived in varied habitats, from swamp to coastal. The fossilized plant remains, however, came from a much wider range, from lowland to mountains. Mixed in with the terrestrial dinosaurs are aquatic reptiles, fish of numerous types, sharks, crocodiles, clams—clearly marine fauna. This layer covers an extensive geographic region. Uniformitarians recognize water was involved in the burial, but assign it to river flooding and meandering. A terrestrial river flood might bury land animals and freshwater fish, but would it also entrap large marine reptiles, fish, etc.? Major, catastrophic flooding of the continents by ocean water better explains the data.

Similarly, marine shellfish often give evidence of having been buried alive in the sediments so deeply they couldn't burrow out. For instance, clams, which normally live underwater and burrow in sediments, are found clumped in great quantities, which is not normal for living clams. The fossils typically retain both halves of their protective shells—tightly closed. They are not in living pose, they are in self-protective pose. Perhaps some dynamic tsunami plucked them from their home on a shallow sea bottom and transported them in vast quantities to another location, where it buried them too deeply and tightly packed for them to escape.

Dinosaur fossils usually consist of just one partial bone, but whenever enough of the carcass remains to reconstruct conditions of death, we can discern the individual animals died by asphyxiation, probably from drowning, with their heads arched back, gasping for air. Paleontologists point out that "all" the rather complete dinosaurs that retain any posture at all died this way. *Archaeopteryx* fossils exhibit this same death pose, too, but how could flying creatures get trapped in mud accumulating so rapidly that they suffocated? They didn't die and then have their fragile bodies trapped in mud; they were very much alive, struggling to survive, and yet were asphyxiated by the mud rapidly accumulating around them.

Over 95 percent of fossils are marine organisms, and they are typically buried in catastrophic deposits on the continents. Conversely, there are essentially no marine fossils buried in a marine setting. They are all buried on land. Normally, when an animal dies in the ocean, it is quickly eaten by scavengers or it decays; seldom does

WERE ANY HUMAN REMAINS FOSSILIZED WHEN THE *TITANIC* SANK?

When the luxury ocean liner the *RMS Titanic* collided with an iceberg in 1912 and sank, it carried 1,517 of its crew and passengers to their watery graves. Rescue crews found numerous bodies floating on the sea, but many more were trapped underwater.

In 1985, the ship was discovered and extensively scoured by remote cameras and submersibles for articles left behind. Thousands of dinner plates and articles of jewelry were recovered, but what of the bodies? None—absolutely none—of the human remains had survived the mere 73 years since the sinking. Even clothing made of cotton or wool had disappeared. Some rubber boots or treated leather shoes remained, but that was about all. Relentless scavengers had devoured every scrap of organic tissue. These included not only sharks, but the

myriad of marine invertebrates inhabiting the ocean floor. Bacteria digested any tiny remains. Nothing can long survive an underwater environment.

Little wonder we find so few remains of the humans and terrestrial mammals that died in the Flood. Dead bodies often bloat in water and float to the surface. Fish of many kinds, not just sharks, feed on them. Any potential fossilization would happen at the ocean bottom where deposition was happening. Mammals and terrestrial animals have a very low "fossilization potential." If complete bodies can't survive the ocean's environment for 73 years, how can they survive 73 million years? Why do such fanciful "stories" survive scientific scrutiny?

When the *Titanic* sank in 1912, it carried over 1,500 people to the ocean bottom. None were preserved as fossils. Similarly, Flood-related human (and land-dwelling mammal) fossils are rare.

it simply sink to the bottom. It must be carried there by water action.

Soft Tissue in Fossils

Fossils typically consist of the altered remains of various hard parts, from wood, to shell, to bone, to teeth. Occasionally, we find the shape of various soft parts preserved by alteration into a more lasting form. But true soft, organic tissue normally decays at a fast rate, in any environment. The rate at which it decays is measurable, and decay happens rapidly. Even under favorable but exotic laboratory preservation conditions, organic tissue is observed to decay quickly. No known natural environment will allow any tissue to last for an excessively long time. Yet such tissue, even dinosaur soft tissue, has occasionally been found.

A remarkable discovery of dinosaur soft tissue was made recently by Dr. Mary Schweitzer. The discovery was made quite by accident when a large dinosaur bone, supposedly 68 million years old, was sawed open. Inside, after acid had been employed to remove the rock casing, soft and stretchy blood vessels and blood cells were exposed. This seems to demonstrate that the bone had relatively recently been alive, although this was not claimed by Schweitzer, who simply presented the evidence. How could organic remains exist after any significant length of time? A frantic attempt was launched by uniformitarians to refute the implications, so great is their commitment to uniform processes and long ages. Real academic persecution ensued from evolutionary zealots. Eventually, Schweitzer's claims were duplicated and validated, and reluctantly accepted.

Once this vanguard instance of soft tissue preservation had been acknowledged, other researchers came forward and revealed their own similar findings, which had not been reported because of bias and fear of opposition. Now the list of reports of soft tissue in "ancient" fossils is long and is rapidly growing. Evidently, either the fossils are not so old, or they were buried under extraordinary conditions…or both.

FOSSIL ANALYSES WITH VERIFIED ORIGINAL SOFT TISSUES

	Publication Date	Brief Description	Evolutionary Age	Publication
			Articles Published in Peer-Reviewed Journals	
1	5/30/1977	Catfish fatty fin in Green River	50MY	H. P. Buchheim and R. C. Surdam, *Geology*, 5: 198.
2	6/14/1992	Osteocalcin in a seismosaur bone	150MY	Muyzer, G. et al, *Geology*, 20: 871-874.
3	9/25/1992	DNA in amber	30MY	Morell, V. et al, *Science*, 257: 1860.
4	6/16/1994	Unaltered amino acids in amber insects	130 MY	Bada, J. L. et al, *Geochemica et Cosmochemica Acta,* 58 (14): 3131-3135.
5	6/16/1994	Dinosaur DNA from hadrosaur bone	65MY	Woodward, S. R., N. J. Weyand and M. Bunnell, *Science*, 266 (5188): 1229-1232.
6	5/19/1995	Live bacteria spores from amber	25-40MY	Cano, R. J. and M. K. Borucki, *Science,* 268 (5213): 1060 - 1064.
7	6/10/1997	Hemoglobin fragments in *T. rex* bone	67MY	Schweitzer, M. et al, *PNAS*, 94 (12): 6291-6296.
8	6/2/1999	Live bacteria from halite deposit	250MY	Vreeland, R. H. et al, American Society for Microbiology, 99th General Meeting, June 2, 1999, Chicago.
9	6/21/1999	Live bacteria from separate rock salts	250MY	Stan-Lotter, H. et al, *Microbiology*, 145 (12): 3565-3574.
10	6/21/1999	Ichthyosaur skin	190MY	Linghan-Soliar, T. et al, *Proc. Royal Soc. B*, 266 (1436): 2367-2373.
11	6/21/1999	Keratin in Madagascar Cretaceous bird	65MY	Schweitzer, M. H. et al, *J. Vert. Paleo*, 19 (4): 712-722 .
12	9/1/2001	*T. rex* collagen SEM scans	65MY	Armitage, M., *Creation Research Society Quarterly*, 38 (2): 61-66.
13	6/26/2004	Live (non-spore) bacteria in amber	120MY	Greenblatt, C. L. et al, *Microbial Ecology*, 48 (1): 120-127.
14	3/24/2005	*T. rex* soft tissue	68MY	Schweitzer, M. et al, *Science*, 307: 1952-1955.
15	7/25/2006	Soft frog, intact	10MY	McNamara, M. et al, *Geology*, 34: 641-644.
16	6/30/2007	*T. rex* collagen	68MY	Scweitzer, M. et al, *Science*, 316: 277-280
17	8/1/2007	Bloody frog bone marrow	10MY	McNamara, M.E. et al, *Geology*, 34 (8): 641-644.
18	4/7/2008	*Psittacosaurus* skin	125MY	Linghan-Soliar, T. et al, *Proc. Royal Soc. B*, 275: 775-780.
19	7/8/2008	Feather melanocytes	100MY	Vinther, J. et al, *Biology Letters*, 4: 522-525.
20	4/30/2009	Hadrosaur blood vessels	80MY	Schweitzer, M. et al, *Science*, 324 (5927): 626-631.
21	8/26/2009	Purple Messel feather nanostructure	40MY	Vinther, J. et al, *Biology Letters*, 6 (1): 128-131.
22	5/19/2009	Primate "Ida" soft body outline	40MY	Franzen, J. L. et al, *PLoS ONE*, 4 (5): e5723.
23	7/1/2009	Hadrosaur skin cell structures	66MY	Manning, P. et al, *Proc. Royal Soc. B,* 276: 3429-3437.
24	10/2/2009	Fungal chitin ubiquitous in Permo-triassic	250MY	Jin, Y. G. et al, *Science*, 289 (5478): 432-436.
25	8/18/2009	Squid ink	150MY	Whilby, P. R. et al, *Geology Today*, 24 (3): 95-98.
26	11/5/2009	Salamander muscle, whole	18MY	McNamara, M. et al, *Proc. Royal Soc. B,* 277 (1680): 423-427.
27	2/25/2010	*Sinosauropteryx* melanosomes	125MY	Zhang, F. et al, *Nature*, 463: 1075-1078.
28	3/10/2010	*Psittacosaurus* skin color	125MY	Linghan-Soliar, T. G. and Plodowski, *Naturwissenschaften*, 97: 479-486. (Same sample analyzed in *Proc. Royal Soc. B*, 275: 775-780.)
29	5/14/2010	Mammal hair in amber	100MY	Vullo, R., *Naturwissenschaften*, 97 (7): 683-687.
30	5/18/2010	*Archaeopteryx* original tissue	150MY	Bergmann, U., *PNAS*, 107 (20): 9060-9065.
31	8/9/2010	Mosasaur blood, retina	65-68MY	Lindgren, J., *PLoS ONE*. 5(8): e11998.
32	11/12/2010	Penguin feathers	36MY	Clarke, J. A. et al, *Science*, 330: 954-957.
33	11/18/2010	Shrimp shell and muscle	360MY	Feldman, R. M. and C. E. Schweitzer, *J. Crustacean Biology*, 30 (4): 629-635.
34	2/7/2011	Chitin and chitin-associated protein	417MY	Cody, G. D. et al, *Geology*, 39 (3): 255-258.
35	4/1/2011	C-14 date of mosasaur (24,600 Yrs)	70MY	Lindgren, J. et al, *PLoS ONE*, 6 (4): e19445.
36	3/23/2011	Lizard tail skin, Green River	40MY	Edwards, N. P. et al, *Proc Royal Soc B*, online.
37	6/8/2011	Type I Collagen, *T. rex* and hadrosaur	68MY	San Antonio, J. D. et al, *PLoS ONE*, 6 (6): e20381.
38	6/30/2011	Bird feather pigment	120MY	Wogelius, R. A. et al, *Science*, online.
			Preliminary Reports Published Elsewhere	
39	8/10/2009	Live yeast in amber	45MY	*Wired Science*
40	4/10/2010	*Australopithecus sediba* brains	1.9MY	*Discovery News*
41	9/27/2010	Lobster shell	"millions"	*Keighley News*
42	10/22/2010	Mosasaur cartilage	80MY	Buchholz, C. C., *Rapid City Journal*

Table 1. Published Reports of Original Soft Tissue Fossils
Papers that were excluded from the list include those with dubious verbiage, especially those which discussed "soft tissues" but failed to specify whether or not the tissues were "original" or chemically altered to a more resistant material. Those papers which specified the latter were also excluded, to the best of the author's ability to discern. The chart demonstrates that a multitude of verified original soft tissue "clocks" have set maximum ages of thousands of years to samples which had all been assigned ages of millions of years.

SIGNIFICANT CHALLENGES TO UNIFORMITARIAN THINKING

Numerous rock types are thought to demonstrate uniformitarian conditions, and associated "millions and millions of years" stories are frequently used to reinforce long-age uniformitarian thinking. However, catastrophic/global Flood thinking usually does a better job of explaining even these pieces of evidence. Just as the various rock categories imply conditions for their formation quite different from modern processes (i.e., uniform conditions), so individual rock layers often require past environments and/or events quite different from those we experience. The partial listing below will illustrate this point.

Salt Deposits

As we all know, seawater contains salt. When seawater evaporates, thin films of salt minerals are left behind, including gypsum, anhydrite, and common table salt, or halite. Today, extensive layers of salt are found of great thickness and covering wide geographic areas. Considered by uniformitarianism to be solely due to evaporation of seawater, can these major geologic deposits be better understood within a global flood context?

The standard interpretative story is that salt layers imply long ages in which salty water repeatedly became trapped in lagoons and then evaporated, leaving the salt behind. Over great ages of repeated fillings and dryings, the salt minerals supposedly built up into thick and wide deposits of pure salt. But today's salt deposits that are known to be from evaporating seawater abound with impurities, and are quite different from major salt deposits in the geologic record. Modern salt deposits are observed to be thin and heavily contaminated with other minerals, wind-blown dust, plant fragments, etc. Conversely, the world's great salt layers are relatively free of contaminants, ready for use on roads, or easily cleanable and appropriate for human consumption.

Furthermore, salt beds of the past often cover immense areas. One salt bed from New York to Ohio covers an estimated 600,000 square miles and is hundreds of feet thick. How many times must an enclosed basin have been filled and then evaporated to produce such volumes of salt? A similar question arises regarding the extensive salt layer underlying the Mediterranean Sea.

Geologists admit there are essentially no modern counterparts to these ancient environments. Modern-day saltwater springs observed on the floor of the Red Sea might be a possible analogous source for salt, but these deposits are local in their extent. The scale of past events dwarfs those of the present.[25]

Can the evaporation model, or any model constrained by uniformitarian thinking, explain the great volumes of relatively pure salt, without other sediments, chemicals, organisms, etc.? There must be a more satisfying story to tell. Surely, something very different happened in the past, something of great lateral extent and of great geologic potential—maybe something like a worldwide flood.

Creationists have proposed a hydrothermal model for salt bed origin, with immense volumes of super-saturated, hot brines extruded into the cold ocean from below during the Flood.[26] Some have speculated that salt volcanoes may have operated that intermittently "erupted" hot salt brines into the cold ocean, where salt precipitated out into layers. There is no comparable modern analog for this, either, but at least it responds to the data. The Bible clearly sets the stage for something like this to happen. During the great Flood of Noah's day, "all the fountains of the great deep [were] broken up" (Genesis 7:11), spewing hot liquids into the deep oceans. This no doubt included magma, but perhaps also hot water containing dissolved chemicals, including salt-saturated brines. These superheated, super-saturated waters would have lost their ability to retain their load when they encountered the cooler oceans, resulting in great layers of precipitated salts. There would be little opportunity for contaminants to enter. Today, only the layers of salt remain. They could better be termed precipitates rather than evaporites.

Buried Coral Reefs

Another favorite uniformitarian challenge to global Flood catastrophism is the frequent occurrence of underground reef-like formations interspersed among the geologic strata. Today, "living" coral reefs are well-studied. Marine invertebrates such as corals and clams often live in underwater communities. When they die, they leave behind their hard parts, consisting primarily of calcium carbonate, which are cemented by microorganisms into the reef complex. Reefs typically grow slowly. So-called fossil reefs are often associated with commercial oil deposits. Applying uniformitarianism

DID MODERN COAL SEAMS FORM IN A PEAT SWAMP?

Most geologists are trained to think from an uniformitarian perspective that present uniform processes operating throughout the past account for all present rock units. This concept considers coal to be the altered remains of plant material accumulated in a peat swamp. Would the peat we observe accumulating in modern peat swamps make a good coal?

Today's peat swamps sport extensive vegetation growing in shallow water or on saturated high ground. Nowhere can laterally extensive flat surfaces be found in a swamp. The decaying organic material collects in the stagnant, acidic water and takes on a rather "coffee grounds"-like texture with the wood and bark quite decayed, thoroughly penetrated by roots and animal burrows.

Let's compare this with a typical coal found in the geologic record. Modern coal seams usually show an extremely regular geometry. Often, a knife-edge contact between the coal and the layers above and below can be seen. Most often the adjacent layers are shale or limestone, both "marine" deposits that necessitate environments of deposition quite different from a terrestrial swamp. In uniformitarian thinking, this involves repeated downwarping and subsequent uplift.

The coal matrix is typically very fine-grain, but surrounds abundant sheets of altered bark, recognizably different from the rest, giving coal a layered look. Seldom are roots present. Thin "clay partings" are almost always seen within the coal, often laterally extensive. They can be traced and correlated—some for miles. The seams are usually of rather constant thickness, and the now-flat bark sheets are consistent with the width and height of a tree. Although some variation does exist in all these parameters, coal appears different from a modern swamp peat, except for its high organic make-up.

The accompanying photograph shows two coal seams visible in a road cut near Price, Utah. Observe the sharp contacts between the coal and the adjacent layers. If a swamp existed above sea level, but then was inundated by the sea to receive overlying marine sediments, then uplifted to become a swamp again, and the cycle repeated, wouldn't there be some erosional channels or variation in peat thickness? How could the seams be so flat and of constant thickness, and how could there be such precise contacts above and below?

The creation model calls for extensive pre-Flood vegetation mats ripped up by floodwaters and then floating on the open Flood ocean, decaying and collecting on the submerged continental shelf as peat layers. Heat turned it into coal. Modern-day peats do not seem to be of the same character as modern-day coals. Perhaps the creation model of decaying plant material collecting under a large floating mat of vegetation during the Flood can account for coal. The great Flood of Noah's day provides a better explanation.

If coal is metamorphosed peat that formed in a swamp, as taught by uniformitarians, it should have uneven surfaces. But coal seams often exhibit flat surfaces and other features incompatible with a peat swamp origin.

leads to the conclusion that long times were required for the growth of large fossil reefs. However, there is a good creationist response to this challenge.

First, we should note that "reefs" found within the geologic strata are typically much smaller than and quite different from modern reefs. The "foreset" and "backset" slopes are interpretive, and really only appear as reef geometry on maps with exaggerated vertical scale. Furthermore, usually only small, broken fragments of reef-forming organisms are found detached from one another and yet bound together in a limey matrix, comprising a structure not organically bound as it is in a living reef.

Next, we should note that the growth rate of modern corals is extremely variable, with documented cases of rapid and extensive growth under conditions of abundant nutrition and protection from storms. Cases of enhanced growth are known around recent structures, such as when a mature reef surrounds a sunken ship. The size of the resultant reefs might point to growth rates many orders of magnitude greater than normal growth rates today in a stable reef. The quick-growing "new" reef appears to have grown to match its environment. Similarly, some reefs are dominated by algae, and given unusual, nutrient-rich conditions, an algal bloom can cause the volume of alga to continue to double in short order. We can surmise that the great floodwaters would have been extremely rich in necessary nutrients.

A better interpretation for ancient reefs might be that reef-forming organisms growing before the Flood were dislodged from their habitat, transported by moving water, and deposited with other sediments when conditions were right.

Stalagmites and Stalactites

Caves of all sizes can be found around the world. Guides, who often have little scientific training, are all too willing to point out stalactites clinging to a cave's roof and stalagmites built up from its floor. They are expected to merely pass on the standard uniformitarian thinking to their guests. Stories of "millions and millions of years" are oft repeated. In fact, many will testify that visitors expect to be amazed by the stories of long ages. They would feel cheated if such tales were missing or altered.

Again, uniformitarian thinking dominates, while facts

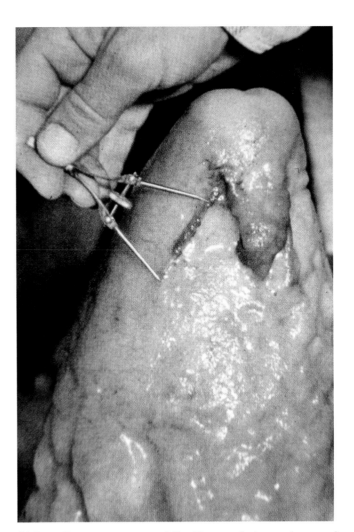

Stalagmites can grow rapidly. Here, a bat was encased within the rock before it could decay.

are minimized. In the standard view, cave features grow slowly, thus the stories perpetuate. Caves, being underground, usually have lots of groundwater seeping through the rock, having percolated down from rainwater above. Most caves have formed in limestone, made primarily of calcium carbonate, which is easily dissolved by slightly acidic water. The cave itself is etched within sedimentary rock, leaving an underground opening and allowing mineral-laden water to drip down from above or be transported through.

In the open cave, the water sometimes evaporates, leaving small amounts of dissolved minerals behind. At present, significant time is usually required to build up any appreciable quantities, but what if rates and conditions were different in the past? What if acidity was higher, or the temperature of the water or air was different, or the rock more easily dissolved? Uniformity of these and other possible conditions is assumed, and is indeed crucial to the calculation of time required. But, cave owners can frequently point to a feature in their

Silicified wood in the Petrified Forest in Arizona. More appropriately termed a petrified log jam, this area could not represent a once-standing forest. None of the trees show a root system, and all the bark has been abraded off.

cave that has formed rapidly, even during their own tenure. Uniformity doesn't always hold, even in the present. And conditions change as often as the weather changes, implying that any set of parameters cannot last long enough to build up large cave formations.

Petrified Wood

From roadside curio shops to classrooms nationwide, we learn of petrified wood being formed over the customary "millions and millions of years." It is true that petrified wood samples are found in strata dated by uniformitarianism as millions of years old, but are the layers really so old and does it take long ages to petrify wood?

As a matter of fact, wood can petrify quickly. Several

An upright stump in the Petrified Forest in Yellowstone National Park. The series of layers were rafted in by a series of mudflows. The tree ring patterns match between the layers. The layers do not represent separate standing forests.

patents have even been granted for ways to petrify wood artificially, even commercially. Wood normally petrifies when hot, silica-rich water is injected into it, filling up the pore space between individual cells, isolating them from decay and bacterial action. Silica when solidified becomes quite hard, thus the wood "turns" to stone. The injection can happen quickly by artificial or natural means, as long as the conditions are met.

Silica-rich water develops primarily in places where volcanic deposits cover the ground. Volcanic ash includes various clays that are loaded with silica. Rainwater releases the silica from the clay and then dissolves it. Deeply buried wood is naturally subjected to overburden pressure that is able to emplace the silica-containing groundwater inside the wood.

Alternatively, wood can petrify more slowly as it decays. Mineral-rich water removes decayed cell remnants, leaving tiny empty spaces into which silica or other minerals settle. Eventually, the entire specimen is replaced. Different parts of the tree decay at different rates, while water content and color may change season by season. This often preserves the tree ring structure. This, too, can happen rapidly, even while the tree still lives. Sometimes the death of the tree is by petrifaction, as silica replaces and surrounds the living cells in the roots, thereby halting organic activity.

Out-of-Order Strata

The geologic column illustrates conventional thinking regarding the passage of time throughout the ages as represented by the strata. While creationists reject the dates and question some of the interpretations of the column, it does represent reality in a relative sense. For instance, in general, wherever Ordovician and Cambrian strata are present in the same geographic location, the Ordovician strata will overlie the Cambrian. But this is not always the case. Sometimes the normal order is reversed. Geologists usually explain such reversed order as the result of one layer being thrust over the other, or overthrusting.

Radioisotope dating seldom comes into play in dating sedimentary rock, because the rock has been eroded from some other rock and then transported and redeposited. Obviously, the sediments are "contaminated" and not useful for dating. Assignment of a stratum's age and thus where it fits in the column is primarily a function of its fossil content, with the "age" assumed

NIAGARA FALLS

The formation of Niagara Falls provides a good comparison of uniformitarian vs. catastrophic thinking. Charles Lyell, in early attempts to defend and shore up his proposal of uniformitarianism and great ages, used Niagara Falls as a centerpiece. The falls are on the Niagara River, where outflow from Lake Erie travels downriver for seven miles before emptying into Lake Ontario. Nearer Lake Erie, the river flows over the Niagara escarpment, where it forms the Canadian and American falls. Headward erosion has caused the falls to move upriver to its present location, leaving the gouged-out Niagara Gorge behind, about seven miles (or over 35,000 feet) long.

The lip of the falls is rather hard limestone, while the shale underneath erodes easily, undercutting the limestone cap rock. Early farmers had watched the falls move upriver for years. They claimed it retreated at about five feet per year. Thus, at present rates it would have taken about 7,000 years (a biblically compatible age) to carve the gorge. But Lyell needed a slower rate to claim the gorge was much older. So, even though observations contradicted him, he claimed it was eroding at only one foot per year and thus had taken 35,000 years to carve. In his mind, and in the mind of many readers, Niagara Falls proved the Bible wrong. But it was Lyell and his calculation that were wrong, based on a wrong assumption of the erosion rate.

Heart Mountain in Wyoming. The strata here are upside down, with the older layers on top of the younger. The older are interpreted to have slid rapidly into place from miles away.

from evolution's timetable. While creationists of earlier decades felt that a sediment sequence found in the "reversed" order was an artifact of the Flood's idiosyncrasies—with fossils of varied "ages" being deposited by sedimentary considerations, not through evolutionary development—more complete knowledge (including data gathered from thousands of oil wells) has demonstrated that the strata really are overthrust in places. Over the years, they have been the subject of much research, with some of the very best research having been done by creationists.

Some of the overthrust sheets are of great thickness and extent, and have evidently been transported and/or raised quite a distance. How can they be moved? Strict uniformitarian thinking has handled the problem poorly, and in recent years dynamic catastrophic conditions have been suggested as moving agents. A currently accepted "uniformitarian" theory explaining the Heart Mountain overthrust in Wyoming (similar to many such out-of-order sequences) calls for an extensive thrust sheet to have slid "older" Paleozoic strata over "younger" Tertiary strata for scores of miles over nearly flat terrain at speeds approaching 60 miles an hour!

But rock sheets of this large size are too weak to be either pushed or pulled. How could this be done? The theory that seems best to explain the evidence involves simultaneous tectonic shaking, uplift, and rapid sliding by gravity—a mega-quake coupled with internal pore pressure lubricating the slide surface. On this point of mighty forces and quick times, creationists/catastrophists tend to agree. Details could be quibbled over, but surely overthrusting required dynamic forces to accomplish.

In Glacier National Park, the overthrust block was supposedly already 900 million years old at the time of sliding, according to uniformitarian thinking, and should have been quite hard and brittle. There should be an extensive layer of broken debris at the slide contact, even if lubricated. But upon inspection, the rubble layer is rather thin. A better interpretation would note that one or both of the layers may have been unconsolidated and still saturated when moved, thereby reducing friction and providing a lubricant. This would probably have taken place late in the Flood year, as the continents were being uplifted and the strata were still soft. Tectonic episodes would have been frequent and intense, and the freshly deposited strata would still have been saturated and pliable. Only catastrophism over short timeframes can satisfy the requirements and allow the thrust to produce the structures we see.

THE GLOBAL FLOOD

In Glacier National Park, older Precambrian strata are thrust over younger Cretaceous strata. While the rocks fossils seem "out of order" at first glance, they have been relocated from their prior "proper" location. This overthrusting should have resulted in a zone of broken and ground-up rock, but little is present. The forces required were intense, related to catastrophic plate tectonics. Only an event like the great Flood could have accomplished it.

Catastrophic Deposition of Mega-breccias

Sometimes we find sedimentary deposits containing large cobbles or boulders known as "clasts," broken pieces of some other rock that have somehow been transported to their present location. To transport sand grains requires moving water—the larger the grain, the more rapid the water implied. But what do we make of the very large clasts found in the geologic record? Some individual clasts have areas measured in square miles. How did they get there?

There are several known mechanisms to move large rocks, some intuitive and some surprising, but all require at least a local, energetic, non-uniform event. One way is by turbidity currents, known primarily from a famous historical example. In 1929, sediment on the underwater continental slope off Grand Banks, Newfoundland, became unstable and slid downhill over a slope of less than three degrees. The saturated sediment avalanched down at initial speeds of at least 60 miles per hour. The sediment was suspended in the turbulent flow and prevented from settling. We know the speed because there were numerous telephone cables crossing the Atlantic in those days that were timed as each one broke. Before the slide was over, it had extended out

430 miles and deposited a thin sedimentary bed two to three feet thick over 40,000 square miles.

No one really knew exactly what happened because it was underwater and out of sight, but decades later, when submarines and underwater cameras were able to venture there, geologists were able to plot the size and character of the deposit. They labeled this new type of deposit a "turbidite," one formed by turbulent waters. Much to their surprise, the new turbidite had exactly the same features as many known deposits in the Appalachian Mountains that had previously been interpreted as products of slow and gradual deposition. Eventually, the new concept forced reinterpretation of up to 30 percent of the sedimentary deposits on land as turbidites, and more are being reinterpreted all the time. The new science of catastrophism had blossomed.

Very large clasts, up to 40 inches in diameter and weighing thousands of pounds, are known to exist in some turbidite deposits. If large boulders are movable with the local catastrophes of today, what would be the result of the much greater, continental-scale catastrophes associated with the global Flood?

Mega-breccias are defined as sedimentary deposits containing conspicuous angular fragments of rock in excess of one meter in diameter. They can be produced not only by turbidites, but also debris flows and gravity slumps. In the Death Valley area in California, some of the clasts are up to five miles by 30 miles. These are noted in sediments considered by creationists to be due to the initial bursts of Flood activity, as the "fountains of the great deep" broke open. The past of our planet has been catastrophic, indeed.

Huge blocks were moved intact by major forces that no longer operate on earth.

ASTROBLEMES

Planet earth has often been visited by encounters from outer space—not alien invaders, but meteorites and comets. These normally bring in only tiny amounts of ice and exotic rocks and minerals, but large impacts in the past exploded onto earth with the energy equivalent of multiplied nuclear blasts. We have all seen photographs of the major impact crater in Arizona, Barringer Crater, but other craters are much bigger, too big to be seen from the planet's surface. They can only be recognized from high altitude. Still others can only be inferred by remote sensing of strata far underground. The accompanying chart lists several big ones, showing their size. One thing we can surely say is that God has at His disposal numerous powerful tools to bring about His will on earth.

Creationists suppose that numerous such impacts must have affected earth during the great Flood, adding to

its horror. Think of the tsunamis generated by large bodies of rock hurtling through space at great speeds and crashing into the ocean. Perhaps the earth passed through an asteroid belt or a dirty patch of space and was bombarded throughout the Flood year. Such impacts may have been the trigger that started the Flood and the breakup of the fountains of the great deep. Most of these impacts would have landed in the ocean and left no visible trace, but others left their mark, particularly as the floodwaters retreated and the continents were exposed.

RADIOISOTOPE DATING

Perhaps the most convincing argument for an old earth involves radioisotope dating. Utilizing the fact that certain elements are radioactive—spontaneously decaying from one atom to another at measureable rates (such as radioactive uranium atoms decaying into stable lead atoms)—uniformitarians claim the time of origin of certain rocks can be dated. Several different atoms that decay by several different nuclear decay paths are used for dating. For instance, uranium 238 decays through a chain of daughter elements into lead 206 by alpha and beta decays, in which radioactive alpha particles consisting of two protons and two neutrons (equivalent to a helium nucleus) or beta particles (consisting of electrons) are emitted.

Sedimentary rock, the kind that contains most fossils, cannot be directly dated by this method, since it consists of eroded and redeposited minerals from previous-

EARTH'S LARGEST ASTEROID IMPACT CRATERS

Name/Location	Crater Diameter (Km)	Asteroid Diameter (Km)
Ishim/Kazakhstan	350	20.8
Aredefort/South Africa	140	7.4
Sudbury/Ontario, Canada	140	7.4
Popigia/Tayrmyr, Siberia	100	5.0
Puchezh-Katunk, Russia	80	3.9
Manicouagan/Quebec, Canada	70	3.4
Siljan, Sweden	52	2.4
Kara/Nenetsia, Russia	50	2.3
Charlevoix/Quebec, Canada	46	2.1
Araguainha/Dome, Brazil	40	1.8

A listing of sub-surface impact craters that struck earth during the Flood, recognized by remote sensing.[27]

HOW DID THE VERTICAL COLUMNS AT DEVIL'S TOWER FORM?

Visitors often marvel at the beautiful columns of rock standing at places like Devil's Tower in Wyoming. There, a mountain of rock rises from the ground in a series of regular, multi-sided columns, extending 867 feet into the air. Columns seem so precise that fanciful legends have grown up around them.

These huge columns consist of once-molten igneous rock that was intruded into other sediments from below and was later covered with more sediment. As hot, molten magma cools and solidifies, it shrinks in volume and fractures along vertical planes, with volume considerations orienting the parallel fractures into five- or six-sided polygons. Hardened basalt is usually much harder than surrounding sediments, which often expose the columns when they erode.

A persistent scientific objection to the biblical doctrine of the young earth has arisen over this issue, however, claiming that the necessary cooling time for such immense volumes of basalt would take far longer than the mere thousands of years allowed in Scripture. Once again, good scientific research provides an answer, and it has to do with water.

While much heat is removed by simple conduction from the basalt to the surrounding rock or air, a surprising amount of heat is removed by water. Water is present within any magma body, and as this superheated water flashes to steam and exits the lava, it carries much heat away with it.[1] Furthermore, as rain or surface water penetrates to the hot layer, it too heats, turns to steam, and escapes, cooling the lava. Experiments and observations have shown this convection of heat to be the key. Measured rates of cooling from the surface to the interior exceed several feet per month. The vertical joints that form the distinc-

Devil's Tower in Wyoming. Melted magma cracked into polygons as it cooled and shrank. The origin of this landmark is controversial, but it probably was injected into Flood sediments. When the surrounding rock layer eroded, it was left exposed.

tive columns facilitate the migration of water in and steam out of the rock.[2]

1. Andrew A. Snelling and John Woodmorappe, 1998, The Cooling of Thick Igneous Bodies on a Young Earth, *Proceedings of the Fourth International Conference on Creationism*, R. E. Walsh, ed., Pittsburgh, PA: Creation Science Fellowship, 527-545.

2. Andrew A. Snelling, 1991, The Formation and Cooling of Dikes, *Creation Ex Nihilo Technical Journal*, 5 (1): 81–90.

ly existing rock. It no longer constitutes an original and datable specimen, though sometimes the cementing material can be dated. All radioisotope dating methods are only applicable to igneous or metamorphic rocks, those which were previously in a hot, molten condition. Cooling of the molten magma from a liquid into a solid starts the "clock" ticking at zero, according to the theory. By measuring the amounts of both the "parent" isotope and the "daughter" isotope (the amount resulting from the decay of the parent), and knowing the rate of change of parent into daughter (given in terms of the "half-life" of the element), an apparent age can be calculated. The concept is elegant. The measurements are precise, and the theory and governing equations are correct. What could go wrong?

The results are interpreted under certain overarching assumptions, and here is where the concept sometimes goes awry. First, it must be assumed that the rate of decay of radioactive isotopes has never changed at any point in the past. Second, it must be assumed no parent material, daughter material, or intermediate products have ever been added to or taken away from the specimen throughout its entire history. It must have been completely closed to the environment throughout time. Third, when the specimen was first formed, it must have had no daughter isotopes present, or the amount of daughter must be able to be determined. Only then can we be certain that when first "born," the specimen's "age" was zero. All three assumptions must be correct for the method's results to be accurate.

How could any scientist in the present be certain of things that occurred millions of years ago? All of these assumptions seem to rely on precise knowledge about the remote past. But are they true? Only if the assumptions are accurate will the calculation be meaningful. As it turns out, these assumptions have proven to be the "Achilles' heel" of radioisotope dating. Research has shown that not only are the last two assumptions often not satisfied, but the first is simply wrong.

Constant Decay Rate: The decay rate (or half-life of isotopes) has proven to be quite stable to environmental changes in the present. Many experiments have attempted to change it, from application of pressure and chemicals to bombardment by high energy particles, with minimal effect. The question is not, however, is it stable in the present, but was it stable throughout the past, before measurements could be made?

When the experts at the Institute for Creation Research and the Creation Research Society launched an eight-year joint research initiative called Radioisotopes and the Age of the Earth (RATE) to investigate this, they discovered that multiple lines of evidence show that the rates of decay had been different during episodes in the past. The scientists found signatures of greater, more energetic decay. Daughter isotopes formed much more quickly then than they do today, as seen by present concentrations of elements and decay "scars."

Accelerated decay could have been accomplished by a nearby supernova bathing the earth in cosmic radiation, or some other as yet unknown mechanism. The decay rate hinges on certain properties of matter, and the RATE scientists concluded that on certain occasions the Creator of all of nature (even atoms) must have altered the way it operates.

Creation scientists do not simply invoke miraculous explanations for solving difficult problems. They recognize and accept that nature operates in accordance with invariant natural law. But on those occasions when Scripture specifically states that the Creator/Lawgiver was acting supernaturally, we have the liberty to investigate the results. Certainly, we are told that during the creation week He was utilizing processes no longer in operation. During the great Flood, He was also operating supernaturally, perhaps using processes we would recognize, but at rates, scales, and intensities far outside today's "uniform" limits.

In a creationist understanding, the timing for the first instance of rapid formation of daughter products was during the early part of the creation week. It occurred after the initial creation of the rocks; before present-day natural law was in place, certain atoms were less stable. Atomic decay at this stage was not necessarily a bad thing, for God was still in the process of forming and shaping His creation into its ultimate "very good" form, using whatever processes He chose.

Furthermore, there are biblical hints and geological evidence that the natural parameters that govern such decay might have been again accelerated during the great Flood, for rocks deposited during the Flood contain hints of more rapid decay. The obvious conclusion was that at these two times when the Creator's supernatural power was being expressed, certain natural "constants" were temporarily changed. God the Creator and Lawgiver has the prerogative to operate outside natural law

RADIOHALOS

As uranium atoms decay into lead, they go through a series of decay steps, several of which utilize beta decay. Each step gives off a different level of energy going out in all directions, and that energy damages the crystal structure surrounding it—often biotite, a form of mica found in granite rocks. An inclusion may contain billions of atoms, each of which contributes to the damage when it decays. The end result is a series of concentric spheres surrounding the cluster. These are seen as a series of concentric circles on a planar sheet of mica. Each element in the decay chain has its own characteristic halo diameter.

While uranium 238 (U-238) has an extremely long half-life (4.51 billion years), some of the intermediate steps proceed quite quickly. Polonium (Po) isotopes are especially unstable, decaying with half-lives from days to microseconds. A complete Po sphere would not take long to form. Yet a granite melt requires time to solidify and will not record a halo unless hard. Sometimes "orphan" polonium halos are found without the parent uranium present. How could rapidly decaying isotopes be within a slow-forming crystal? Full U-238 halos are always found nearby, necessitating much radioisotope decay.

Creationists recognize these igneous rocks to have been emplaced after the Flood had deposited sedimentary layers. Following deposition of the sediments, a liquid igneous mass intruded and hardened. As part of ICR's RATE initiative, scores of granite specimens were collected from around the world and scoured for the microscopic halos. Tens of thousands were counted, from all levels of the geologic column. Note that one of the intermediate products in the decay chain is highly mobile radon gas easily moved by steam jetting from hot saturated rocks. Note also that at the center of the Po halos is an empty hole, not lead atoms.

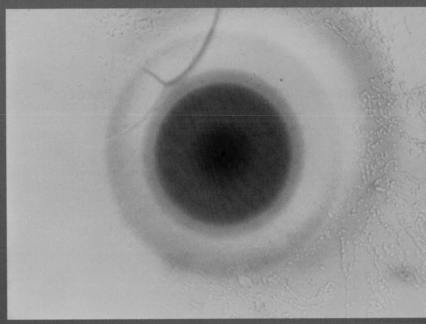

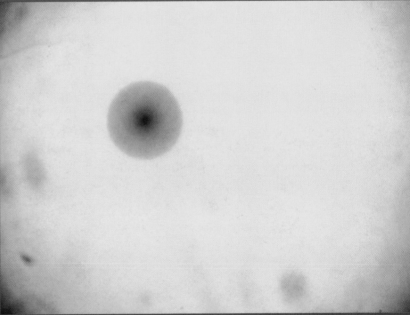

The energy released by the decay of each radioisotope is distinct from all others. It leaves a ring of discoloration in the surrounding crystal. Some rings are from extremely short-lived isotopes. They have no uniformitarian explanation.

These mutually inconsistent situations are fully impossible within uniformitarianism. The only conceivable way to explain the facts is to propose rapid movements of decaying radioactive atoms coupled with accelerated decay episodes.

LOCATION	EXPECTED	MEASURED
Hualapai basalt	200 yrs.	1.6 my
Mt. Etna basalt	2,100 yrs.	.25 my
Mt. Etna basalt	29 yrs.	.35 my
Mt. Lassen basalt	85 yrs.	.11 my
Sunset Crater basalt	950 yrs.	.27 my
Kilauea basalt	<200 yrs.	21 my
Kilauea basalt	<1,000 yrs.	3 my
Kilauea basalt	<1,000 yrs.	30 my
Kilauea Iki basalt	40 yrs.	8.5 my
Mt. Stromboli	38 yrs.	2.4 my
Hualalai basalt	200 yrs.	22.8 my
Rangitoto basalt	<800 yrs.	15 my
Mt. Erebus	17 yrs.	1.6 my
Mt. Etna basalt	37 yrs.	.7 my
Medicine Lake obsidian	<500 yrs.	12.6 my

Historical volcanos that have extruded "datable" lavas. When dated by the standard technique, all date millions of years older than their actual ages.[28]

when He desires, and the evidence indicates He has done so at least during the times specified in Scripture. The discoveries made by the RATE scientists were published in 2000 and 2005 in a two-volume technical report titled *Radioisotopes and the Age of the Earth*.

Some speculate that God allowed accelerated decay to happen at the time of the Curse, when God judged all creation because of Adam's rebellion, but this can't be rigorously supported. Genesis 3:17 does tell us, "Cursed is the ground for [Adam's] sake." But a sudden burst of radioisotope decay would have released lethal doses of radiation, and that didn't occur, according to the scriptural account. It must have happened at a different time, probably before the creation of life, or during the great Flood when the thick covering of water would have shielded the remaining life from harm.

Maintenance of a Closed System: The second assumption concerns whether the system has been contaminated by outside atoms or the leaching out of atoms within. Is it possible to guarantee pristine conditions throughout the entire time that uniformity assumes? The times proposed are exceedingly long, according to standard thinking, far longer than man's supposed tenure on earth. Can a rock be isolated from the environment for millions or billions of years, and can we be sure?

Consider the fact that water can dissolve even large at-

oms like uranium or lead. That is why such strict guidelines exist for the sampling of drinking water, checking for contaminants like lead. Contamination is surpassingly difficult to avoid. Consider also that groundwater penetrates everywhere, through wells, into basements, into soil, and deep inside the earth. No location is immune. It is also true that researchers try to notice telltale signs of past contamination, and reject suspect specimens, but is it reasonable to claim that a particular sample has been isolated when so many others have not?

This would especially be the case if the world was inundated by a global, planet-altering deluge in the days of Noah. The waters were marked by unusual chemistries, high energies and temperatures, etc. What location escaped its influence? Was any rock or location spared alteration by the Flood's waters? Could anyone today be certain his or her specimen was uncontaminated?

Often when an attempted dating effort produces an age-date that couldn't be right from anyone's perspective, perhaps too old or embarrassingly recent, an otherwise honest uniformitarian researcher will explain it away by claiming unnoticed contamination. The professional radioisotope literature is full of such claims. If so many are tainted, can we be confident in any specimen?

Starting Conditions: Perhaps a more telling assumption involves the starting conditions. This amounts to the claim that a specimen "born" in historic times should date "too young to measure." This one is directly testable, for volcanic eruptions occur today in which fresh rocks are solidified from magma. We often know from observation the precise day the lava flowed, and precisely when a molten lava field cooled and hardened. Thus, we know the exact "birthday" for the rock from which a particular specimen comes. Seldom, however, does the radioactive date agree with the observed age, casting doubt on the technique's accuracy. Recently formed rocks have been dated by the standard methods, using these same assumptions, and often the ages calculated are embarrassingly high. The point is, when the method can actually be checked, it fails measurably. Why then should we give it any credence when we cannot check it?

Multiple Dating Techniques

There are actually several dating techniques that are routinely used. The uranium-lead method was the "granddaddy of them all," and has always been the standard by which others are calibrated. For certain types of rock, other methods are employed, such as potassium-argon, rubidium-strontium, neodymium-samarium, and isochrons and isotope ratios developed from these methods. Each is thought to be most appropriate for a particular type of rock, but sometimes multiple methods are used on the same rock. Obviously, their results should agree, but seldom does this happen. The results are often discordant, sometimes even bizarre. This is not to say the results are completely meaningless, but if they don't reflect accurate ages, what are they telling us?

The RATE initiative discerned certain patterns in the ranges of isochron ages when the same rocks were dated by several different methods. Those that decay through beta decay tended to give younger dates than those that undergo alpha decay. Furthermore, those parent isotopes that are relatively heavier (having a larger atomic weight) surprisingly produced older dates than the less heavy ones. Those with a longer half-life (a slower decay rate) tended to give older dates also. Applying multiple dating methods to the same rock would predictably indicate varied ages for the several methods—different in a predictable way. It seems the "deck is stacked." You can actually "prove" a rock is a particular age by the choice of method. Certainly, radioisotope dating as invoked by uniformitarianism does not speak with an authoritative voice.

In summary, radioisotope dating is based on three assumptions, two of which are not provable at best, and the other demonstrably false in practice. Specimens inherit seeming age from surrounding rocks and are easily contaminated. Rocks are seemingly "born" old. The decay rates have been found not to be constant. Because claims that rocks are millions or even billions of years old logically depend on this assumption of constant decay rate, its falsification fatally undermines them.

Testing a single rock often produces discordant ages between methods, and ages that are obviously recognizably erroneous. While the theory is robust and the measurements precise, the use of it leads to error, especially when it is shown that bias resides in the methods. This important result of creationist research should be of tremendous encouragement to Christians to hold fast to scriptural truth, particularly in regard to the age

of the earth and its physical history. Research continues to discern what the patterns actually mean, but whatever the studies eventually show, the method certainly should not cause a Christian to doubt God's inerrant Word

Carbon-14

The best known and probably the least understood radioisotope dating method is carbon dating. Most non-specialists mistakenly think that carbon dating has proved the earth to be millions and billions of years old. But perception sometimes differs from truth.

Carbon dating works like this. In the upper atmosphere, incoming cosmic radiation produces fast-moving neutrons that impact a nitrogen-14 (N-14) atom, altering it into a carbon-14 (C-14) atom, which is radioactively unstable. Eventually, this C-14 atom will decay back into an N-14 atom. Soon after a radioactive carbon atom forms, it usually combines chemically with oxygen to become carbon dioxide, which may be metabolized into a plant. All plants take in carbon, and since about one carbon atom in a trillion is radioactive, all plants possess this small level of radioactivity. Plants are part of the biosphere—a necessary link in the food chain for most other organisms. Plants are eaten by animals that may then be eaten by other animals. In time, every plant and animal has this same low level of radioactive carbon in its cells. It ceases to take in C-14 when it dies, yet decay goes on. In principle, by measuring the amount of C-14 left in the remains, one can estimate how long ago the plant or animal died. Of course, this method is only applicable to (carbon-based) organic materials, from flesh to bone to wood, etc., whose C-14 levels are in equilibrium with the C-14 in the atmosphere. No one would ever use carbon dating to date a rock, for it can only date once-living things.

Carbon-14 spontaneously decays back to nitrogen at a measurable rate. This rate is much faster than any of the other unstable atoms mentioned earlier that are commonly used for dating rocks. Carbon-14 decays so rapidly that essentially all the radioactive carbon will have turned back into nitrogen in no more than about 100,000 years. Each 5,730 years (one half-life of C-14), half of the radioactive carbon atoms will decay into nitrogen. (Compare this with the half-life of uranium 238, measured today at 4.5 billion years.) Eventually, all will have decayed. Measuring the amount remaining in a dead specimen allows the length of time

Radioactive carbon-14 decays so fast, none would remain after 100,000 years or so. However, it is found in rocks thought to be millions or hundreds of millions of years old according to uniformitarianism. Every coal seam or limestone layer (hundreds of millions of years old), every dinosaur bone (tens of millions of years old), and even every diamond (crystalline carbon, billions of years old) contains C-14. All "date" just a few thousand years old, just like they should according to the creation/Flood model.

since death to be calculated, or the time elapsed since the organism stopped replenishing its C-14.

Despite the seeming precision, the method has its flaws. Historically dated bodies or objects provide a reality check, and quite frankly, carbon dating is known for its

inaccuracy. It most often finds application in archaeology, and is thought to be useful for about the most recent 3,000 years (i.e., since the time of King David) if calibrated properly. Archaeologists may routinely use C-14 to date the timbers in a tomb, or grain stored in a clay pot, or papyrus in a scroll, but they never trust its results unless they can be matched with dates gathered through other historical means. If the C-14 date disagrees with a known historical date, they discard the C-14 date and keep that derived from historical means.

Even though C-14 can't be used to date rocks, the method does have something to say. Surprisingly often, fossils found in the strata record still retain original bone or wood. For instance, dinosaur bones have sometimes been discovered that have resisted alteration and still retain datable bone protein. While uniformitarians know not to date an "ancient" fossil, creation scientists have sent specimens to be dated. In each case, the bone's "age" has turned out to be just tens of thousands of years old, not 65 million or 200 million years old as assumed by uniformity. The new, highly precise AMS (accelerated mass spectrometry) method has reinforced this. The fossils in the rocks, and thus the rocks themselves, are evidently not so old.

Similarly, limestone rock (calcium carbonate) contains carbon, as does marble (metamorphosed limestone). Uniformitarianism dates these rocks using methods other than C-14 as hundreds of millions of years. In each case, the age determined from C-14 is just a few tens of thousands of years, not hundreds of millions or billions of years. Coal, altered plant material, has likewise been well analyzed, and every time the isotopic makeup of a coal seam is determined, it always contains C-14, despite the fact that most coal seams conventionally are thought to be 50 to 300 million years old. When dated, every specimen, from numerous coal deposits around the world and assayed in standard laboratories, always yields dates of just a few tens of thousands of years old. Seems like every fossil and rock type is really quite young.[29]

A remarkable discovery was made by the RATE scientists. They found C-14 is also present in diamonds, a crystalline form of carbon. Diamonds are thought to have formed deep inside the earth, where pressures and temperatures are quite extreme. Diamonds, however, are different in that they are not the altered remains of organic material. They never were alive. They don't breathe air or eat plants. Furthermore, the carbon atoms in diamonds are so tightly packed, no outside contamination is possible. Gathering diamonds from around the world, RATE found low levels of C-14 present in each of them, enough to date the diamonds at just a few tens of thousands of years old. They are not yet old enough to be C-14 "dead." Yet diamonds are thought by uniformitarian standard thinking to be perhaps billions of years old, far too old to have retained even a single atom of C-14. The evidence shows that they, too, are "young."[30]

If the earth were old, the rates of C-14 production in the atmosphere and decay on the surface should have produced a steady state by now, with formation equaling decay. Calculations show this equality would be reached in less than 100,000 years, but there's a problem. Measurements show that the number of C-14 atoms is growing faster than they decay. All known C-14 would build up at present rates in about 50,000 years. This disparity can readily be seen when a series of tree ring series is dated, forcing a calibration curve to be derived. Even this calibration curve fails for older and older specimens, however.

Carbon dating results need some calibration in a creation/Flood/young earth sense, as well. Scripture places the creation of all things, including the atmosphere, less than 10,000 years ago. Plants and animals before the Flood lived in an environment quite different from the present, and their fossils reflect that difference. Flood considerations are even more drastic, insisting the entire atmosphere was "washed clean" just 5,000 years or so ago. According to Flood thinking, there was essentially no C-14 in the atmosphere at the end of the Flood, and all of it has built up since then and is still building up. Experience has shown that fossil specimens deposited during the Flood year usually "date" around 40,000 years or so, with many exceptions.

Despite its weaknesses, carbon dating stands tall among radioactive dating methods, and is thought to be the most accurate, yet its results point to a recent deposition of rocks and fossils and soundly contradict uniformitarianism. The evidence shows that things were quite different in the past, and the rock and fossil records are only a few thousand years old.

SCIENTIFIC EVIDENCE THAT THE FLOOD WAS GLOBAL IN EXTENT

The Word of God claims to be the record of the One who was present throughout the past and who recorded accurate history. He Himself sent the great Flood to destroy the planet because of man's rebellion. We have established that the Bible unequivocally asserts that the great Flood was global in extent. In the preceding chapter, we documented that the Flood was a hydraulic and tectonic cataclysm that brought about great geologic changes to the earth. We now press on to investigate whether the geological evidence supports the Bible's claim that the Flood was geographically global.

Obviously, Scripture doesn't give us all the details. For instance, it doesn't mention the Grand Canyon and how it was formed. We must take the biblical report of the past, combined with geological data we can study, and fill in the blanks as best we can. Understanding that we can't go back in time to observe the actual events, we must ask: Do the physical results of past processes support or deny the reconstruction of history built on a plain-sense reading of Scripture? Many inferences could be drawn from both the biblical data and the physical evidence, but all should be done in submission to the authority of the biblical record. There we find our starting place, the basic framework on which to hang our geological conclusions.

In this chapter, we feature geographical and geological evidence left behind by the Flood of Noah's day. Was the Flood global in extent as well as catastrophic in intensity, as Scripture indicates? Keep in mind that a global flood, while impacting the entire planet, was

probably not acting in the same way at all times at all places on the globe. There were, no doubt, numerous and varied episodes during the Flood that would produce a myriad of geologic results, including those due to storm-driven waves coming and going, unrestrained tides coursing across a barren planet seemingly devoid of terrain above sea level, multiple tsunamis sweeping over submerged surfaces from all directions, land masses shifting about and colliding, etc. In one part of the world the Flood might be eroding a land mass, while in another part it would be depositing sediment.

These events would not have each been global in scope at every instant, but overall their combined devastation would be global. However, individual processes would have been operating on at least regional or hemispherical scales, in contrast to the local, uniformitarian scales of today. We can measure the geometry of the geological products of the Flood, the results of past geological processes, and determine if their causes were extensive or local, catastrophic or uniform. We can compare which view of the past better matches the data in the present.

The best way to investigate this difficult issue is first to study individual rock strata and discern their origin as best we can. Once the individual pieces are gathered, we can attempt to solve the larger puzzle.

We can begin by studying the familiar rock layers in the general area of Grand Canyon in the southwestern United States. In many ways, these strata are representative of many others, and they are certainly more accessible. For simplicity, let us begin with the lowest layers of Grand Canyon strata, i.e., the ones many creationists interpret as deposited before the Flood, and work our way up through early Flood rocks to the canyon's rim, and then beyond. We can continue on to the beautiful realm of mid-Flood Zion National Park, then the likely later-Flood Bryce Canyon. Along the way, we can observe several other important layers outcropping nearby. These are all easily seen by geologists and vaca-

tioners.

ROCKS DATED AS PRECAMBRIAN

Several sets of rock have been identified in Grand Canyon. The lowest rocks, visible only in the Inner Gorge, are non-bedded igneous and metamorphic rocks. These contain no fossils at all. Evolutionists date them to the time before life evolved, while creationists generally consider them to be from early creation week, i.e.,

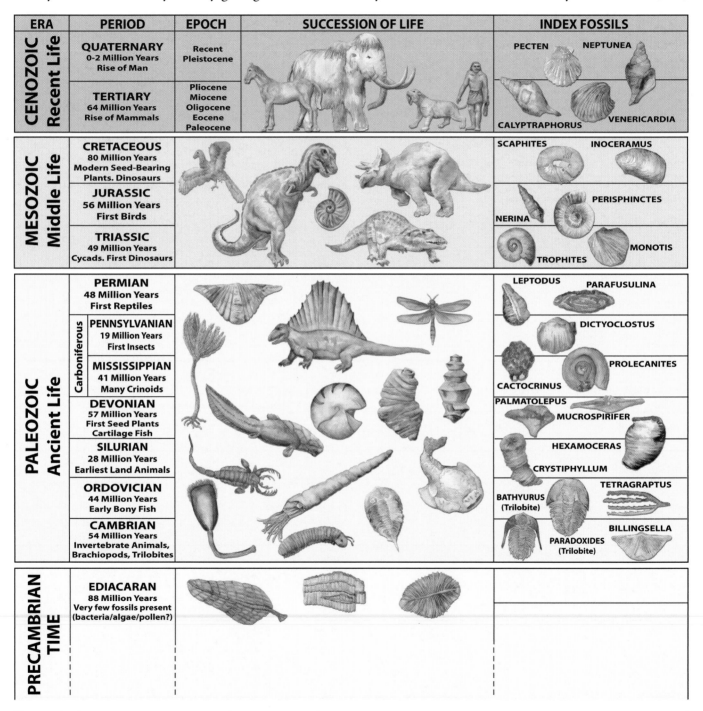

ERA	PERIOD	EPOCH	SUCCESSION OF LIFE	INDEX FOSSILS
CENOZOIC Recent Life	**QUATERNARY** 0-2 Million Years Rise of Man	Recent Pleistocene		PECTEN NEPTUNEA CALYPTRAPHORUS VENERICARDIA
	TERTIARY 64 Million Years Rise of Mammals	Pliocene Miocene Oligocene Eocene Paleocene		
MESOZOIC Middle Life	**CRETACEOUS** 80 Million Years Modern Seed-Bearing Plants. Dinosaurs			SCAPHITES INOCERAMUS NERINA PERISPHINCTES
	JURASSIC 56 Million Years First Birds			TROPHITES MONOTIS
	TRIASSIC 49 Million Years Cycads. First Dinosaurs			
PALEOZOIC Ancient Life	**PERMIAN** 48 Million Years First Reptiles			LEPTODUS PARAFUSULINA
	Carboniferous — **PENNSYLVANIAN** 19 Million Years First Insects			DICTYOCLOSTUS
	Carboniferous — **MISSISSIPPIAN** 41 Million Years Many Crinoids			CACTOCRINUS PROLECANITES
	DEVONIAN 57 Million Years First Seed Plants Cartilage Fish			PALMATOLEPUS MUCROSPIRIFER
	SILURIAN 28 Million Years Earliest Land Animals			HEXAMOCERAS CRYSTIPHYLLUM
	ORDOVICIAN 44 Million Years Early Bony Fish			BATHYURUS (Trilobite) TETRAGRAPTUS
	CAMBRIAN 54 Million Years Invertebrate Animals, Brachiopods, Trilobites			PARADOXIDES (Trilobite) BILLINGSELLA
PRECAMBRIAN TIME	**EDIACARAN** 88 Million Years Very few fossils present (bacteria/algae/pollen?)			

The geologic column according to uniformitarianism. Fossils are arranged in Periods supposedly spanning hundreds of millions of years. Creationists generally accept the fossil and rock order implied in the column, but deny the great ages assigned to them. The fossils shown reflect the assumed evolutionary order and are not necessarily as found. Actually, vertebrate fossils are quite rare, while **95 percent of fossils are invertebrates essentially equivalent to animals living today.**

before God created life. They were likely altered by the enormous forces unleashed later in the week as the Creator completed His work.

These rocks were eventually overlain by a variety of sedimentary strata. The only possible fossils in these layers are of microscopic, single-cell organisms. These sedimentary layers probably speak of the time during Day Three of creation week when God called the continents up out of the world ocean. Great forces were at work, deforming and altering the original created materials as the Creator embellished them into continents or perhaps one single supercontinent. No life was then present. This was immediately followed by the creation of plants, also on Day Three, and later the creation of animals on Days Five and Six.

Vishnu Schist

In Grand Canyon, several of these early rock units bear mention. The first is the dark and foreboding Vishnu Schist and related rock units. It can be correlated with similar metamorphic rocks across the North American plate, partially forming the core of the continent. One wonders just how such huge rock masses could have been metamorphosed on such a grand scale. Some poorly understood mechanism utilizing intense heat and pressure must have altered original Day One rocks into their present state. Uniformity proposes the sediments were deeply buried for long ages. These conditions might engender the necessary high heat and pressure to metamorphose sediments, but are these parameters possible on the immense scale implied by the mysterious-looking Vishnu Schist? Laboratory equipment can produce essentially the same rocks using more normal temperatures and pressures, especially starting with an appropriate watery mineral gel.[1] Extremely hot water under great pressure acts as a catalyst to start and speed up the process. This enables

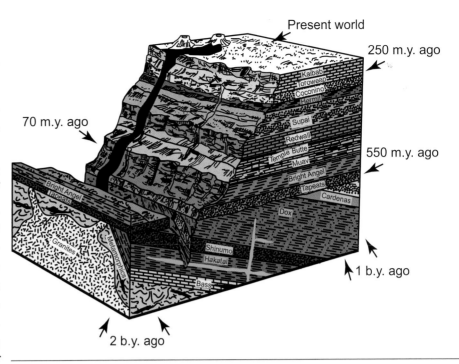

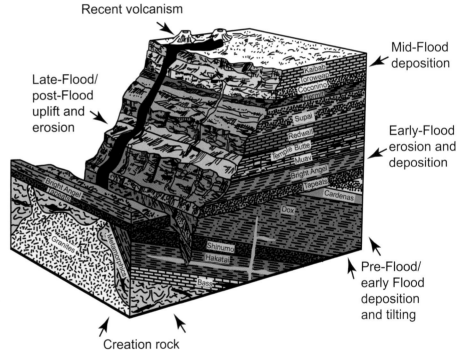

What do the rocks say? Nothing—rocks don't talk. They must be interpreted. On top is the uniformitarian view of Grand Canyon rock strata. Creationists interpret them differently. Same data, different interpretations. Which is more credible? Which is more consistent with Scripture?

the recrystallizing process to proceed rapidly. But what can accomplish it on a continental scale?

Processes operating during the creation week were anything but uniformly natural. In fact, they were supernatural. Creationists suspect that the original Day One and Day Three rocks may have themselves been altered during the Day Three continental uplift. Occurring so

The Zoroaster Granite intrudes into the overlying Vishnu Schist. The metamorphic Vishnu dates from the creation week, while the igneous Zoroaster probably was thrust upward in semi-molten form during the great Flood.

rocks we observe. Requiring an intense, global cause, no mechanism of today will suffice. The forces involved during the creation week followed by those in operation during the great Flood of Noah's day, however, would be adequate to do the job.

Zoroaster Granite and Other Granites

Pinkish streaks of Zoroaster Granite can often be seen injected into the Vishnu Schist. These rocks at least date from a time subsequent to the emplacement of the host rock, having squeezed up like toothpaste into cracks in the Vishnu. The now rocky "toothpaste" must have been pliable, thus in a hot molten condition when injected. Although in Grand Canyon the granite zones are of varying sizes, sometimes rather large, in other places granite forms the cores of entire mountain chains, evidently having bubbled up like hot wax in a "lava lamp." Uniformitarians call for great lengths of time to accomplish this, but creation researchers point out that the presence of water can dramatically speed up this process.

PALEOZOIC STRATA

Opinions differ on specifics, but most creationists contend the majority of Precambrian rocks were deposited and/or metamorphosed before the great Flood. The strata of greatest interest stem from the Flood, and are the primary subject of this book. The period of time between creation and the Flood (1,656 years, according to the best manuscripts) probably enjoyed only calm geological activity, but certain geological processes must have operated capable of depositing minor sediment amounts. For instance, rivers flowed into the sea, carrying eroded sediments and depositing them offshore. Some of the canyon's rock layers date from that quiescent period. These were eventually covered by Flood sediments.

Let us consider the strata in and around Grand Canyon, applying Flood considerations to their origin. The two diagrams on page 145 illustrate how each of the two camps, uniformitarians and catastrophists, might interpret the array of geological data in Grand Canyon. Remember, both sides have the same rocks and fossils to study, but creationists and evolutionists interpret

rapidly, intense heat and pressure must have been generated, able to "cook" the rock into what we now call schist. Ancient, similar rocks found on all continents show evidence of such stress and rapid movement. It was all according to the Creator's plan, and the end result was not destroyed rock, but a hard and durable foundation for the continent, suitable for His "very good" purpose.

Similar metamorphic processes operate today on a limited scale, such as adjacent to an active fault, but normally the metamorphosed zone is quite local, just inches in scale, not at all comparable to the continent-wide history differently based on their widely different assumptions. Which option holds more closely to Scripture, and which best handles the geological evidence?

Pre-Flood rocks are typically labeled as from the Precambrian system, although some of the uppermost Precambrian layers may have been from the early bursts of the Flood. The Flood commenced with great tectonic upheavals—the breaking open of the "fountains of the great deep" (Genesis 7:11). This introduced massive volumes of water and steam to the surface, some with high mineral content and/or rare chemistries and high temperatures. No doubt, magma chambers spewed out their contents. This mix of material would have not only been deposited, but it would also alter any rocks it contacted. Today we can observe hardened lava flows that erupted at that time, such as the Cardenas Basalts, coupled with faulted and tilted layers of fossil-free, pre-Flood sedimentary rock, including the Shinumo Quartzite. These sediments have much to teach us regarding the creation, pre-Flood periods, and early Flood events, but our attention will focus primarily on the overlying Flood strata, assigned in conventional circles as from the Paleozoic Era and times following.

Under normal circumstances, moving water rushing over a landscape will erode it. We see this happen today when spring floods overflow the Mississippi River Valley. Eroded canyons sometimes result, scoured out in an episode of brief terror. However, when the flowing water carries a high sediment load, continuously supplied from upriver, it will deposit sediment as the water velocity lessens. The conditions must be conducive. The main key is the presence of abundant sediment in the water and a place to receive it.

We can clearly see the ferocity of the Flood's initial activity when we examine the rocks. In Grand Canyon, the first thing on the record is a mighty episode of erosion, an unconformity. Here, the underlying metamorphic, igneous, and sedimentary rocks are beveled off to an amazingly flat surface. One rock type overlies a very different rock type at this interface, separated in only a few places by a thin disrupted zone. Uniformitarians consider the time represented by this erosion episode to be many millions of years, but such a view does not match the observation. A long period of erosion would almost certainly result in a thick rubble layer, stream channels, or at least an undulating surface, with pro-

The Great Unconformity between the basement metamorphic rock and the overlying Paleozoic fossil-bearing rock.

nounced highs and lows. Except for a few places where a hard, resistant Shinumo boulder is lodged near the erosion surface, the erosion plane exhibits little relief. The better explanatory model postulates dramatic incursion of energetic waters, able to carry along large boulders, which first leveled the terrain and then deposited its sediment load, beginning with the largest boulders. The erosional surface has aptly been named "The Great Unconformity," for it is indeed "great," extending across the continent.

Tapeats Sandstone

The lowest layer of generally flat-laying strata has been named the Tapeats Sandstone. It can be traced throughout the canyon and correlated with strata in surrounding states. It has been assigned to the Cambrian system, supposedly dated some 515 to 520 million years old. In most places in the canyon, it represents the earliest Flood deposit. This pancake-like rock varies from 125 to 325 feet in thickness throughout the area, and consists of quartz sand grains cemented into hard rock, with larger grains and even cobbles and boulders clustered at the very bottom.

These larger grains and rocks can only be transported by very energetic water movements. As moving water slows and curls back onto itself, larger and more dense material drops out first, and then coarse sand settles to the bottom, followed by medium-size sand grains, then fine sand grains—a series of diminishing size. Over time, these sand grains harden into sandstone as cement binds the grains together. In the presence of adequate cement, the sediments harden into sedimentary rock rather quickly, not requiring the "millions and millions" of years we normally hear about. For instance, the concrete in a sidewalk could be called a man-made rock, with varied sand and rock ingredients rapidly cemented together by the added "cement." Today, the Tapeats is a very hard rock and stands as a vertical, dark brown cliff. Complete body fossils are rare, but trackways of trilobites and worm burrows have been found.

Even though Grand Canyon might seem large when you're there, it covers only the northwestern corner of Arizona. Mapping the lateral extent of the Tapeats, however, produces a surprise, for the "pancake" layer extends across Arizona into New Mexico, up into

Immediately above the Great Unconformity is a layer of bushel-basket-size boulders and other cobbles.

Utah, into Colorado, and farther. It is reliably correlated with beds in Montana, Wyoming, Illinois, Pennsylvania, Michigan, up into Canada, and around into Greenland and Europe. At least continental in scope, it can be labeled hemispherical, far different from any local deposit uniformity might propose.

The Tapeats has been interpreted by uniformitarian considerations to be from a shallow-marine, near-shore environment, with beach sand accumulating amid high-energy waves. Much like the St. Peter Sandstone discussed earlier, its thickness is tiny compared to its width. Traditionally, uniformitarians have attributed the immense lateral extent of this blanket sand to a migrating beachfront—at one time here, moving over time to there. After millions of years of migration, it took on its thin, wide geometry. Is this valid? The unconformity below this "blanket sand" shows that erosion had beveled the underlying strata to an extremely flat surface, on which this relatively thin layer of sand was deposited. If great time had been involved, wouldn't there be more elevated highs and eroded river valleys, more thickening and thinning? Isn't there a better explanation?

In recent decades, many geologists have reinterpreted this layer as having been deposited by a rapidly moving sandy mudflow, perhaps by a turbidity current or underwater landslide. This continent-wide deposit would have required a series of sandy flows, one after the other, each one encroaching farther and farther inland. The area covered by the Tapeats is immense, continental or hemispherical in extent. This rock unit is far too large in area to have been a migrating beachfront. Its catastrophic signature hints at a single cataclysm with multiple surges but with little elapsed time. Such an event is beyond the scope of human imagination, let alone experience. Uniformity surely doesn't address it.

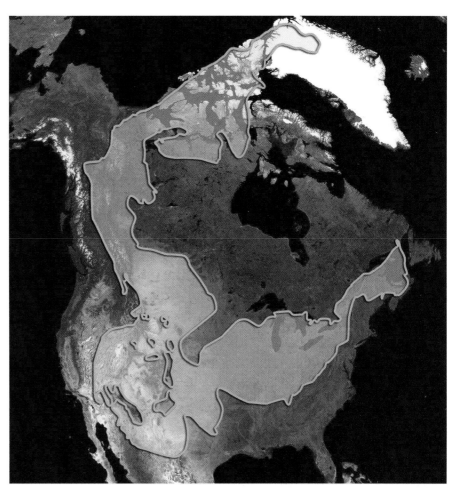

The Tapeats Sandstone, the lowest member in the Sauk Megasequence, covers a semi-continental area and is now understood by many geologists to be due to a series of dynamic underwater mudflows. Creationists consider it to be one of the earliest deposits of the great Flood. Catastrophic deposition on a regional scale equals evidence for the global Flood.

Bright Angel Shale

Overlying the Tapeats Sandstone is the drab green and brown Bright Angel Shale, nearly 400 feet thick, consisting of even smaller-grain particles of silt and clay. It too is designated Cambrian. The Tapeats is dominated by large sand grains at its base and finer sand nearer its top. The deposition of the Bright Angel can be considered a continuation of the ever-more-fining upward sequence of particle size of the Tapeats. Noticeable beds of dolomite and limestone are locally present, interspersed with the tiny silt and clay particles in the shale. While the underlying Tapeats stands as a cliff, the combination of layers in the Bright Angel can be easily eroded, resulting in a slope that can be recognized as a noticeable bench within the canyon.

Fossils of marine invertebrates pepper the layers. Trilobites are here, sometimes found complete, but more often ripped into pieces, so much so that they have merited the term trilobite "hash." Water was deeper and the current was slower when this sediment was laid down. The Bright Angel Shale covers approximately

GAPS IN THE GEOLOGIC COLUMN

The geologic column—that presentation of the rock record that places rock strata into various ages—can be intimidating. Because it seems authoritative and we see it so frequently, we sometimes place more faith in it than it actually deserves.

Without a doubt, rocks and rock strata can be characterized by placing them on the column. While many incorrect notions are imbedded in this diagram (most particularly the "absolute" ages given), rock layers really do usually line up the way the drawing presents them. This visual illustration can be a useful tool, especially when considering one rock's age "relative" to another. But the rock layers are frequently dated by their fossil content, arranged in the erroneous evolutionary order. How much credence should the Christian creationist place in it?

It might help to consider the rock layers in Grand Canyon, since they are so well known and studied in creationist literature. Obviously, the layers rest one on top of another, with no gaps between them. Schematic drawings present them this way, but while the layers are dated consecutively, they are not dated one right after the other. Often there are lengthy time gaps postulated between the layers. The rock record of those time periods is missing. These gaps, called "unconformities," represent either a period of non-deposition or of erosion.

If the old earth view is correct, then the record is woefully incomplete. Most Grand Canyon strata are dated in the supposedly 300 million-year-long Paleozoic Era, but of the

seven periods within that era, only five are represented in Grand Canyon. More importantly, if the upper and lower surfaces of each stratum are dated by questionable uniformitarian means and plotted on a vertical line showing the entire Paleozoic Era, less than ten percent of the total time postulated by evolutionists is represented! It better represents brief episodes of deposition within the great Flood of Noah's day.

The geologic column as normally presented should not be considered accurate history and should be recognized as a statement of evolutionary old earth dogma. There is some truth contained in the geologic column, but not as it is normally taught. Its implications can never justify doubting God's truth as recorded in Scripture.

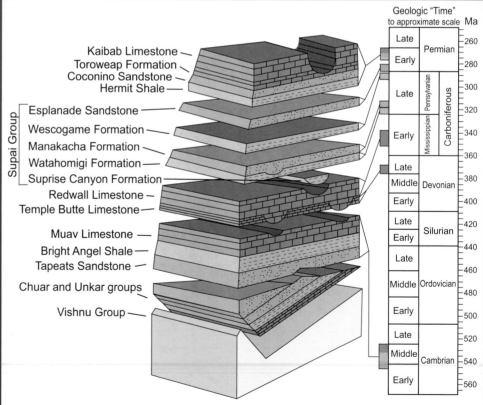

The rock layers in Grand Canyon represent only a small portion of the total time postulated by uniformitarians. Their "evidence" for evolutionary time is the space between the layers! They interpret each period as representing many millions of years, but the strata are better understood as brief episodes of deposition during the great Flood of Noah's day.

the same large area as does the Tapeats. Normally fine particles of shale and clay require long times and calm waters to be deposited, but under conditions of abundant and continuous supply, a bottom-hugging slurry can quickly result in thick deposits. Thus, two beds, one on top of the other, result, but they are actually growing laterally farther and farther inland.

Muav Limestone

Capping the Bright Angel, a yellow-brown muddy layer called the Muav Limestone can be found transitioning with the formation below it. It consists of hard, resistant limestone, and forms prominent cliffs throughout the area, again of Cambrian age. Floodwater was even deeper and velocities were slower when it was deposited, allowing extremely fine particles to agglomerate and settle, and dissolved chemicals to be precipitated, thus continuing the series of fining-upward sedimentation. Fossils here are not abundant, but some trilobite trackways have been found. Again, it covers approximately the same area as does the Tapeats and Bright Angel.

The Tonto Group

The three formations discussed above—the Tapeats Sandstone, Bright Angel Shale, and the Muav Limestone—are considered a "package," a continual sequence of sediments resulting from the transgression of the ocean onto the land. Geologists of all persuasions recognize this sequence, and have named it the "Sauk Sequence." The area covered by Tapeats would be essentially the same for any and all of the three individual beds. The sequence has been called a *megasequence*, which is followed by another megasequence, and then another. The upper and lower limits of all megasequences ignore the Period or Era boundaries of the standard geologic column designations, illustrating the ad hoc nature of the column. Each represents one great dynamic incursion of the ocean onto the land.

To simplify the story, when shallow but powerful water first encounters the land and water energies are greatest, erosion is extensive. As velocities lessen and begin to curl back, only large boulders and cobbles can be deposited. As the water velocity tapers off with increasing depth and wider area, larger and then smaller sand grains drop out, then finer particles, and finally chemical precipitates. As transgression progresses, three zones are deposited laterally and essentially simultaneously. As shown in the accompanying diagram, as the transgression moved inland, the zones took shape as linear beds, one on top of the other. In the first stage, larger particles are carried out by stronger currents where they are deposited, then smaller ones as current slows. Meanwhile, smaller particles are transported even further out. All were deposited virtually simultaneously, as their lateral extent progressed. In Grand Canyon, this series has been named the Tonto Group, all assigned to the Cambrian system.

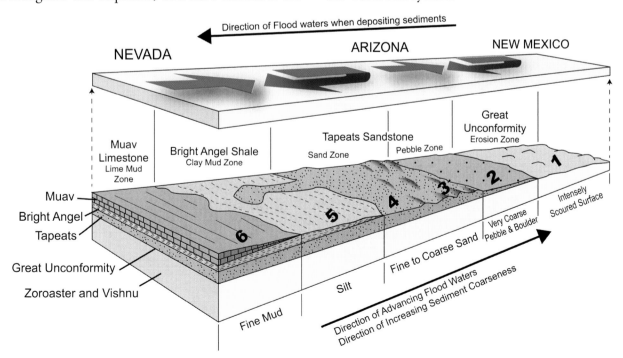

Strata laid down side by side. As an energetic turbidity current or mudflow encounters land, it first erodes, and then deposits large boulders, then sand and smaller particles, ending up in a vertical series of layers.

Consider that rapid marine transgression of water over the pre-Flood continent eroded a great unconformity and then deposited the Sauk Megasequence of layers. As the transgressing waters lost their initial energy, they began to curl back and return to the ocean from which they had come, eroding the recently deposited strata. Another transgression was soon to follow, and the sequence repeated.

Creationist Guy Berthault, a French scientist, has demonstrated the deposition of such a sequence using a large laboratory flume. Employing a wide channel, varying water depths, and a continual supply of coarse and fine sediments, he actually filmed two discrete layers of sediments accumulating simultaneously, growing laterally side by side. Larger grains were continually deposited on the lower end of the flume, followed by smaller grains on top. Continued flow repeatedly duplicated the sequence adjacent and immediately downstream until continual layers were deposited. The layers were not deposited sequentially one after the other, but continually and simultaneously.[2] He has produced an explanatory film, excellent for classroom viewing, which shows these principles.[3]

Remember, below the horizontally bedded Tapeats lies a distinctive, strikingly horizontal erosion surface. The underlying pre-Flood rock had been beveled off to leave a flat horizon, onto which the Tapeats was laid. The Tapeats is overlain by the Bright Angel Shale and then the Muav Limestone. Each of the three Tonto layers is found throughout the length of the canyon and extends (with different names) across the continent and sometimes even beyond. All this deposition began with the striking erosional event, the Great Unconformity—a great unconformity indeed.

Another far-ranging unconformity bounds the upper extent of the Tonto Group at the top of the Muav, making this series of fining-upward sediments (Tapeats–Bright Angel–Muav) a distinct package of sediments. It is truly enormous, at least semi-continental in extent, bounded by major unconformities. A megasequence is defined by such regional unconformities above and below.

An oceanic transgression that rapidly covered much of North America could not be a "uniform" event, eroding and depositing great volumes of sediments, for nothing of this character or magnitude happens today, nor has it ever been observed by scientists. We observe tsunamis and turbidity currents, but never such rapid erosion followed by the dumping of such vast quantities of sediments over such a large area. Certainly, no gradual inundation of the land by slowly rising oceans could accomplish such extensive erosion of hard rock, transport and deposition of large boulders over long distances, as well as deposit such an extensive volume of varied sediments. The energy levels involved are unimaginable, but we see the evidence. Would not an energetic global flood, such as the great Flood of Noah's day, be implicated?

The major erosional unconformity that is evident stratigraphically above the Sauk Megasequence (above the Muav Limestone) is almost as instructive as the Great Unconformity below. Remember, the Sauk Megasequence is at least semi-continental in area, and so were the layers that came after, including the St. Peter Sandstone described in the preceding chapter. But the St. Peter is not present in Grand Canyon, nor are several other layers that followed. Some not-insignificant amount of time must have elapsed between the Muav and deposition of the layer that actually is above, for much happened. Evidently there were at least two major erosion and deposition episodes that followed, and the latter has erased much of the evidence of the former. If you follow the Muav to the west, you find sedimentary rock several hundred feet thick overlying it, capped by evidence of further erosion, all of which is missing in the canyon. Several layers once existed there that are now gone from the area.

Interestingly, the "double" erosion overlying the Muav did not produce a mature drainage pattern, but a surface with only moderately undulations in a few places, with the few minor lows now filled in with the next-higher formation, the Temple Butte Limestone. Uniformitarianism postulates that the time that passed between the erosion ending the Sauk and the deposition of the strata resting above would be lengthy, on the order of 130 million years, plenty of time to develop a drainage system, with streams and rivers, valleys and hills. Where can we see the well-developed landscape implied by such a long time? It does not exist.

Megasequences

Six or more megasequences comprise the entire Phanerozoic (fossil-bearing) geologic column, at least on the continental interiors or the cratons. The continental margins were due to plate movements, both concurrent and subsequent. Since rapidly moving water can accomplish much geologic work, while stationary water does little, this concept bears promise as the primary character of the great Flood of Noah's day.

Each sequence begins with a basal sandstone containing sand grains of lessening diameter as you move upward (or forward in time) through the layer. This is typically covered by shale or siltstone composed of tiny particles, which in turn is covered by extremely tiny, precipitated particles. The lowest megasequence is, as we have seen, the Sauk Megasequence, which was followed by an erosional unconformity. The overlying megasequence is called the Tippecanoe Mega-

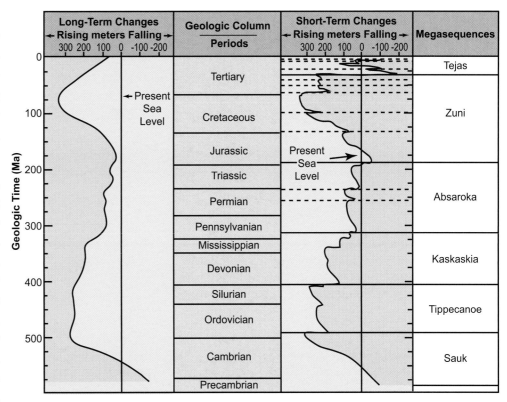

Fossil-bearing strata come in packages called megasequences. Progressing up the strata package, sandstone is first encountered, then shale, then limestone, each consisting of finer particles than the previous layer. Each megasequence is characterized by an extensive erosional unconformity, and is completed by another unconformity. The next sequence follows that.

sequence. At its base lies a significant sandstone bed, and above it lie shale and limestone beds, just as they did in the Sauk, also followed by an unconformity. It has been recognized across much of the northern hemisphere, but is entirely missing, evidently eroded, in Grand Canyon.

The Tippecanoe Megasequence spans the Ordovician and Silurian systems, dated from about 500 to 400 million years ago, according to mainstream thinking. Its lowermost, coarse-grain, blanket sandstone, the St. Peter Sandstone and its correlating equivalents, is capped by shale and limestone, just as is the Tapeats in the Sauk sequence. It, too, is ended by a regional unconformity.

Erosion ending the Tippecanoe Megasequence not only completely removed the Tippecanoe sediments in the Grand Canyon region, but also gouged out a few low areas in the underlying Muav (the uppermost Sauk formation). Some of these low depressions are now filled with a somewhat purplish, sandy, dolomitic limestone named the Temple Butte Formation. This limestone has a quite fine-grain, micritic texture (with tiny, silt-

size grains) that is not like the coarser aragonite limestones (with larger clay-size grains) of today. Coupled with the overlying Redwall Limestone, it represents the end stages of the Kaskaskia Megasequence, the third major transgression of the ocean onto the land.

Often, limestone strata contain many fossils, but few are found in the Temple Butte Formation. It is the only layer in the canyon that has been assigned to the Devonian system, conventionally dated by uniformitarians at about 370 million years old. But an evolutionary arrangement of fossils must have been used for assigning the dates. The passage of time is not evident between the Temple Butte Limestone and the overlying Redwall Limestone, yet they are assigned to different Periods—Devonian and Mississippian, respectively—supposedly tens of millions of years apart. Completely missing are strata of both the Ordovician and Silurian systems, totaling some supposed 72 million years. They were either not deposited here or, more likely, eroded. The area was underwater and deposition could normally be expected. Or, as creationists might suspect, the transgressing floodwaters temporarily regressed oceanward, producing an extremely flat surface, other than these few low places now filled with Temple Butte. Normally, a mature erosional surface might sport a well-developed drainage pattern, appearing on a map as dendritic (tree-like) drainage, but none can be seen here. Uniformitarians often describe the Temple Butte strata as in-filled delta distributaries, but what delta today accomplishes such "flat" erosion and such a milieu of channels? Where is the evidence of the missing 72 million years?

Between the Temple Butte and the Redwall Limestone lies an extremely flat disconformity, and above them another unconformity is inferred. It too is extremely flat, with no evidence of life zones, either submarine or terrestrial. In isolated areas, the Surprise Canyon Formation is present, but in most locations, no features produced by surface water action such as sinkholes or caves have been found in the top surface of the Redwall Limestone. It doesn't look like much time elapsed between the formations.

Redwall Limestone

One of the most noticeable features in Grand Canyon is the 500-foot-thick red cliff about halfway between bottom and top, appropriately called the Redwall Limestone. The reddish color is not endemic to the rock itself, for when freshly broken it exhibits a natural light gray color. Rather, the red color has seeped down from red shales in the overlying Supai Group of formations and stained the gray limestone.

This red stain can itself be instructive, for it takes some years to thoroughly cover and soak into the Redwall. If the miles-wide canyon were continually widening over millions of years, portions of the rock surface would always be rather newly exposed and fresh limestone could be seen. But only in side canyons, after flash flooding or an earth tremor has caused a rock fall, does the true color appear. Few "new" features can ever be seen. The canyon as a whole could best be considered a museum of past processes, not ongoing present processes as demanded by uniformitarianism.

Contrary to popular expectations, few fossils are found in most Grand Canyon strata. Conversely, fossils of many invertebrate animals are found in several horizons within the Redwall. Most important are the estimated billions of two-foot-long nautiloids recently discovered oriented in a particular direction by water current. This was a mass kill zone, as powerful currents overwhelmed a living community and buried them together. As mentioned earlier, Dr. Steve Austin of ICR, reasoning from a catastrophic platform, investigated these important fossils, and inferred an estimated billions more, where uniformitarian scientists had missed them. He traced them across several states, documenting an amazing "death event."

The Redwall Limestone also contains abundant chert nodules made almost entirely of silica, which testifies to extremely hot waters (perhaps the "fountains of the great deep" of Genesis 7:11) involved in its formation. Its matrix consists of quite pure fine-to-coarse limestone and dolomite, with only minor amounts of clay and quartz. The Redwall consists of extremely fine-grain calcite, not the aragonite of today's lime sediments, indicating a high-energy environment and history. Uniformitarians often cite the Redwall Limestone as the prime example of limey detritus accumulating in a calm sea, ignoring the billions of two-foot-long nautiloid fossils. This massive kill zone, covering a vast area, instead requires catastrophic conditions.

Dynamic water movement is also called for by the enormous carbonate cross-beds present in the Redwall, requiring deep, fast-flowing water currents. This formation was not deposited in calm seas, as is often taught. It is assigned by uniformitarianism to the Mississippian system, spanning from about 320 to 340 million years old, but creationists would date it to somewhere in the early to middle stages of the Flood.

The Kaskaskia Megasequence

The Temple Butte and the Redwall Limestone represent the end stage of the third fining-upward sequence of beds known in geology. The Kaskaskia Megasequence supposedly spans the time period from about 400 to 320 million years ago, according to uniformitarian thinking. Clastic sediments such as sandstone and shale, expected to have been deposited prior to the limestones, either weren't deposited or were all eroded in the Grand Canyon area, but are found in other locations. As before, the package is bounded by major unconformities above and below. The three megasequences discussed so far (the Sauk, Tippecanoe, and Kaskaskia) run consecutively, each a fining-upward sequence closely followed by the next erosive episode and the next fining-upward megasequence. The fourth such sequence, the Absaroka, includes all the rest of the strata in Grand Canyon, from the Surprise Canyon Formation and the Supai Group up to the Kaibab

The reddish Supai Group, the source of the red color in the Red-wall Limestone, totals about 1,000 feet in thickness. It is composed of sandstone, siltstone, shale, and limestone, with no known local source. Uniformitarians feel the color might imply iron oxidized in a terrestrial source, but the flat, extensive layers argue instead for marine origin.

Limestone. These strata probably represent the middle stage of the Flood.

Surprise Canyon Formation

This mixed lithology unit is similar in its limited extent to the Temple Butte Formation. It is less than 100 feet in thickness at most exposures. The Surprise Canyon Formation was indeed a surprise, for its distinctive appearance was noted by chance from a helicopter. It likely represents the first pulse of the Absaroka Megasequence in the canyon. Uniformitarians assign it to the latest Mississippian and/or the earliest Pennsylvanian systems, with an assumed age of about 320 million years. It is only present in a few locations.

Supai Group

The Supai Group of sandstone, siltstone, shale, and limestone overlies the Redwall in most locations, separated from it by another unconformity. It (and occasionally the Surprise Formation) signals the start of the Absaroka Megasequence. Consisting of four major formations, the Supai totals over 1,000 feet in thickness, all rather reddish in color. Uniformitarians assign the group to the Pennsylvanian through the lower Permian time, from about 315 to about 285 million years ago. As expected, no regional unconformity is present between the Supai's layers, but some have suspected minor unconformities. Uniformitarians typically propose

slow and gradual deposition to have continued unchecked.

Such a reddish color today normally comes from oxidation of minerals in a terrestrial environment where oxygen is freely available. In this case, uniformitarians consider the Supai Group strata to be from an extensive delta, but several features argue for a marine origin instead. Deltas are typically local features, with pronounced high and low areas. The wide area covered by the Supai Group does not indicate a deltaic environment. In places, its "deltaic" sandstone intertongues with marine limestone, invalidating a strictly land-based origin.

Marine fossils lace the deposits, as well. Large-scale cross-bedding indicates deep and wide flowing water, not river or delta sedimentation. The Supai is rather flat and featureless, having no deltaic distributaries or channel systems, making it unlike any delta on earth today, and thus due to a cause unlike any today. Furthermore, the lack of a nearby source for the varied sediments demands a far-away source and a far-from-normal level of energy and flow of water to emplace them.

Hermit Formation

Immediately above the Supai lies the reddish-brown Hermit Formation, consisting of siltstone, claystone, and fine-grain sandstone, as well as marine limestone, totaling some 300 feet in thickness. It, too, is thought by uniformitarians to represent a delta or river floodplain, but it exhibits dominant marine characteristics as well, covering an extensive area. No delta of today looks like this. It has been labeled by uniformitarians as Permian in age, some 280 or so million years old.

A major unconformity and change in rock type caps the Hermit, normally signaling the end of a megasequence, but here the details are unclear. The next overlying stratum is the well-known Coconino Sandstone, appearing to be the typical basal sandstone of a new megasequence. Perhaps it is. The Absaroka has been subdivided here by some uniformitarian observers, who have proposed several short transgressions and regressions. From a Flood geology consideration, we can at the very least think of the Coconino as a major new transgressive "pulse" within the Absaroka.

Understand that God's main purpose for the Flood

Although the traditional interpretation of the Coconino Sandstone is that it started out as desert sand dunes, it is better understood as underwater sand waves. On its dune faces are amphibian tracks that could only be preserved under water. The "sand dune" heights and slope are also better explained by underwater deposition.

was to purge the sinful, wicked, violent world of its inhabitants. Remember that while standing water may be harmful, moving water does the greater "purging." Whether transgressing onto the land or regressing off the land, moving water would accomplish a job that standing water could not. The strata, rightly considered, are a record of dynamic moving water, capable of accomplishing God's intention. Water coming and going would accomplish God's purpose quite well.

Coconino Sandstone

The cream-colored bed sitting conformably above the Hermit is the important Coconino Sandstone, known for its prominent cross-beds. Resistant to erosion, it forms a recognizable, whitish-colored, ribbon-like cliff throughout the canyon, close to its rim. Uniformitari-

ans have long used this stratum to "disprove" Flood geology, for it is interpreted as fossilized wind-blown sand dunes. Obviously, there couldn't have been a large, dry desert right in the middle of the Flood.

Enormous cross-beds, up to 30 feet high, dominate the deposit, and do indeed remind one of desert sand dunes. However, the end may be in sight for this primary argument used against Flood geology. Despite its prominence in anti-creationist literature, uniformitarians have done little research here following their initial designation. Recent research funded by ICR has found strong evidence that the Coconino cross-beds are best interpreted as underwater sand waves (very large ripple marks).[4] There is much at stake here. An enormous desert in the middle of a huge flood is inconceivable, and thus incompatible with the Flood of Genesis. Conversely, water-deposited sand dunes of this magnitude are incompatible with uniformitarianism.

The angle of repose of loose desert sand is up to 34 degrees, but the cross-beds typically have dips of about 25 degrees, more like giant underwater sand waves. Furthermore, tiny amphibian or lizard tracks can often be found on the tilted bed faces. Lizards might walk around in a desert, but their tracks would hardly be preserved. Recognizable footprints require wet conditions and quick cementation before they smear or blow away. Interestingly, the tracks are always trending up the underwater "dune" slopes, as would be the case if they were made by frightened animals escaping from rising water. We can thus infer they were deposited under water, not in dry desert air. These features have led many to change their long-cherished opinion and consider the underwater alternative. But there is a problem that hinders many uniformitarians from even considering the evidence.

The smaller, but similar, features (i.e., ripple marks on a beach) obviously result from shallow, high-energy waves. The much larger "ripple marks" in the laterally extensive Coconino must have also been formed by high-energy water such as extremely large and wide currents. The dominant sand grain size itself insists on high velocity water to transport them. The excessive height of the cross-beds demands deep water, but normally water flows slowly at depth. Deep water flowing at a high velocity over a laterally extensive area stretches the imagination. Such a suite of dramatic conditions seemingly forces a careful scientist to conclude that an

PALEOCURRENTS

A creationist colleague of ICR, Professor Art Chadwick, has spent years collecting nearly 500,000 measurements of paleocurrents, directions of water currents employed in past depositional events as published in the standard geological literature. These data points came from 15,000 locations, more than ever before collected. He plotted their location, current direction, and "age" as assigned by mainstream thinking, and arrayed them graphically on computer plots. One can see the dominant current direction in Virginia, or France, etc., at any period of "time" on the geologic column. To see them in sequence is almost like seeing a graphical animation of the Flood itself.

In Dr. Chadwick's words:

> We have verified the stable southwesterly [i.e., the currents were from the northeast] pattern of paleocurrents across the craton [continental interior] documented by others (Potter and Pri-

or, 1961; Seeland, 1968) and have chronicled its persistence with some variation throughout the Paleozoic. In the Mesozoic the currents exhibit increasing variability and shift from predominantly westerly [i.e., from the east] to predominantly easterly [i.e., from the west]. By mid Cenozoic there is no discernable direction continent-wide pattern, reflecting expected tertiary basinal sedimentation. These patterns and transitions must accompany major changes in global current trends.[1]

There are clear dominant trends indicating current directions that were stable on a global scale. Uniformity of geological processes and rates relies on local, "normal" currents to transport sediments. One might suppose a variety of current directions would have predominated over time, but the data indicate otherwise.

1. Arthur V. Chadwick, 1993, Megatrends in North American Paleocurrents, *Society of Economic Paleontologists and Mineralogists Abstracts*, 8: 58.

unimaginable catastrophe must have been raging at the surface, something like the hypercanes discussed earlier. Such a storm or complex of storms is beyond the limits of "slow and gradual" uniformitarian processes and rates, and thus any change of thinking on their part is slow, despite the clear evidence.

Near Grand Canyon Village, the Coconino Sandstone averages about 300 feet thick, but it varies up to 1,000 feet thick to the south, where there is indisputable evidence the sediment was water-deposited, not as dunes but as flat beds. As with all the individual beds in Grand Canyon, the Coconino covers vast territory, at least 200,000 square miles over the states of Arizona, Utah, New Mexico, Colorado, Texas, Kansas, and Oklahoma. Similar beds of the same "age" are found on other continents as well. No desert of this magnitude exists today, thus standard uniformity-based thinking cannot apply. The Coconino was not a desert. Something catastrophic and regionally active was needed.

Consider the Hermit Formation and the Coconino sandstone and the completely different sedimentary environments they imply, according to uniformity. The Hermit is thought to be a vast delta, hosting a thriv-

ing community of varied plants and animals living near the coast. The overlying Coconino was a desert, they claim, with sparse life and arid conditions. The entire area surrounding and including the Hermit would have to be raised in elevation far enough to become this enormous, dry desert. This extensive uplift is thought by uniformitarians to have required at least 10 million years. Remember, the Hermit was supposedly an offshore deposit that was slowly uplifted. Wouldn't extensive drainage channels have been produced as the waters drained? Where are the mountains and valleys that the uplift must have produced? Where is the pronounced topography? Is there any real evidence of millions of years? The expected support cannot be seen. Cannot good scientists refrain from repetition of the "millions and millions of years" mantra long enough to consider the evidence?

The contact between the Hermit and the Coconino is knife-edge sharp. The abrupt change in particle color, size, and type impresses one that it was due to a sudden change in sediment and sedimentary conditions. No gradual shift in conditions could account for such a stark difference. No erosion pattern developed in the upper Hermit surface, even though it must have been exposed or near to the surface for much of that time. There is no channeling, no worm burrows, no animal tunnels, no root penetration, nothing to indicate the passage of millions of years. Evidently, the time is needed to satisfy uniformitarian dating only, but it is not demanded by the evidence.

The real data imply rapid, catastrophic deposition, with a sudden change in sediment source and depositional conditions, and with minimal time involved. Both layers are conventionally dated as Permian, but geological uniformitarianism and biological evolution demand a gap between them. This contact has been dubbed a paraconformity, for it looks conformable, but a time gap is called for to satisfy uniformitarianism—one not supported by the evidence.

Toroweap Formation

A similar change can be seen at the top of the Coconino Sandstone where so-called desert sand dunes inter-finger with a marine limestone. How can a desert deposit inter-finger with a marine deposit?

In many places, the whitish cliff-forming ribbon of Coconino abruptly gives way to a more easily eroded sandy limestone, covered with vegetation. As does the Coconino, the Toroweap covers a vast, several-state area. This gray, fossiliferous limestone is usually about 250 feet thick, and consists of a rather pure limestone near the center, while containing a higher percentage of sand near the top and bottom. Laterally, it varies a great deal, with a thick sandy zone nearly identical to the Coconino in Arizona's nearby Walnut Canyon. Hydraulic conditions and sediment content must have been rapidly changing during deposition. It is hard to imagine a natural environment changing so quickly from the Coconino "desert" to an underwater (early Toroweap) one—that is, from deltaic to desert to offshore, back to

The contacts between Grand Canyon strata are characteristically flat, even though tens of millions of years are postulated between their deposition.

This fossil is from the Kaibab Limestone formation. As worms burrowed through recently deposited mud, fragile trace fossils remained. This "bioturbation" must have been accomplished before the sediment hardened, and would destroy all sedimentary structure in the mud. Sediments harden into rock quickly. Since most sedimentary rocks abound with sedimentary structure, they could not have been exposed to bioturbation for long before the next layers were deposited.

desert again, and then back to underwater—all with minimal erosion and no signs of time passing.

Kaibab Limestone

Approximately 300 feet of impure, resistant limestone rims the canyon, containing numerous broken fossils of marine invertebrates, chips of which can easily be found along the rim trail. Along with the underlying

Supai Group of varied beds, the Hermit Formation, the Coconino Sandstone, and the Toroweap Formation, the Kaibab Limestone is conventionally dated as within the middle Permian system, around 275 million years ago.

Altogether, the Supai through Kaibab layers comprise the fining-upward Absaroka Megasequence (perhaps divided into two at the Coconino). Predictably, the Absaroka is bounded by regional unconformities above and below. The strata are widespread, and each of the individual beds requires catastrophic conditions for deposition. Marine invasion of the land brought dynamic, wide-ranging deposits of varying sediments, to be followed by devastating erosion. That sounds like major flooding.

Several thousand feet of sediments were once perched atop the Kaibab, but most are all eroded from the canyon area now. This extensive stack of layers forms the Grand Staircase to the north and will be briefly discussed below. In turn, they host favorite tourist locations Zion Canyon and Bryce Canyon. Together with Grand Canyon strata, they give us a good summary of the workings of the great Flood.

Mesozoic Sediment

The strata change in character and fossil content above the Permian system. Throughout the underlying Paleozoic strata, only marine fossils and deposits are preserved. Virtually all fossils everywhere are of marine origin, but some of the later sediment originated on land and contains some fossils of land-dwelling plants and animals. This includes strata designated as Mesozoic, thought by uniformitarians to date from about 65 to about 250 million years ago, but in Flood geology thinking dates to the time when Flood incursion was toward its maximum. There was more to come, however, before God's justice was completely satisfied. This supposed "Mesozoic" Era would have followed the time of Grand Canyon "Paleozoic" strata deposition. Tertiary "time" followed the Mesozoic, and Quaternary "time" followed that. Each period of the Flood left its own characteristic deposit behind.

Obviously, erosion of the canyon's strata could not have been accomplished until after the deposition of the strata, but how much later? Studying the strata provides a clue, and when we do we see that erosion of the canyon itself was only the last episode of much greater erosion that included the later strata, too. The Kaibab Limestone is stratigraphically overlain by numerous Flood layers, seen in Utah to the north, which have been removed from the canyon's rim.

Geologists who study the canyon no longer consider it to have been eroded by the Colorado River over 70 million years, even though this is still taught to non-specialists and impressionable students. Discovery that a solidified lava rock found on the south side of the canyon had erupted from a volcano on the north rim proved that the eruption and lava flow had occurred before the canyon was eroded. The river and canyon would have interrupted the flow of magma. To their surprise, when the basaltic rock was radio-dated by the standard dating method for this type of rock (based on the faulty assumptions discussed above), it was found

Monument Valley, a region of the Colorado Plateau.

THE YOUNG EARTH

Both good science and the Bible point to earth's catastrophic past. Geological data demand dynamic solutions to origins questions and do not allow uniformitarian ones. Did you know both science and the Bible also teach the young age of the earth? Numerous points have already been aired in these pages, but let us consider a few more. They will not only point to recent creation, but demonstrate the bankruptcy of uniformitarian thinking. Consider:

Salt in the ocean: The oceans grow saltier each year as rivers bring in more dissolved salts. Knowing the ocean's volume and average salt concentration, we can calculate how much salt is there. We can measure how fast it arrives, and how fast it is removed. Evolution teaches that life evolved in a salty sea about three billion years ago. But at present (uniform) rates, even in one billion years the ocean would be so choked with salt that life would be impossible. Uniformitarianism is incompatible with the ocean's salt makeup.

Erosion of the continents: The volume of the continents above sea level is known. Uniformitarianism considers them to have risen from the sea hundreds of millions of years ago. We can measure how fast the continents are eroding. In some places the land is rising, but at far slower rates than it is eroding elsewhere. At present rates, all the continents would be gone in just a few million years, yet they are still here. There shouldn't be any sedimentary rock left, no fossils, no granitic core—it should all be gone. Uniformitarian thinking doesn't explain the facts.

Helium in the atmosphere: When an atom of uranium-238 (or thorium) undergoes alpha decay into a lead atom through a series of decay steps, it ejects eight alpha particles, which are essentially helium atoms (two protons and two neutrons = a helium nucleus, to which electrons attach). Helium's light weight causes it to rise through pores in the rocks and eventually enter the atmosphere. Sensitive sensors can measure how much helium is in the atmosphere, as well as how much enters it. If present rates have continued for the supposed previous millions of years, there should be lots more helium than is currently there.

Helium in the rocks: A similar calculation can be made regarding helium content in rocks of "known" uniformitarian age that contain radioactive uranium. By knowing the rate of decay, we can calculate how much helium should be present. Tiny, slippery helium atoms leak out through rock's pores over time, faster than they are generated. If the rocks are as old as the standard view supposes, the helium should have mostly escaped. Instead, way too much is still present. Helium is still building up! It looks like the rocks are not so old after all.[1]

Soft-sediment deformation: Sediments harden into rock rather quickly in the presence of an adequate cement binding the particles together. The sediments can later be deformed through folding or faulting. Often, the sediments give evidence of still being soft and pliable when deformed. It appears there was not enough time between deposition and deformation to harden the sediments, even though uniformitarianism often assigns dates to the two processes many millions of years apart.[2]

Sediments in the ocean: As the continents erode and sediments are carried downstream, they build up on the ocean floor. If the continents have been eroding for hundreds of millions of years at their present rate, there should be a predictable amount there. With submarines and drill cores, we have been able to observe that there is not nearly as much sediment as uniformitarianism requires. All of the sediment currently there would accumulate in a time far shorter than uniformitarianism predicts.[3]

Human history: Real history is human history, during which reliable eyewitnesses observed and recorded events. True history began with the invention of writing, agriculture, and human society around 5,000 years ago, according to historians. Bible-believers recognize this as about the time of the Flood. Except for the biblical account, only various traditions survive from before then. Any thoughts of times before 5,000 years ago are based on either biblical revelation or on the concept of uniformitarianism, and that concept has proved to be inaccurate and based on false assumptions about the unseen past.

1. John Morris, 2007, *The Young Earth*, Green Forest, AR: Master Books, 87-89.

2. Steven A. Austin and John D. Morris, 1986, Tight Fold and Clastic Dikes as Evidence for Rapid Deposition and Deformation of Two Very Thick Stratigraphic Sequences, *Proceedings of the First International Conference on Creationism*, R. E. Walsh, C. L. Brooks and R. S. Crowell, eds., Pittsburgh, PA: Creation Science Fellowship, Inc., 3-13.

3. Ariel A. Roth, 1998, *Origins: Linking Science and Scripture*, Hagerstown, MD: Review and Herald Pub., 263-266.

to be much too young to fit the long-repeated, unifor-mitarian story, and the "age" was revised down to less than five million years.[5]

MOENKOPI FORMATION

Remnants of two of those mostly eroded layers can still be seen nearby. One is several miles south of the canyon at Red Butte, and the other at Cedar Mountain as seen from Desert View Tower on the east end of the park. Although they look somewhat like volcanoes, these conical-shape hills are merely leftovers of the mighty erosion episode that removed most of the overlying strata and laid bare the upper surface of the Kaibab.

Both Cedar Mountain and Red Butte are made up of the easily eroded Moenkopi Formation, an intermingled reddish mudstone/siltstone/sandstone. Originally, the Moenkopi was over 300 feet thick, as can be seen in outcrops to the north. It escaped being scoured off in a few places by the vagaries of swirling water. The rest of the extensive Moenkopi layer is completely gone,

and several more layers above it. But since the upper surface of the Kaibab is noticeably flat and featureless, what type of regional erosion would leave behind such a terrain? This breathtaking scouring must have been accomplished by what the U.S. Army Corps of Engineers researchers call "sheet erosion" that employed rapidly moving water everywhere flowing at about the same depth.

Conventional thinking places the Moenkopi in the early Triassic system, some 245 to 250 million years ago, but creationists consider the layer to have been laid down when the Flood was nearing its height. This was a time of continual catastrophic shifting of the continental plates, with sea level rapidly adjusting. Could this vast sheet erosion episode have occurred when the oceans regressed? Such sheet erosion, with deep water flowing at high velocity, can erode down to the same level throughout an area and not leave eroded channels. That matches the terrain surrounding Grand Canyon. But that was not the only erosion going on. The strata are complicated in this part of the column, with unconformities riddling the area and distorting

Tightly folded strata at Split Mountain, California. The sediment layers, which are quite hard now, must have been soft when they were deformed. Soft sediment deformation argues strongly for a short time between deposition and deformation.

the record.

Shinarump Conglomerate

Capping the Moenkopi on Cedar Mountain is a most remarkable deposit. Included within the Chinle Formation discussed below, the Shinarump Conglomerate is "dated" as belonging to the Triassic Period. Consisting of an enormous layer of hard, chert pebbles that have no local source and thus must have been brought in from afar, it baffles researchers. The standard interpretation of this deposit is that it is due to the action of a braided stream. Today, braided streams lazily migrate back and forth through a nearly flat streambed. But consider that this deposit averages 50 feet thick and covers over 100,000 square miles in area. The pebbles are large enough to require fast-flowing water to transport them over the necessary long distance. There is no environment on earth today remotely comparable to this. The deposition of a thin, uniform bed of sand and gravel of such size differs markedly from anything uniformitarian thinking can propose, certainly quite different from the braided streams we know today, even at flood stage. Hydrologists can only postulate rapid sheet flow of gravel-bearing water, depositing its load as the velocity slowed. Dated as Middle Triassic, a 15 million-year hiatus is inferred between deposition of the Moenkopi and the Shinarump, but the Moenkopi's upper surface doesn't bear record of this.

Chinle Formation

The series of Moenkopi Formation and Shinarump Conglomerate is unconformably overlain by shale, muddy sandstone, and volcanic mudflows that comprise the Chinle Formation, usually several hundred to 1,000 feet thick. Petrified Forest in Arizona is the upper member of the Chinle Formation. This popular display of abundant petrified wood would more aptly be called the Petrified Log Jam, for no hint of a standing forest remains. The logs are never in standing position, but strewn about over a large area, with their long axis in a preferential direction, showing placement by moving water.[6] Aggressive movement by water abraded all the twigs and bark, yet quickly buried the logs, leaving intricate tree rings preserved.

In addition to the petrified logs, fossils of dinosaurs, amphibians, ferns, and marine life of many types are present. The Chinle deposit of shale and sandstone is essentially a huge volcanic deposit mixed in with flowing mud, implying eruptions on a large scale. The volcanic component contains much silica, necessary to petrify wood. The Chinle has been assigned to the Middle Triassic and conformably overlies the Shinarump. It correlates with deposits of varying names and characteristics over much of the American West, including at least the states of Arizona, Nevada, New Mexico, Utah, Colorado, Kansas, Oklahoma, and Texas.

Returning to the megasequence concept, not all sequences are represented in their entirety in all locations. Erosion has taken a toll on the rock record, removing parts of it. The upper layers of Grand Canyon strata are within the Absaroka Megasequence, while the more fine-grain Moenkopi, Shinarump, and Chinle Formations have been largely removed in the canyon by the major erosion episode closing the Absaroka. Marked by a general fining-upward sequence—major sandstones at the bottom, finer clastics above—from Supai to Kaibab, it is completed by major unconformities above and below. In Flood thinking, these important rock layers represent the Flood nearing its maximum height and extent, before it finally began to wane.

The next overlying megasequence is the Zuni Megasequence, spanning the "dates" from about 190 million to about 35 million years ago, according to uniformitarian reckoning. The Zuni incorporates the important Jurassic, Cretaceous, and Early Tertiary systems (including essentially all the dinosaur "era" in evolutionary terms), but in Flood thinking it saw the maximum and early waning of the Flood. Much Flood devastation was still to come, as the waters rapidly drained off the rising continents, accompanied by continuing, rapid, and catastrophic plate movements, mountain range uplift, and large volcanic eruptions. This megasequence is perhaps the most complex, and some researchers have divided it into three lesser sequences. Much of the evidence has been removed by erosion, either the bounding erosional episodes or intermediate ones.

Creationists might consider this period of the Flood as the time when the floodwaters maintained their position on the land. The waters were in no sense stagnant, but were coming and going, all the while continuing their devastation. Remember, the primary goal of the Creator/Judge was to annihilate rebellious and violent mankind. Continued ocean transgressions and regressions would have accomplished that purpose much better than standing water.

Zion Canyon

Within the Zuni Megasequence, several important individual layers should be mentioned that are visible in spectacular Zion Canyon. The multicolored siltstones and sandstones of the Moenave and Kayenta Formations with the important Navajo Sandstone combine to represent the clastic zone beginning the sequence. Missing in Zion Canyon, but prominent nearby, is the Wingate Sandstone, famous for exposures in Arches National Park and elsewhere. Together, these layers comprise the Glen Canyon Group, which measures up to 2,000 feet in thickness. They are assigned by uniformitarians to the Jurassic system, supposedly some 200 million years old.

Navajo Sandstone

To the casual observer, the Navajo Sandstone appears much like the Coconino Sandstone. Both are interpreted as desert sand dune fields, but similar questions arise in both. Here, dunes are stacked upon previous dunes to a height of many hundreds of feet. These are most recognizable at Checkerboard Mesa, where multiplied dozens of "dunes" are stacked up in a prominent hillside. In sand dune fields with which we are familiar, the dunes seldom stack at all, as the dominant wind direction continually relocates and redeposits the sand. Thus, an unlikely combination of conditions must be postulated to account for the stacking of multiplied dunes.

As before, the angle at which the cross-beds rest is much more compatible with an underwater environment than a desert environment. The typical sand grain size in the Navajo requires fast-flowing water, and the measured dune height implies deep water was involved. Surely, the "fossilized" dunes are more reflective of underwater sand waves, and would be acknowledged as such were not the conditions needed so extreme. Furthermore, the deposit covers an extensive area, several hundred miles in radius, far larger than most modern

The Navajo Sandstone in Utah, like the Coconino Sandstone and for much the same reasons, is better interpreted as giant underwater sand waves rather than desert sand dunes.

sand dune fields. Rapidly flowing water at depth never occurs today for such a large area. A mighty catastrophe is required to explain the data. These strata were eroded in the Grand Canyon vicinity by the frightening sheet erosion that exposed the Kaibab Plateau.

Interestingly, the dinosaur fossil-bearing Morrison Formation lies within the Zuni Megasequence but is not exposed here. Dinosaurs somehow escaped death until several months into the Flood. Perhaps they were better swimmers/floaters than mammals and other land creatures, but this stage of the Flood was also marked by immense volcanic eruptions. We typically find dinosaurs buried by flowing mud choked with volcanic debris, their remains surrounded by plant and animal fossils from mixed environments. Few, if any, survived the Flood much longer.

Bryce Canyon

Tourists who visit Grand Canyon and Zion Canyon often also visit the nearby Bryce Canyon. This majestic spectacle exemplifies what erosion due to Flood runoff would look like. The soft, easily eroded siltstone here was deposited late in the Flood after the regionally extensive layers of Flood strata were laid down. As the Flood waned, the continents were being uplifted and water was draining back to the sea. The retreating floodwaters rushed over the not-yet-fully hardened sedimentary deposit. Floodwaters may have ponded

Bryce Canyon in Utah rests in the Zuni Megasequence.

here while post-Flood rainwater collected. Seeming "lake" deposits dot the region. Perhaps a ponded lake here suddenly failed, and the clay and silt of the Brian Head and Wasatch Formations slumped away. The lake had likely been held in place by a natural dam. As we all know, when a dam fails, it fails catastrophically.

Bryce Canyon is not really a canyon at all, but the remnant, semicircular edge of such a lake. Its rapid failure has left numerous beautiful spires and columns that give the "canyon" its charm. Slow erosion, such as is occurring today, dismantles the spires; it requires extraordinary circumstances to create new ones. Present processes do not explain Bryce Canyon.

The Tejas Megasequence

Strata in and surrounding Bryce Canyon are dated in the first half of the Tertiary Period and are placed in the Tejas Megasequence, as are the several layers stratigraphically above it. This megasequence is noticeably shorter and involved shallower water depths than those preceding it. Creationist researchers have not yet reached consensus regarding its place in time, variously

putting it in the Flood runoff stage or in the early post-Flood period. Much remains to be learned about this dynamic and enigmatic period of earth history.

MEGASEQUENCE DATA COMPILED

This lengthy recitation of stratigraphical evidence regarding megasequences in the American Southwest serves a summary purpose. It is not intended to replace the standard terminology already in use, but to give a "Flood-ish" stamp on concepts long overrun by uniformitarian thinking. Geologists conceived and developed the megasequence concept (Laurence L. Sloss and others) by considering outcrop characteristics, coupled with drilling logs and cores, compiled onto regional subsurface maps, but the concept has been dramatically extended and amplified by oil exploration technology. Seismic exploration tools can now "look" underground and study what has never been seen on the surface. Keep in mind that these sequences have been recognized right across the continent and even onto other continents, especially in the Northern Hemisphere where data are good and studies plentiful. Truly, these large-scale patterns represent reality, and their regional/continental scope speaks also of global causes for the strata. Megasequence details are yet somewhat controversial among creationists, but the global extent of ocean transgressions and regressions and the fining-upward nature of the deposits speak eloquently of the Genesis Flood.

The semi-continental sequences were all consecutive marine transgressions onto the land, with deposition interrupted only by widespread erosion. Essentially, each stratum records violent devastation of the continents by ocean waters. Each rock layer is best understood to be of catastrophic origin. Virtually each one contains fossils, dead things buried in watery graves. Together, the consecutive megasequences represent everything, all the strata units, in all stages of the Flood.

The Tertiary Period, toward the end of the Flood, saw great geologic activity. This geologic "period" may have seen more sedimentation than any other, with the possible exception of the Cretaceous.[7] Can this be the waning stages of the Flood or post-Flood residual catastrophism, as some have proposed? It also saw extensive volcanism,[8] greater than any other Period. Surely, it was a time of intense geologic activity. Investigation is continuing among creationist researchers, and no consensus has yet been reached, but only the great Flood had the scope and power to accomplish so much.

THE QUATERNARY PERIOD

The one geologic Period not included in any megasequence is the Quaternary, the time during which the post-Flood Ice Age developed. This was also a time of lots of water activity, from increased rain and snowfall and the resulting runoff, to saturated Flood deposits dewatering. Major storms were common, not only in the north where snow was building up into glaciers, but throughout the lower latitudes. This was not a universally cold period all over earth, but storms were fierce and summers weren't warm enough to fully melt winter snows. The glaciers moved across freshly deposited Flood strata, scraping them off and filling streams with eroded material, which then collected in low areas or was transported to the new oceans.

Land animals migrated from the mountains of Ararat around the world, aided by land bridges connecting all continents, with the possible exception of Aus-

tralia. These bridges were eventually drowned when the glaciers melted, separating the continents. Meanwhile, great herds of large animals were free to roam and multiply prolifically. Mammoths, particularly associated with the Ice Age, thrived in numerous areas, from Florida to Siberia. When sudden storms hit, large herds were sometimes trapped and died. Now we find multiplied thousands of mammoth bones buried in the surface deposits. They were not caught in Flood activity, but in post-Flood storms. Only a few dozen mammoths were frozen with flesh intact, and these unlucky individuals were seemingly trapped on river ice or mudslides along the banks of modern rivers. Their carcasses lie entombed in the sediments covering Flood strata.

Scripture informs us of the great Flood of Noah's day, and it informs us in no uncertain terms that there was only one such Flood, yet we have just studied evidence for six (maybe subdivided into a few more) major marine inundations of ocean water onto the continents, interspersed with regional erosion—a complex of comings and goings of the water. No sooner did the waters expend their energy on the land than they rolled back out to sea, only to be reenergized and return to do more damage.

In Scripture, we read of the power and devastation of the great Flood of Noah's day, and that it far surpassed our experience and probably even our imagination. With waters "prevailing exceedingly" over the land, covering even "the high mountains" for several months, causing the death of "all flesh in whose nostrils is the breath of life, of all that lived on dry land"—how can we comprehend it? These are military terms, implying a complete "conquering" of the land. In confirmation and expansion, geology reveals the Flood involved a continual flooding, with tsunami-like waves of water rushing inland multiple times, and then rushing back out until nothing survived and the continents were fully judged.

Scripture speaks to this, too. In Genesis 8:3, we read that "the waters returned from off the earth continually." The Hebrew verb translated "returned" is used again in the same verse where a combination verb form is translated "continually." In some sense, the "returning" was a continual returning. In verse 7, the same word describes the raven's actions as it flew "to and fro," implying a cyclic "coming and going." It finds usage

THE GRAND STAIRCASE

Grand Canyon is only the last notch of a much larger canyon stretching from northern Colorado to southern Arizona. The north flank of Grand Canyon is overlain by the Vermillion Cliffs, made up of the Chinle and Kayenta Formations, and the White Cliffs are made up of the cross-bedded Navajo Sandstone. That is overlain by the Grey Cliffs, all of which make up Zion Canyon strata units, which are overlain by the Brian Head and Wasatch Formations, giving Bryce Canyon its unique charm.

Creationists generally attribute Grand Canyon and strata designated as Paleozoic to the beginning phases of the great Flood, and ascribe Zion Canyon and strata from the Mesozoic to the middle stages during which the Flood was at its maximum. During the Cenozoic, the waters began to wane. On at least a regional scale, all of the strata deposition required intense, catastrophic forces—the great Flood of Noah's day!

The accompanying diagram illustrates the successive layers and their vertical relationship.[1] Grand Canyon shows the continent-spanning Tapeats Sandstone, deposited during the first burst of the Flood by dynamic water action. The Redwall Limestone, in which billions

Grand Canyon possesses deposits left during the early Flood, while Zion Canyon has those from the middle Flood, and Bryce Canyon the late (and post) Flood. The individual layers, not all of which are pictured here, are typically of vast extent and of catastrophic origin—the signature of the Great Flood of Noah's day.

of two-foot-long nautiloid fossils were discovered by creationists, prove the deposit could not have been due to gradual processes. Likewise, the Coconino Sandstone is an underwater sand ripple deposit, not a series of desert sand dunes. Zion Canyon places the Navajo Sandstone in its proper context among marine deposits with marine fossils, not as a terrestrial deposit. Bryce Canyon can best be considered a failed lake bed full of ponding floodwaters. It all fits inferences gained from biblical information. The Grand Staircase, shown in this figure, could be considered Exhibit A for the Flood model of geology.

1. Adapted from Figure 4.12 in Austin, S. 1994. *Grand Canyon: Monument to Catastrophe*. Santee, CA: Institute for Creation Research, 69.

again in verse 9, when the dove was first sent out. It vainly searched for a resting place on land but found none, eventually returning to Noah. An amplified literal translation of verse 3 might be: "And the waters retreated from off the earth, restlessly and/or continually turning back." As the raven went and returned (to and fro), having found no immediate place of rest, and the dove searched in vain for rest and returned to its starting place, so did the floodwaters.

Perhaps this back and forth, restless motion could simply imply tidal action, but something even more

dynamic seems in view. Evidently, Scripture is communicating that as the Flood rose and "prevailed exceedingly" (Genesis 7:19), it literally "conquered" the land and its inhabitants. This is a powerful verb meaning "to overcome all opposition." The great Flood did more than rise and maintain its position over the land. Things were more complicated than that. It continually assaulted its goal.

Perhaps some human or animal inhabitants could manage to survive the first or second onslaught, but soon there came the next. Scripture is clear that no air-breathing, land-dwelling animal survived (most marine creatures and plants succumbed, as well), but several watery "attacks" were necessary to accomplish the complete purpose. We are not told all the details in Scripture. Geology fills in the blanks.

Certainly, there was a time or times when the whole earth was covered by the floodwaters, but there may have been some land exposed during various stages somewhere, as floodwaters came and went. The study of the megasequences above indicates just that. The waters were continually encroaching farther and farther onto the land, one transgression after another, coming and going until all was covered, and God's justice finally satisfied. And then it began to "abate." The strata, rightly considered, are a record of dynamic moving water, capable of accomplishing God's intention.

Today, the floodwaters have returned to the deep ocean basins. In order for the waters to have drained off the continents, a receptacle must have been prepared. The total volume of water on earth didn't change, but the distribution of the topography must have changed, with continents and mountain chains rising and ocean basins lowering. A literal translation of an Old Testament reference to the ending of the Flood reveals that the mountains rose, the basins sank down (Psalm 104:8-9). The new topographic highs and lows allowed the waters to collect in the newly formed ocean basins.

A process was used to accomplish this redistribution of mass. According to Genesis, it took some seven months. Intermediate stages witnessed an ever-deepening sea level. There is much evidence for an intermediate sea level before the waters had completely drained into the oceans. There are flat-topped sea mounts, scoured by wave action far below such action today. There are eroded canyons and bays that extend far into the sea, far below the reach of erosion today, and other puzzling phenomena. The continents retain a similar but opposite record, such as raised inland shorelines documenting a dropping sea level. The implications of the geologic record confirm the biblical record.

A Big Picture Look at the Sediments

Compiling the sedimentary and stratigraphical data from the American Southwest, particularly from the Grand Canyon, Zion Canyon, and Bryce Canyon areas, reveals some stunning conclusions. In general, we see that the relative "ages" of the canyons assigned by uniformitarians are in the proper order, with Grand Canyon representing the Paleozoic Era (the oldest, or earliest in the Flood), Zion Canyon representing the mid-Flood Mesozoic, and Bryce Canyon the Tertiary (the youngest, or latest in the Flood). As mentioned, not every layer is exposed in all three canyons, but when assembled into a time-based series, like boxcars in a train, they line up in this order. When drawn in stratigraphic sequence, they demonstrate why the area is called the Grand Staircase. Note that the layers cover a vast area, much of the American West. Few areas are as well-studied and as complete as this.

In general, the rocks speak of rapid, catastrophic deposition. The geologic column is a graphic record of repeated marine transgressions, incursions of the ocean onto the land, interspersed with regressions as the water rushed back into the oceans. Little time is needed for the entire column. The record shows what Genesis tells us, that the floodwaters were washing "to and fro" over the land. There is nothing about the "column" that should cause the Bible-believer to doubt the truth of the Genesis record.

Some say there is no scientific evidence for the great Flood of Noah's day. To this we can only ask, "What evidence are you looking for?" All the stratigraphical evidence, the geological evidence, the fossil evidence, etc., speak of a watery judgment of life that can best be understood as resulting from the great Flood of Noah's day—just as described in Genesis.

THE MESSAGE OF THE FLOOD

As we saw in chapter 1, man's thinking in the "latter days" will be dominated by a wrong philosophy, the belief that God never has and never will intervene in the affairs of this world. This overarching concept claims that things have never been any different than the way they are today. Far more than mere adherence to natural law for the operation of things in the present world (i.e., modern uniformity of processes and rates), it becomes a philosophical application of unchanging natural law in the present to the unobserved past and future. It becomes the "religious" perspective known as uniformitarianism.

To a uniformitarian, God did not create earth, nor did He send a flood of judgment on earth. Things have continued for millions and billions of years just as we see them today. Furthermore, there will never be a time in the future when the Creator exercises His authority over creation. To a committed uniformitarian, things have always been and will ever be "uniform."

But the Bible offers a very different history. We have seen the prominence of the great Flood of Noah's day's in Scripture. Biblical writers, inspired ultimately by the Holy Spirit of God, the Creator and Judge of all creation, described it in unequivocal terms as global in extent and devastating in impact. They placed great significance on its purpose and function as God's instrument of judgment on the sinful actions and rebellious attitudes of mankind.

God had created all things, including man. He had blessed man with every physical and emotional com-

fort, including intimate fellowship with Him. God had given man a meaningful life, with rewarding responsibilities. As Creator, He has the authority over His creation and the right to set up guidelines for life.

Yet man rejected these undeserved gifts and guidelines. Soon after the perfect creation, with every reason to shun sin and its sure consequences, Adam chose to rebel, opting to believe Satan's lie that man can make his own choices and determine his own destiny—that man can, in essence, become as God. God responded in righteousness and fairness when He sentenced Adam to the just penalty of death—not only physical death, but spiritual death, eternal separation from Him and all goodness and righteousness. Sin's penalty must be paid.

Unfortunately, it wasn't long after Adam rejected God that his descendants' sinful appetite increased. Mankind rebelled to a degree comparable perhaps only to the rampant sin of our day, for the wickedness in "the days of Noah" just before the great Flood is compared to the wickedness in the "latter days," likely our days (Matthew 24:37-39; Luke 17:26-27). In Noah's day, God sent the great Flood as the instrument of His holy justice, a punishment for man's sin.

God is who He is, whether or not man responds properly. He graciously didn't leave it up to us to discover His nature and character. He directly communicated these things to Adam, and today His Book clearly reveals who He is and what He is like. In Scripture, we see Him first of all described as a holy God, neither able to sin nor to abide sin in His presence. As a God of justice, He has declared to us, as He did to Adam, the penalty for sin. In His holy economy, "the wages of sin is death" (Romans 6:23).

The Bible also tells us something that we know from experience: "All have sinned, and come short of the glory of God" (Romans 3:23). Indeed, "there is none righteous, no, not one" (Romans 3:10). We all deserve God's righteous judgment. No one escaped God's justice during the great Flood unless they accepted His gracious provision for their salvation in the Ark of Noah. In just the same way, none can escape God's wrath and punishment for his own sin today. Yet in His mercy, love, and grace, God has provided a way of escape through the sacrificial death of His only begotten Son, our Lord Jesus Christ.

God the Son took upon Himself the form of a man, came to earth to experience man's condition, yet resisted all sin. As perfect man, He had no penalty of His own to pay, thus he could choose to die in place of another. He willingly died in man's stead: "Christ died for our sins" (1 Corinthians 15:3). As fully God, i.e., God the Son, Christ's death was fully sufficient to pay for the sins of all mankind, for all time. His death paid an infinite penalty and satisfied the claims of infinite justice for all condemned men.

As His life was slipping away on the cross, Jesus declared, "It is finished" (John 19:30). All that was necessary to redeem mankind had been done, and He dismissed His spirit. For three days, He lay in the tomb, but then in glorious victory He rose from the grave, having conquered sin and its penalty, death. As risen conqueror, He offers us forgiveness for our sins, resurrection, and eternal life. There is no more penalty to be paid. Now He offers us the same eternal life He earned and intended for man all along.

The question then arises, "If Christ has done it all, what is there left for me to do?" The answer: Nothing. No work to accomplish. No penance to perform. God only requires that we believe that we are worthy of the death penalty for our sins, and that Christ's death on the cross sufficiently paid our own death penalty. We may choose to serve Him and do good works, but we do so out of a heart of love for Him for all he has done for us, not to gain His forgiveness and salvation. That is a free gift.

Settle it forever, then. Affirm to God that you agree you are a sinner deserving His justice, and that the penalty for your sin—your rejection of the holy, sinless God and His authority over your life, and the sinful choices you have made—warrants the death penalty. Recognize that Christ has paid that penalty in full. Place your confidence in that transaction. God asks for us to come to Him and receive His forgiveness for our sinful actions, thoughts, and attitudes. Request and receive forgiveness on the basis that the penalty has been fully paid. Accept the fact that justice has already been served.

When we ask in faith, recognizing our desperate need and unreservedly believing that these things are true, God responds with forgiveness, restoration, and reconciliation. He adopts us into His family and makes us His children—children of God. He grants us a meaningful life in this world, and everlasting life in the next.

What a glorious future awaits us. Our eternal home will not be governed by the "uniform" laws we now live under. We will experience creation as He intended it to be. Man's relationship with his Creator will be fully restored. All will be "very good" once again.

NOTES

INTRODUCTION

1. John C. Whitcomb and Henry M. Morris, 1961, *The Genesis Flood: The Biblical Record and Its Scientific Implications*, Phillipsburg, NJ: Presbyterian and Reformed Publishing Company.

2. Andrew A. Snelling, 2009, *Earth's Catastrophic Past*, Dallas, TX: Institute for Creation Research.

CHAPTER 1

1. Donald E. Chittick, 1984, *The Controversy: Roots of the Creation-Evolution Conflict*, Portland, OR: Multnomah Press.

2. Henry M. Morris, 1984, *The Biblical Basis for Modern Science*, Grand Rapids, MI: Baker Book House.

3. John Morris, 2007, *The Young Earth*, rev. ed., Green Forest, AR: Master Books.

CHAPTER 2

1. Terry Mortenson, 2004, *The Great Turning Point: The Church's Catastrophic Mistake on Geology—Before Darwin*, Green Forest, AR: Master Books, 12.

2. Henry M. Morris, 1988, *Men of Science, Men of God*, Green Forest, AR: Master Books.

3. Charles Darwin, 1839, *Voyage of the Beagle*, London: Smith, Elder, quoting from chapter 9 under the entry dated April 26, 1834.

4. This project was undertaken within ICR's RATE (Radioisotopes and the Age of the Earth) research project. See Steve Boyd, 2005, Statistical Determination of Genre in Biblical Hebrew: Evidence for an Historical Reading of Genesis 1:1-2:3, *Radioisotopes and the Age of the Earth: Results of a Young-Earth Creationist Research Initiative*, Larry Vardiman, Andrew A. Snelling and Eugene F. Chaffin, eds., El Cajon, CA: Institute for Creation Research, and Chino Valley, AZ: Creation Research Society.

5. R. M. Cornelius and John D. Morris, 1995, *Scopes: Creation on Trial*, El Cajon, CA: Institute for Creation Research.

CHAPTER 3

1. See Henry M. Morris, 2000, *Biblical Creationism: What Each Book of the Bible Teaches about Creation and the Flood*, Green Forest, AR: Master Books. This book reviews every Scripture passage that deals with creation matters or God as Creator, showing that there is no hint in all of Scripture of evolution or old earth thinking.

2. Henry M. Morris, 1985, *Scientific Creationism*, Green Forest, AR: Master Books.

3. Henry M. Morris and John D. Morris, 1996, *The Modern Creation Trilogy*, Green Forest, AR: Master Books.

4. John C. Whitcomb, 2011, *The Early Earth*, 3rd ed., Winona Lake, IN: BMH Books.

5. Bill Cooper, 1995, *After the Flood*, Chichester, UK: New Wine Press. This book documents migration of the nations as they traveled the world.

CHAPTER 4

1. Steven A. Austin, 1981, Springs of the Ocean, *Acts & Facts*, 10 (8).

2. Michael Oard, 2009, How many impact craters should there be on the earth?, *Journal of Creation*, 23 (3): 61-69; Carl R. Froede, Jr., 2002, Extraterrestrial

Bombardment of the Inner Solar System: A Review with Questions and Comments Based on New Information, *Creation Research Society Quarterly*, 38 (4): 209-212.

3. Thomas D. Ice and James J. S. Johnson, Using Scriptural Data to Calculate a Range-Qualified Chronology from Adam to Abraham, with Comments on Why the "Open"-or-"Closed" Genealogy Question Is Chronometrically Irrelevant, presented March 1, 2002, at the Evangelical Theological Society Southwest Regional Meeting in Dallas, Texas.

4. Henry M. Morris, 1984, *The Biblical Basis for Modern Science*, Grand Rapids, MI: Baker Book House, 385-396.

CHAPTER 5

1. E. A. Truax, 1991, Genesis According to the Miao People, *Acts & Facts*, 20 (4). Mr. Truax, who spent most of his life working for the Lord among the Miao people, provided this creation account (as he translated it) to Dr. Henry Morris many years before *Acts & Facts* began publication.

2. Tim F. LaHaye and John D. Morris, 1976, *The Ark on Ararat*, Nashville, TN: Thomas Nelson, 231-242.

3. G. Pinches and F. Hommel, 1910, The Oldest Library in the World and the New Deluge Tablets, *Expository Times*, 21: 369. Pinches' editorial marks were omitted for clarity.

4. Source: Dr. Bill Cooper, The Earliest Flood Tablet, Pamphlet 382, May 2011, published by the Creation Science Movement, Portsmouth, UK.

5. E. A. Speiser, 1992, Atrahasis (Accadian Flood Myth), in James B. Pritchard, ed., *Ancient Near Eastern Texts Relating to the Old Testament*, 3rd ed. w/ supplement, Princeton: Princeton University Press, 105-106.

6. Personal correspondence with Dr. Michael Arct, tree ring expert, April 16, 1986.

CHAPTER 6

1. There are many contributors to our understanding of these issues, but the most complete are *Noah's Ark: A Feasibility Study* by John Woodmorappe, and *The Genesis Flood* by John Whitcomb and Henry Morris.

2. John Baumgardner, 2005, Recent Rapid Uplift of Today's Mountains, *Acts & Facts*, 34 (3).

3. Cliff Ollier and Colin Pain, 2000, *The Origin of Mountains*, New York: Routledge, 304-306; John Morris, 2005, When Did the Mountains Rise?, *Acts & Facts*, 34 (3).

4. John Baumgardner, 1986, Numerical Simulation of the Large-Scale Tectonic Changes Accompanying the Flood, *Proceedings of the First International Conference on Creationism*, R. E. Walsh, C. L. Brooks and R. S. Crowell, eds., Pittsburgh, PA: Creation Science Fellowship, Inc., 17-28; Steven A. Austin et al, 1994, Catastrophic Plate Tectonics: A Global Flood Model of Earth History, *Proceedings of the Third International Conference on Creationism*, R. E. Walsh, ed., Pittsburgh, PA: Creation Science Fellowship, Inc., 609-621; John Baumgardner, 2003, Catastrophic Plate Tectonics: The Physics Behind the Genesis Flood, *Proceedings of the Fifth International Conference on Creationism*, R. L. Ivey, Jr., ed., Pittsburgh, PA: Creation Science Fellowship, 113-126; John Baumgardner, Runaway Subduction as the Driving Mechanism for the Genesis Flood, *Proceedings of the Third International Conference on Creationism*, 63-86.

5. Ibid.

6. Mayr, Ernst, 1969, *Principles of Systematic Zoology*, New York: McGraw-Hill

Book Co., 11-12.

7. John Woodmorappe, 1996, *Noah's Ark: A Feasibility Study*, Dallas, TX: Institute for Creation Research, 7.

8. Ibid, 13.

9. Tim F. LaHaye and John D. Morris, 1976, *The Ark on Ararat*, Nashville, TN: Thomas Nelson.

10. S. Maxwell Coder, 1986, *Jude: The Acts of the Apostles*, Chicago: Moody Press, 84-93.

11. S. W. Hong et al, 1994, Safety Investigation of Noah's Ark in a Seaway, *Journal of Creation* (previously called *Technical Journal*), 8 (1): 26-36.

12. Michael Oard, An Ice Age within the Biblical Time Frame, *Proceedings of the First International Conference on Creationism*, 157-166.

13. Steve Shilling et al, 2004, Posteruption glacial development within the crater of Mount St. Helens, Washington, USA, *Quaternary Research*, 61 (3): 325-329.

14. See Tas Walker, 2002, The Black Sea Flood May Evaporate Completely, *Journal of Creation* (previously called *Technical Journal*), 16 (3): 3-5.

CHAPTER 7

1. See Derek V. Ager, 1993, *The Nature of the Stratigraphical Record*, 3rd ed., New York: Wiley.

2. Robert H. Dott, 1983, Episodic sedimentation—How normal is average? How rare is rare? Does it matter?, *Journal of Sedimentary Petrology*, 53 (1): 5-23.

3. Michael Oard, 2004, *The Missoula Flood Controversy and the Genesis Flood*, Chino Valley, AZ: Creation Research Society Books.

4. Steven A. Austin, ed., 1994, *Grand Canyon: Monument to Catastrophe*, Santee, CA: Institute for Creation Research, 106-107.

5. See John Morris and Steven A. Austin, 2003, *Footprints in the Ash*, Green Forest, AR: Master Books.

6. See Harold G. Coffin et al, 2005, *Origin by Design*, Hagerstown, MD: Review and Herald Pub.

7. Morris and Austin, *Footprints in the Ash*, 67; Steven A. Austin, 1996, Excess Argon within Mineral Concentrates from the New Dacite Lava Dome at Mount St. Helens Volcano, *Creation Ex Nihilo Technical Journal*, 10 (3): 335-343.

8. Steve A. Austin, 1991, Floating logs and log deposits of Spirit Lake, Mount St. Helens Volcano National Monument, Washington, *Geological Society of America, Abstracts with Programs*, 23 (5): 85.

9. For fuller documentation, see Austin, *Grand Canyon: Monument to Catastrophe*, and John Morris, 2000, *The Geology Book*, Green Forest, AR: Master Books, 10-19.

10. Adapted from Austin, *Grand Canyon: Monument to Catastrophe*, 34.

11. Juergen Schieber, John Southard, and Kevin Thaisen, 2007, Accretion of Mudstone Beds from Migrating Floccule Ripples, *Science*, 318 (5857): 1760-1763.

12. Donald R. Prothero and Robert H. Dott, 2004, *Evolution of the Earth*, Dubuque, IA: McGraw-Hill, 291.

13. S. A. Weil et al, 1979, National Uranium Resource Evaluation: Chattanooga Shale Conference, U.S. Department of Energy.

14. Steven A. Austin, 2003, Nautiloid Mass Kill and Burial Event, Redwall Limestone (Lower Mississippian), Grand Canyon Region, Arizona and Nevada, *Proceedings of the Fifth International Conference on Creationism*, R. L. Ivey, Jr., ed., Pittsburgh, PA: Creation Science Fellowship, 55-100.

15. William A. Hoesch and Steven A. Austin, 2004, Dinosaur National Monument: Jurassic Park or Jurassic Jumble?, *Acts & Facts*, 33 (4).

16. Roger Sigler and Van Wingerden, 1998, Submarine Flow and Slide Deposits in the Kingston Peak Formation, Kingston Range, Mojave Desert, California: Evidence for Catastrophic Initiation of Noah's Flood, *Proceedings of the Fourth International Conference on Creationism*, Pittsburgh, PA: Creation Science Fellowship; Steven A. Austin and Kurt P. Wise, 1994, The Pre-Flood/Flood Boundary: As Defined in Grand Canyon, Arizona and Eastern Mo-

jave Desert, California, *Proceedings of the Third International Conference on Creationism*, R. E. Walsh, ed., Pittsburgh, PA: Creation Science Fellowship, 37-47.

17. Ager, *The Nature of the Stratigraphical Record*.

18. John Morris, 2012, Volcanoes of the Past, *Acts & Facts*, 41 (6): 15.

19. Andrew Snelling, Regional Metamorphism within a Creationist Framework: What Garnet Compositions Reveal, *Proceedings of the Third International Conference on Creationism*, 485-496.

20. Andrew A. Snelling, 1994, Towards a Creationist Explanation of Regional Metamorphism, *Creation Ex Nihilo Technical Journal*, 8 (1), 51-77; Andrew A. Snelling, Regional Metamorphism within a Creationist Framework: What Garnet Compositions Reveal, *Proceedings of the Third International Conference on Creationism*, 485-496.

21. Austin, *Grand Canyon: Monument to Catastrophe*, 83-111.

22. Diagram modified from Ariel Roth, 1988, Those Gaps in the Sedimentary Layers, *Origins*, 15 (2): 75-92.

23. John Baumgardner, Catastrophic Plate Tectonics: The Physics Behind the Genesis Flood, *Proceedings of the Fifth International Conference on Creationism*, 113-126.

24. John Morris and Frank Sherwin, 2010, *The Fossil Record*, Dallas, TX: Institute for Creation Research, 40-41.

25. Stef Heerema, 2009, A Magmatic Model for the Origin of Salt Formations, *Journal of Creation*, 23 (3): 116-118; Neil C. Mitchel et al, 2010, Submarine Salt Flows in the Central Red Sea, *GSA Bulletin*, 122 (5-6): 701-713.

26. John Morris, 2002, Does Salt Come from Evaporated Sea Water?, *Acts & Facts*, 31 (11).

27. Modified from Steven A. Austin, 1993, *Mount St. Helens Field Study Tour Guidebook*, Santee, CA: Institute for Creation Research, 47.

28. Andrew A. Snelling, 1999, "Excess Argon": The "Archilles' Heel" of Potassium-Argon and Argon-Argon "Dating" of Volcanic Rocks, *Acts & Facts*, 28 (1).

29. John Baumgardner et al, Measurable 14C in Fossilized Organic Materials: Confirming the Young Earth Creation-Flood Model, *Proceedings of the Fifth International Conference on Creationism*, 127-142.

30. Larry Vardiman, Andrew A. Snelling and Eugene F. Chaffin, eds., 2005, *Radioisotopes and the Age of the Earth: Results of a Young-Earth Creationist Research Initiative*, El Cajon, CA: Institute for Creation Research, and Chino Valley, AZ: Creation Research Society, 614.

CHAPTER 8

1. Andrew A. Snelling, 2006, Confirmation of Rapid Metamorphism of Rocks, *Acts & Facts*, 35 (2).

2. Guy Berthault, 1986, Experiments on Laminations of Sediments, Resulting from a Periodic Graded-bedding Subsequent to Deposit, *Compte Rendus Académie des Sciences, Paris*, 303: 1569-1574. Guy Berthault, 1988, Sedimentation of a Heterogranular Mixture: Experimental Lamination in Still and Running Water, *Compte Rendus Académie des Sciences, Paris* 306: 717-724. See further discussion in Austin, *Grand Canyon: Monument to Catastrophe*, 38.

3. Berthault, Experiments on Laminations of Sediments, Resulting from a Periodic Graded-bedding Subsequent to Deposit; Berthault, Sedimentation of a Heterogranular Mixture: Experimental Lamination in Still and Running Water.

4. John Morris, 2010, The Coconino Sandstone: A Flood or a Desert?, *Acts & Facts*, 39 (7): 15.

5. Steven A. Austin, ed., 1994, *Grand Canyon: Monument to Catastrophe*, Santee, CA: Institute for Creation Research, 83-110.

6. Arthur V. Chadwick and Leonard R. Brand, 1974, Fossil Tree Orientation in the Chinle Formation, *Origins*, 1: 22-28.

7. Roy D. Holt, 1996, Evidence for a Late Cainozoic Flood/post-Flood Boundary, *Creation Ex Nihilo Technical Journal*, 10 (1): 128-167.

8. Ibid.

CREDITS

IMAGES

Harold Coffin: 104BL

Creation and Earth History Museum: 125 (ammonites slab)

Creation Research Society (*CRS Quarterly*): 129

Fotolia: 16, 21, 24, 37, 41, 42, 48, 52, 58, 61R, 63, 84, 85, 97, 120T, 131, 140, 159, 164, 168

Carl Froede: 56

Google Earth: 80B

Heritage Auctions, Inc.: 122, 125MB, 125B

Institute for Creation Research: 137, 145

iStock: 21, 38, 44, 51, 66, 69, 73, 78, 87, 91, 93, 98, 100T, 109, 115B, 132, 140

John Mackay: 61L

Dr. John Morris: 17 (adapted from Don Chittick), 19 (adapted from Don Chittick), 26, 74, 102, 104L, 107, 113, 117, 120B, 121, 125T, 128, 130, 135, 140TL, 140ML, 146, 147, 148, 155, 156, 158, 161, 163

NASA: 32, 40, 53, 76, 80T, 120M, 142

National Oceanic and Atmospheric Administration: 54

National Park Service: 133

Public Domain: 26 (Charles Darwin), 30, 47, 70, 124

Roger Sigler: 114, 134

U.S. Bureau of Reclamation: 101

U.S. Geological Survey: 104R, 155

Vision Forum: 26

Susan Windsor: 20 (from Henry M. Morris), 22 (adapted from USGS), 35 (HMM), 36 (HMM), 59, 81, 90, 92, 94, 100B, 108, 111, 112, 115T, 116, 119 (after Roth), 144, 149, 150, 151, 153, 166, 167

T: Top
M: Middle
B: Bottom
R: Right
L: Left

ADAPTED ARTICLES

John Morris, 1991, Are Plants Alive?, *Acts & Facts*, 20: (9).

John Morris, 1990, Did God Create with Appearance of Age?, *Acts & Facts*, 19 (9).

John Morris, 2005, In the Early Earth, Were All the Months Exactly Thirty Days Long?, *Acts & Facts*, 34 (12).

John Morris, 1999, Where Was the Garden of Eden Located?, *Acts & Facts*, 28 (12).

John Morris, 2004, How Soon After the Flood Did the Earth Return to Equilibrium?, *Acts & Facts*, 33 (10).

John Morris, 2006, Why Did God Give the Rainbow Sign?, *Acts & Facts*, 35 (1).

John Morris, 2012, Tree Ring Dating, *Acts & Facts*, 41 (10): 15.

John Morris, 2003, Did Noah's Flood Cover the Himalayan Mountains?, *Acts & Facts*, 32 (9).

John Morris, 2008, A Providential Wind, *Acts & Facts*, 37 (4): 13.

John Morris, 1990, How Could Fish Survive Noah's Flood?, *Acts & Facts*, 19 (7).

John Morris, 2010, Dinosaurs According to Their Creator, *Acts & Facts*, 39 (10): 16.

John Morris, 1992, Why Don't We Find More Human Fossils?, *Acts & Facts*, 21 (1).

John Morris, 1993, Was There Really an Ice Age?, *Acts & Facts*, 22 (8).

John Morris, 2009, Sedimentary Structure Shows a Young Earth, *Acts & Facts*, 38 (7): 15.

John Morris, 2004, Were the Huge Columbia River Basalts Formed in the Flood?, *Acts & Facts*, 33 (5).

John Morris, 2008, Surface Features Require Rapid Deposition, *Acts & Facts*, 37 (12): 13.

Brian Thomas, Fossil Analyses with Verified Original Soft Tissues, posted on icr.org July 21, 2011.

John Morris, 2003, Did Modern Coal Seams Form in a Peat Swamp?, *Acts & Facts*, 32 (8).

John Morris, 2012, Gaps in the Geologic Column, *Acts & Facts*, 41 (2): 16.

John Morris, 2012, The Grand Staircase, *Acts & Facts*, 41 (4): 14.

INDEX